INTERNATIONAL ENCYCLOPAEDIA
OF
ISLAM

Vol.-4

Principles of Islam

INTERNATIONAL ENCYCLOPAEDIA OF ISLAM

Vol.-4

Principles of Islam

Editor

A.H. Qasmi

ISHA BOOKS

DELHI-110 033

International Encyclopaedia of Islam
(*Religion*)

ISBN: 81-8205-320-X (Set)

ISBN: 81-8205-324-2

Published in 2006 in India by
Isha Books, D-43, Prithviraj Road,
Adarsh Nagar, Delhi-110 033

Printed at : Rajdhani Printers, Delhi.

Contents

Preface

Man is a social creature. It is the society where he learns how to live in this vast cosmos. Apart from society, people are divided into different castes, cultures and creeds. All these factors go in developing a man's personality. Of all the factors, mentioned above, religion is most important.

There exist about more than two thousand religions in the world today. A religion is regarded as a sacred institution, which governs a man's life here and hereafter and teaches him how to lead a happy and prosperous life.

What's unique to Islam is its endowment to humanity from the divine creator or the Almighty. It is not a set of principles and dogmas scribed by a scholar or thinker. It was sent on the earth circa fifteen hundred years ago, but its principles and preachings hold good even today. Besides showing humanity a straight way to the eternal success, it also has a say in various other walks of human life, such as economy, politics, human rights, social relations, judiciary, marriage and so on and so forth.

Another distinguished feature of Islam is that apart from being the latest religion, it is also the last one. That is to say, whatever is there in Islam, it is valid upto to the doomsday. Now, there will not come any other religion till the Day of Judgement. Therefore, it is the most powerful and as well as the most human-nature-friendly.

Given the present global scenario, there was being felt a dire need to bring out such a mini-encyclopaedia of Islam which may cater to the maximum needs of man in the least possible sheet of paper.

The present series is an humble attempt in the same direction. It comprises ten volumes which cover all the major disciplines of human life like, Prayer, marriage, justice, human rights, social justice and so on.

We are sure that the endeavour would prove to be a capsule of treasure of knowledge about Islam, prepared perfectly. Nevertheless, considering the adage 'to err is human', we would be obliged if the readers suggest some improvements for further editions.

Editor

1

Historical Backdrop

Primitive man lived in a world which he did not understand; he was surrounded by all sorts of dangers, many of which he could not see or comprehend; so it is no wonder that he jeared nature. When he did so and conceived them as being more powerful than he, it was only natural that he should attempt to obtain their goodwill and to get them to aid him, or at least not to injure him. Primitive man thus began to worship the objects of nature that impressed him most or that he feared most. If he lived in a country where the rays of the sun were welcome, it followed that he would worship the sun. If he lived near a volcano or great waterfall, primitive man would be impressed by it and worship it.

The same would be true of any high mountain, large river, huge tree, great rock, or any animals which were feared, such as the tiger, lion, alligator, or any animal upon which man depended for food or raiment, such as the cow, bear, or buffalo. If the rain brought prosperity, it might be worshipped. On the contrary, the thunder, lightening, or tornado might be worshipped through fear. The sea and fire have been common objects of worship. At a later stage animals and other objects of nature were worshipped. This was not, however, the original type of nature worship but a later development of it.

Primitive man could not realize the full meaning of death, and could not think of the person who died as leaving this world entirely. He thought that the spirit must be simply leaving the body or going upon a journey, and that it was, therefore, apt to return. Dreams might have increased this belief in spirits; in fact, Spencer declared that belief in spirits came from dreams. This conception of death, supplemented by dreams, led primitive man to believe that the spirit was able to leave the body and the dwell at a distance from it, or upon death to come back and perhaps enter into some object of nature, as a tree or animal, or to return to his old hut.

Sometimes the savage would look upon this spirit as a friend and sometimes as an enemy, depending largely upon whether the person was liked or jeared in life. Efforts were made to appease the ill will or gain the goodwill of a spirit by means of prayers, offerings, praise, and even flattery.

Development and Cultivation

While many of these customs and actions seem strange to us, the theory is logical enough. The belief in spirits seems to have been almost universal, at least the belief that the spirit lived after the body was gone. Herbert Spencer, imagining that religion originated from this belief, worked out his famous "ghost theory" of the origin of religion. He suggested that a savage, because of overeating, or from some such cause, might have a dream, perhaps of going on some hunting expedition, and yet he told next morning by his wife or by someone else that he had not stirred from his hut, but had tossed about all night; that he might see his reflection in the pool of water; and that in this way he would come to the natural conclusion that he had a double, which could leave him at will, especially when he slept.

From this belief in a double personality came ancestor worship. Animal and nature worship also originated in this way, according to Spencer, as a development of ancestor worship. In fact, Spencer attempted to show that all religions originated in this fashion. The theory was, of course, built upon too narrow a foundation, for while possibly some religions began in this manner, it is preposterous to assert that all religions were thus evolved. Ancestor worship still survives in many countries, most noticeably in China, simply because the people have not emerged as yet from this stage. In some countries it preceded nature worship, at least in certain forms, but as a rule ancestor worship came later, being an outgrowth of nature worship.

In fetish worship, an object is idolized because it is supposed to be the residence of a spirit or god. In this way any striking object of nature or any unusual object might be worshipped; it might be carried around as a kind of talisman. This type of religion might be called a combination of the preceding two; it is an outgrowth of them.

Worship of Supreme : The worship of a supreme, all-powerful being was sometimes found among primitive men. This at first took the form of polytheism, or the worship of several gods, but it gradually changed to monotheism through the calling out of the minor or less important gods. Sometimes this supreme being was merely a mountain, a tree or the sun, but it stood out as supreme over other deities. Gradually, this belief became loftier and purer, the worship of the lesser divinities being abandoned. This gave the foundation for the highest form of religion.

When a savage looked upon a god as a person, he naturally thought that the god needed food and other necessities of life; so he offered them. Sometimes these sacrifices were destroyed entirely. In countries where cannibalism was, or had been, practised these sacrifices might take the form of human beings, generally slaves or children. Hindu mothers even today frequently throw their babies into the Ganges as offerings. The early Greeks before starting upon a great expedition would sacrifice a beautiful girl, and the Spartans allowed their children to be flogged to death before the temple of Diana. The sacrifice of animals succeeded human sacrifice. In this way, especially among the Jews sacrifices took the nature of a sign of atonement for sins, or as a means of warding off punishment.

Concept of Prayer : Prayer is the logical attendant of sacrifices. It is the method of telling what is the object of making the sacrifice, it states the request that is made of the gods. Its importance increases with the rise of the religion.

Because of the religious association, objects connected with worship attain an air of sacredness, especially the fetishes, temples and places of worship. Any object or ceremony or service connected with religion becomes invested with sacredness. This still continues, and at times has become more pronounced with the progress of religion.

Vitally, related to and infinitely confused with early religion was magic. Professor Thomas takes that magic with the savage is of higher importance than religion. In nearly every tribe there was some person or persons similar to the witch doctor or the medicine men of the American Indians, whose function was to interpret signs, foretell the future, exercise power over the spirits, either in warding off calamity or in bringing things desired, cure the sick, and do those things which were beyond the power of the average man. As the religion became elevated, it gradually purged itself of these impurities, although most religions are not yet entirely clear of them.

Formerly, religion was of greater social importance than it is today; it absorbed more of the life of the savage. The gods had to be consulted before any important event took place, even after the state of savagery was passed. The Romans would never undertake any war or military expedition or engage in any battle unless the signs were favourable. The king or chief was also high priest at first, and in that stage church and state were one; it was not until very recent times that they became separated particularly in Christianity. Religious dances formed an important feature in religion. Religious feasts were held in times of harvest, and on other special occasions.

The moral effect of religion was chiefly in the way of producing tribal solidarity, and in restraining the tendencies to excess. It would tolerate those things which were of help to the tribe, and forbid those things which were injurious. It developed tribal loyalty, obedience to the chief, observance of tribal customs, and submergence of individual interests to tribal interests. In practice it acted as a strong conservative force, checking and discouraging individual initiative and independence. On the other hand, it was a hinderance to reform and gave little chance for original thinking; in fact it discouraged it. While the primitive religion held the individual from excess, it often was an impediment to progress.

Of the three seats of early culture, Chaldea (or Early Babylon), Egypt, and China, Chaldea was in all probability not only the earliest but the centre from which the other two spread out. The Hebrews, borrowed heavily from Early Babylon, the Jewish Legal Code being traced back in many particulars to the Code of Hammurabi, which antedated the laws of Jews by many centuries. The people of Early Babylon were cosmopolitan; in fact, Hammurabi, the first great king, ruled a collection of many peoples, who spoke many tongues. As a consequence their religion was not a pure religion but a mixture of many beliefs. There was a belief in spirits; the world was thought to be full of such spirits, which could be controlled only by means of charms and magic. These spirits were supposed to be responsible for all pains and disease as well as misfortune. Nature worship was also interwoven into the spirit worship. There was a vast number of gods, both great and minor. Most of the gods were represented by animal emblems. The religion was too complicated to develop into a real state religion. When Babylon was absorbed into the Persian Empire, it lost its religion, which was not sufficiently developed to survive.

***Earliest Religion* :** The earliest religion which we find in Egypt was the resultant of many still earlier religions. It contained remnants of animal worship, particularly the ibis, cow and cat, and by the fact that those animals were sacred in the provinces in which they were worshipped. Alongside of this was the worship of higher gods, such as the sun, moon and sky. Chief among these gods was *Ra,* meaning "sun". There was a family of gods similar to the Greek family of gods, consisting of *Osiris,* the sun god of *Abydos,* his wife and sister, *Isis,* and brother, Set.

While *Osiris* was the embodiment of height and purity, *Set* was supposed to represent the opposite; he was the embodiment of all evil, particularly the desert, darkness, the hot south wind, sickness, and, what seems strange to us, red hair. Between *Osiris* and *Set* there was constant hostility, and we have the story *of* the death of *Osiris,* the search for the body of *Iris,* and the avenging of the death *of* the son, *Horus.* Egyptian religion approached monotheism through the survival of the stronger gods and the predominance of one god in each city or province. Egyptian temples were residences of the gods, rather than places of worship, images being placed in the temples so that the gods might enter them.

The worship of the gods was celebrated being a public rather than a private function. Egyptian religion included a belief in future existence. The pyramids were erected as tombs for the kings. The belief was that the soul accompanied the sun god to the underworld, where its lot depended upon how its possessor had lived or had treated the god during life. While Egyptian religion was an advance over what had preceded, it showed possibilities of becoming a pure spiritual faith, and embodied in it many ideas of correct living and of duty to neighbours, it became degenerate and corrupt with the decay of Egyptian civilization and the crumbling of that nation as a political state.

However, both the Babylonian and Egyptian cults show how religions develop through the coming together of many religions. The Babylonian and Egyptian religions were too cold and formal to become great, although they exerted some influence upon the development of other religious beliefs.

Ancient Religions

Greek Religions : The religion of Greece passed through the same stages as other religions; however, because of the high state of culture attained, the rapid growth of civilization, and the favourable environment, which stimulated the imagination and the philosophical and religious development, it developed much more rapidly than the religions of other countries. While nature and spirit worship at a certain stage existed in Greece, they were early abandoned. The gods were functional gods and had distinctly human attributes; they had not only human bodies but even human passions; they hated, loved, were jealous, and even stole like human beings, despite the belief that they were endowed with super-human powers. The Greek gods formed a family, Zeus being the father and Hera the mother. The Athenians after establishing a vast number of temples and shrines, erected one to the "unknown god" for the fear that they had omitted one. Each city had its patron god or goddess; also each divinity represented a particular function.

With Greek religion went a belief in a future world inhabited by spirits who received rewards or punishments, particularly the latter. Perhaps the greatest effect of Greek religion was the inspiration it gave to art, specially sculpture and poetry. The religious festivals and games offered an incentive to physical development. While the gods were supposed to be guardians of justice, righting wrongs and meeting out punishments, and in this way to hold men in restraint, the moral effect was almost negligible, for the gods represented the prevailing standards of morals. The Greek religion did not hold out a goal to be attained, such as the Nirvana of Buddhism or the Heaven of Christianity which easily supplanted the Greek religion when the early Christian apostles preached the new faith.

Roman Religion : Rome offers perhaps the best example of the survival of the fittest in regard to religion. Early Roman religion was animistic, the nature spirits were worshipped or appealed to; sacrifices and worship was given in exchange for protection and help as it was bargain or contract, not a feeling of love. There was the worship of *Lares,* or household gods, who were the spirits of the ancestors. This led to the introduction of the worship of defied persons, like *Romulus* and later *Julius Caesar.* Roman religion became a part of the state, no war or enterprise being undertaken without consulting the gods and then not carried out unless the omens were favourable.

The religion was so complicated that it required a priestly class to interpret the will of the gods or the wishes of the spirits. However, the Romans took over almost entirely the Greek worships, especially their conception of the gods, only giving the Greek gods and goddesses Latin names, and carried out their worship to such an extent that many people think of the Roman religion merely as an outgrowth of Greek religion.

However, through competition the best elements of the different religions survived until finally Islam emerged not only as a religion but as a beacon light to humanity. Prior to that a stage had come when Christianity became the dominant religion; increasing in force after the fall of Rome as a world power, it became incorporated into the state and ruled Europe for a long time through the Catholic Church, which later split into the Roman and Greek Catholic Churches.

While there are many religions in the world, five stand out above all others, not only in the number of adherents but in their social influence. To complete this study of the evolution of religion, we must discuss the essential features of Confucianism, Brahmanism, Buddhism, Christianity and Islam.

Chinese Religion : The most influential of the three religions of China—Confucianism, Taoism, and Buddhism—Confucianism is an integral part of Chinese civilization, which has been looking backward for centuries. While named after Confucius, a Chinese sage and philosopher who is supposed to have lived from 550 to 478 B.C., it antedated him by many centuries, for Confucius was chiefly a collector and preserver of the wisdom of the past, although he did add somewhat to it. He collected this knowledge and handed it down in written form, of which there are now preserved five or six books.

To those books is added a second set of classics edited by disciples of Confucius, especially Mencius, which are supposed to contain teachings of Confucius.

The worship of Confucius himself is the chief addition to the worship of the time prior to him. Confucianism in reality is not much of a religion according to the general conception of religion, being more a system of philosophy. There is nothing cruel or revolting or degrading in the worship, no mythology, no idols, no priestly class. Everything is dignified and well arranged. It is essentially a religion of form, in which doctrine counts for very little and action is not governed by any code of ethics. The main thing is to do the proper thing at the proper time in the proper way.

The objects of worship are of three classes :

(a) heaven, the principal Chinese deity, by which is meant the sky—the blue air—which is conceived of as a living force, and worshipped for itself and not as the residence of some other power;

(b) the spirits, all good, generally spoken of in the plural sense, there being one for each object of nature, and conceived of, not as moving around, but as being organized into a priesthood, and worshipped in a body;

(c) ancestors, the worship of whom is the prescribed working religion of each individual. Belief in the future world is centred in the idea of the continuation of the family; it is thought to be the duty of everybody to marry and rear descendants in order to carry on this worship. Tablets are placed in the home to the memory of these ancestors; and to these tablets the spirits of the ancestors are supposed to come when properly invoked. The emperor must sacrifice to all the emperors who preceded him, and the magistrates to all who have held the office before them. This homage is given, not for the sake of peace or aid, but because of gratitude and devotion. The person offering sacrifices prays to be worthy of offering them. There is no self humiliation, for the Chinese take their religion complacently.

Under Confucianism religion is not separated from daily life; it is a ritual fixed by tradition and carried out by custom and habit. As taught by Confucius religion becomes a theory of government and morals. In the way of social influence Confucianism is largely responsible for the complacence of the Chinese; it was one of the causes of the backwardness of China in the past. Closely akin to Confucianism is Taoism, a cult founded by Lao-Tsze, which in its early days consisted by a higher code of morals and self-discipline than Confucianism.

It degenerated, however, into magic and, while it later borrowed the apparatus of religion from Buddhism and became recognized, it has never obtained a vital hold upon the people. Confucianism never grappled with the social problems of the day or attempted to reform things; it has merely tried to hold them as they were. Its effect has been to keep its adherents from advancing. Unlike many religions it has not degenerated or become corrupt, but has remained much the same as it was two thousand years ago.

Vedic Religion : One of the old religions is Brahmanism. It is the direct outgrowth of the anterior Vedic religion, which was brought into India by her conquerors. The Vedic religion was an advance over the previous faith of Babylon, but was a combination of spirit and nature worship. Upon this Vedic faith was based Brahmanism, which cast aside the old ideas of nature worship in favour of an inward subjective religious attitude. New gods were introduced, chief of whom is *Brahma*—the creator, *Vishnu*—the preserver and *Siva*—the destroyer. The conception of *Brahma* is not only an external deity, but is also present in one's own experience. Brahmanism teaches that service to religion is done by getting away from mankind, by isolation and separation of self from the sin of the world. There is no distinction between good and bad deeds, for to be holy one must keep clear from all that degrades or confuses. Salvation is a matter of individual concern, there being no desire to spread the light or to save others. Religion is gained through isolation, to be holy one must be alone.

Connected with Brahmanism are sacred books, including the sacred Vedic literature, supposedly inspired writings, hymns, treatises and law books; there are also the famous laws of Manu, compiled about 2000 B.C., a collection of rules designated to govern the entire Hindu population. There is also required of the Brahmans a complicated system of sacrifices, which have become a matter of form. The social effects have been great, but since only the individual is concerned, group morality has not been fostered. Brahmanism has not attempted to relieve the sufferings of the people or lay hold of the problems of society.

It has allowed the people of India to live in poverty and misery; it has made no attempt to break down the caste system, but on the contrary has upheld it and encouraged it, because the priestly class are on top of the social pyramid. Neither it has attempted to elevate the position of woman; it has held her down. These failures indicate its great weakness, because a religion to be successful must aid humanity. Brahmanism has simply not done it. Its key-note is isolation and self-salvation.

It has, however, paved the way for Buddhism, which was an outgrowth of it and which is the culmination of Indian religions.

Buddhism was originated in India but it has flourished as a religion in China, Japan, Tibet, Java, Sumatra, Siam (Thailand), Burmah and Ceylon (Sri-Lanka) and is divided into northern and southern branches. While considered a revolt from Brahmanism, it is simply the evolution of Brahmanism into a higher form.

Buddhism : Buddhism is a religion without a god, without prayer, without a priesthood, without worship. It is a religion which owes its success not to its theology or to its ritual, for it has neither, but to its moral sentiment and to its external organization. The term "Buddha" means the Enlightened One or the Enlightened; there were supposed to have been twenty-four of these Enlightened Ones before Gautama, the founder of Buddhism, appeared. They were human but were supposed to have reached a super-human condition by passing through periods of renunciation and of compassion for man's suffering and to have entered human life and borne the burden of man's sufferings. It is not negative like Brahmanism, but positive and constructive. One achieves happiness through a life of right living; thus the religion has an extremely high code of morals and ethics. It offers Nirvana, a place of liberation and freedom, which one can reach even before death. The way of reaching it is by a life of self-renunciation and by suppression of the desires and passions. Under Buddhist morality, which includes equality towards all and respect for all living beings, are five rules of righteousness, which resemble the ten commandments; they are binding on all followers of Buddha. They are:

(1) not to kill any living being;

(2) not to take that which is not given;

(3) to refrain from adultery;

(4) to speak no untruth; and

(5) to abstain from all intoxicating liquors.

Devout members and the following:

(1) not to eat after mid-day;

(2) not to be present at dancing, singing, the playing of music, or acting;

(3) not to use wreaths, ointments, scents, or personal ornaments;

(4) not to use a high or broad bed, and

(5) to possess no silver or gold.

Because there is no god, prayers, sacrifices and priests are not necessary. Man must save himself by his own efforts. While under Buddhism there are no priests, there are wanderers who leave home and travel about, teaching and practising the religion. They resemble the monks and friars of the Catholic Church.

Buddhism became marvelously popular because of its simplicity, morality and broad humanity. But because of its openness and freedom it has degenerated, becoming contaminated with magic and superstition in every land where it has gone. It was too lofty to be appreciated, and therefore was not suitable as a working religion to the people with whom it dealt. While a lofty religion, Buddhism even at its best is a sad religion, regarding human life as evil. While having deep compassion for the sufferings of man, it has taken no means of reforming the world, concerning itself only with winning individual adherents; so it has had little social effect, although it has not been reactionary as Brahmanism has been. On the whole, it is an exceedingly free religion, allowing its followers to worship as they see fit or not to worship at all.

Later Religions

Christianity: After discussing these religions, we focus our attention on Christianity. Any treatment of Christianity should be prefaced by one of Judaism, of which it is an outgrowth, but because of lack of space and general familiarity with the principles of Judaism—such a treatment may be omitted. At the time of the coming of Christ, Judaism had become hardened into mere formality and needed rejuvenation. Christianity fulfilled that need by replacing the religion of form by one of love.

When Christianity appeared, the world was in need of a higher religion, hence its rapid rise and influence. It, later, became hardened into too definite a system under the Roman and Greek Catholic Churches, and still later under many of the Protestant sects, perhaps most noticeably under the Puritans and the Church of England, but its constant trend is to throw off the control of individuals and the opinions of a few, and allow greater and greater individual freedom, especially in the Protestants denominations. To sum up, Christianity is the religion proclaimed by Jesus Christ. Its principles are set forth in the New Testament, and its churches abound all over the world. Although Christianity has had a great influence on Western civilization, the West is finding it increasingly difficult to live up to her own Christian principles.

Islam : Islam, last of all the religions but by no means the least, came in the sixth century A.D. as the climax and the crowning glory of all the religions known to this world. It is the eternal source of light to the humanity which was still groping in pitch darkness. The dawn of Islam saw the rays of its light all over the globe like the rising sun and continued as an unending and ceaseless battle against want and hunger, ignorance and disease and a pleothora of problems with which humanity has always been suffering. It aims at establishing a Welfare State. It is a religio-political concept of State in which temporal and spiritual are not kept in water-tight-compartments. It is the very negation of the Christian dogma which preaches: Render unto Caesar the things that are Caesar's and render unto God the things that are God's.

In Islam Caesar and God are not two separate entities. It is not torn by the dualism of state and church whose separation has been deemed an absolute dogma in Christianity. In Islam God and Universe, spirit and matter, church and state, are organic to each other. Man is not the citizen of a profane world to be renounced in the interest of a world of spirit situated elsewhere. To Islam matter is spirit, realizing itself in Space and Time. To sum up, unity of God and catholicity of Islam are the corner stones of this great religion which have made it universal for all times and climes spreading to each and every nook and corner of the world.

World of Islam

The followers of Islam constitute one-fifth of the entire human race. The Muslim world straddles over vast regions of the continents of Asia and Africa. This region has been the cradle of a large number of higher civilizations. Economically, its potential is great. Politically, it is "the great third of the world." And, to crown them all, it is the world of Islam— it is the upholder of a great ideology which is not merely a religion but a way of life. For long Islam has been misunderstood and misinterpreted in the West. It is one of the most queer facts of history that despite West's strides in quest of knowledge and learning, despite the centuries of contact between the world of Islam and the West, Islam is perhaps the best known and the most misunderstood religion in the West.

However, it is a happy augury that now there are welcome moves to develop correct understanding between Islam and the West. This is a very pleasant mission indeed. But this is not possible without a proper understanding of the causes of conflict and distrust which have separated the two. Therefore, a sincere attempt should be made to find out the causes of the discontent, conflict and distrust of several centuries. If we succeed in doing so, new vistas of cooperation and concord will open up to the entire humanity, which in fact will be a great service to the humanity as well as to the religion.

2

Concept of Faith

What is religion? Is it a set of dogmas, mythological beliefs or mere rituals? Is it a mere slogan? Is it a cult? Is it a body of rules and regulations formulated by some individual or group of individuals? Is it ritualistic worshipping and no more? Is it a *mantra* for turning poverty into riches? Is it a money-purchased ticket for paradise? "If it is not all this, then at best it is one's personal affair," the modernist will say and he may further add: "Since it is my personal affair, you need not bother about it".

This attitude has become fossilized over the centuries and has come to be the accepted viewpoint the world over, even in the Muslim countries. You may claim to be a Muslim, well and good. But whether you conform to the basic fundamentals of your religion in actual practice or not, no one bothers. Rather, no one dares to offend you by questioning you about your personal affair. None has a right to interfere in the personal affairs of others. This is the prevailing situation the world over. But has this the sanction of any true religion? Let us examine critically.

Definition and Meaning

First of all let us review how this attitude came to be popular. No true religion ever confines itself to the spiritual aspect of human personality only to the exclusion of its intellectual and temporal aspects. All religions lay down rules for the spiritual as well as temporal guidance of man as much in his relations to society as in his relations to his soul or to the ultimate reality.

Eternal Religion

True religion knows no duality of body and soul. It encompasses man's whole personality in all its manifold aspects and varied relations. Religion deals with man as a whole and supervises all his activities, physical, intellectual or spiritual. In the early history of all great religions this unity of man is observable. It was only later on when ease-loving persons found it difficult to maintain a coherence between their secular and sacred activities that a bifurcation came to be accepted between the two. Religion crystallised into lifeless dogma that could be safely entrusted to the clergy.

The common worldly-wise man was left to do as he wished with little danger of interference from the other side. Religion and politics came to be segregated and the result in Allama Iqbal's words, was barbarism. This cleavage between religion and politics was more pronounced in Christianity where the Church was officially separated from the State some centuries back. Religion was no more a dynamic force in human society. It was just a personal affair of the individual. The hint was quickly picked up by all European nations and with the passage of time the attitude was accepted by the Muslim societies as well when the latter came under European domination and influence.

The result was evident. People lost sight of the true teachings of their religion and the slogan "religion is a personal affair" came to be accepted by all—Muslims and non-Muslims alike. This state of affairs practically put an end to call to do right and dissuade from doing wrong and the sporadic attempts of some zealous religious leaders and workers as well as some good Muslims to bring youth back to religion were often met with ridicule or went unheaded. This ultimately led our society to moral bankruptcy.

The Torn World : The present-day world is torn between the materialistic philosophies of Marxism and Capitalism. It becomes all the more pronounced with the advancement in science and technology. Modern science is materialistic in theory and mechanical in its practical approach. In framing theories about its subject-matter, it relies upon sense perception as the only source of knowledge and considers material phenomena as the only knowable, i.e. scientifically demonstrable, reality. In practice, its main interest is to develop machines, or handle machine-like things, by applying its theories to material objects.

Material Objects : It has the same approach towards human activities. The method applied to the study of material objects is also used, with necessary modifications, to frame scientific theories about human behaviour. An attempt is made, in the light of these theories, to control man as a naturally-built machine. Whatever aspects of human behaviour can be observed through sense perception are accepted as the data of human sciences, but the aspects which are not so observable are rejected or ignored as "unscientific." For example, man's creative experience of self, the visionary experience of a poet or a philosopher, and religious experience of a prophet or a saint are considered to be beyond the scope of scientific inquiry, and without any scientific content. Either their truth is altogether denied as a distortion and unreality as by the strictly materialist philosophy, *or* they are believed, as by the idealist philosophy, to imply a truth which is not scientifically demonstrable.

Modern philosophy, which has developed on the lines of modern science and claims to be "scientific in spirit basing its conclusions on facts rather than religious beliefs," does not fully recognise to be a "hand-maiden" of religion, it has become the interpreter of science. Its new job is to organise the results of various natural and social sciences in a picture of the world as a whole, not allowing any place of importance to religion. Based on "pure" science and pursuing a course independent of religion modern philosophy has been led to two distinct world outlooks, i.e. the dialectical materialist outlook and the Western idealist philosophy.

Materialist Philosophy : The dialectical materialist philosophy totally rejects the truth of religion and believes in the sense-oriented science like a religious faith. True to the materialist and mechanical spirit of science, it views the ultimate Reality as Matter in Motion, i.e., a big moving machine which can be scientifically studied and mechanically handled through human brain, itself a highly evolved matter. However, this big machine is not a single mechanical device, but consists of diverse mechanisms (i.e. motions of matter) which are qualitatively different from each other. These mechanisms, or "forms of motion", as they are called by this philosophy, are classified as mechanical, physical, chemical, biological and social—the quality of individuality missing in them because there is no room for it in a mechanical set-up.

The term "dialectics" is used to associate the element of change and growth with motion, but this does not change the predominantly mechanical character of the material dialectics. A motion of matter, which is devoid of voluntary self or creative individuality, is necessarily mechanical and cannot be called dialectical in the true sense. The true dialectics must involve a creative factor, which alone can make forward movement and dynamic growth possible.

A mechanical motion is one which results from a specific mechanism, i.e., a specific collective arrangement or apparatus of material objects, and not from an inherent creative factor that may be controlling or moving material objects from within. Dialectical materialism is predominantly mechanical because although it recognises an element of growth and change in phenomena, yet it tries to interpret it to be the result of specific material conditions rather than an inherent creative factor that may be moving the matter from within. It denies that the element of change and growth can be injected into the material motion only through a creative will.

For example, it believes that a social movement or revolution is caused by a specific mode of material (economic) conditions and not by the creative will and consciousness of an individual or a group, or by the religious awakening of a people. No doubt, man's will and consciousness are also said to play a role in the social revolution, but this role is merely that of a superstructure, or a by-product, and not that of a prime mover of the revolution.

Even a prophet's message is interpreted to be a by-product of material conditions rather than a revealed Word of God. The failure on the part of material dialectics to comprehend the creative role of will and consciousness is mainly due to an anti-religious prejudice, and the strictly materialistic outlook inherited from science. A socialist form of economic planning, which is the ultimate goal of this philosophy, may force the people to work like a machine, but it can never inspire them to be willing partners in social reconstruction unless it also recognises the creative and determining character of their will and consciousness.

Labour is believed, by the dialectical materialists, to be the prime mover of social dialectics, but the concept of labour is confined to the production of such material and "spiritual" (i.e., of the character of a mere superstructure or by-product) values as are needed for man's material, rather than his creative or religious survival. Moreover, the labour process of the production of material and "spiritual" values, according to this view, can be mechanically controlled through socialistic planning, and does not involve any creative or religious factor that may inspire the individuals to be selfless "co-workers" of God.

Believing that man basically strives to fulfil his material (metabolic-economic) needs dialectical materialism considers him selfish by nature, as also taught by modern science. That is why this philosophy is reluctant to give man's self the role of a free agent—an agent that can decide and direct its own course of action—thus, depriving it of any opportunity to usurp other's rights by its selfish pursuits. The only way to check man's materialist-selfish nature, according to this philosophy, is to make him work under a socialist mode of production where no room is left for self-seeking and exploitative activity and every individual is forced to work, willingly or unwillingly, for collective good. However, it is not quite correct to consider man as basically materialist and selfish "by nature". He can be made a selfless and willing participant in social reconstruction if his religious consciousness is also awakened and recognised as a reality. Having no vested interests to serve, the dialectical materialistic philosophy can very easily see through the religious truth if only it broadens its epistomological outlook to include the religious experience along with the sense perception.

Second World Outlook : The second world outlook, the Western idealist philosophy, does not outright reject the truth of religion like dialectical materialism, but it also bases its conclusions on scientific discoveries rather than religious beliefs. It does not give religion its due place in world outlook and accepts it, at the most, as mere ritualism or another worldly affair of human soul. And that too because religion, in such a position, can be used as an instrument of exploitation, and this philosophy has to serve the capitalist exploitative system by all means, scientific or unscientific.

The Western philosophy is idealistic in so far as it believes that it is man's consciousness and self that determine the course of events and not the course of events—the material conditions—that determine man's consciousness and self. But this idealism is not based on the creative or religious concept of man's self, according to which he is a selfless vicegerent of God on this earth or a spirited selfless worker. Instead, it is based on the narrow scientific concept of man's self which views him as selfish by nature—always running after his material gains and motivated merely by his animal-like instincts. According to this view, every individual has the right to work for his own benefit even at the cost of others' rights.

Such a concept of self gives exploiting classes, as the dialectical materialists rightly allege, a free hand to exploit and the working classes a mental justification for being exploited. True idealism, based on the deeper anti-exploitative nature of man's self can, however, come only through religious consciousness. The Western philosophy remains blind to it partly because of its sense-oriented outlook and partly because of its exploitative interests. It never dares to probe into the revolutionary meanings of religion, which is against all exploitation, and tries to maintain it in its present distorted form. If at all "scientific" investigations are made into religious consciousness, they deal merely with the whereabouts of human soul after death and not with its requirements in this life, which is as real as life after death. The human soul, in these investigations is visualised to be a sort of non-observable material object rather than a directing force which "proceedeth from my Lord's *Amr*".

So the failure of the Western idealist philosophy to comprehend the true nature of "idealism", which should be based on a deeper concept of self, and the inability of dialectical materialism to realise the true nature of dialectics, which should also include the creative and religious aspect, is mainly because of their total allegiance to the sense-oriented science and disregard for religious truth. It is strange that while they claim to be based on facts and to be scientific in spirit they adopt a very unscientific attitude towards religion. They fail to recognise that the religious truth at its own level of experience, is quite scientific, although it may look unscientific, superhuman, supersensible, or even non-existent at the ordinary level of sense experience. "Religion is not physics or chemistry" says Iqbal, "....it really aims at interpreting a totally different region of human experience". The conflict between religion and science, he adds, "is due to the misapprehension that both interpret the same data of experience. We forget that religion aims at reaching the real significance of a special variety of human experience."

Total View : Although religion is a total view of Reality and not sectional and piecemeal like various sciences, yet it has all the characteristics of a scientifically true knowledge and can provide as scientific a world outlook as the modern philosophy claims to do—an outlook which is, however, epistemotogically wider than modern philosophy. Let us now briefly see how and why the religious truth can be called scientific.

The first characteristic of a science is that it is based on experience. And so is religion. As Iqbal writes: "Religion is essentially experience—known in this sense by the unfortunate name of mysticism and recognised the necessity of experience as its foundation long before science learnt to do so. It is as critical of its level of (religious) experience as naturalism (science) is of its own (sensory) level". But whereas science excludes religion from its limited view of reality, religion being an expression of the whole truth, does not reject science as a true form of knowledge and establishes the truth of sense perception as a part of man's total knowing self besides his religious faith.

The second characteristic of the scientific truth, based on sense perception is that it is communicable and verifiable. Being a special inner capacity of varying stages (the prophetic experience being the highest stage, unattainable by saints and ordinary individuals), religious experience also reveals a truth which can be communicated and verified. If that was not so, prophets and saints would never have been able to communicate their message and there would have been no individuals and communities following and verifying the truth of their message. The religious communities could not be organised on the basis of a mere blind faith. Religious experience, no doubt, is primarily subjective, but its contents can be made objective through words and deeds and verified to be true by others, according to their capacity.

The third characteristic of the scientific truth is that it can successfully be put into practice because it corresponds to the real nature of things. "The question whether objective truth can be attributed to human thinking," says Karl Marx, "is not a question of theory, but is a practical question. In practice, man must prove the truth of his thinking". The only proof of the truth of an idea a scientific theory or an ideology, according to modern philosophy, is provided in practice, i.e., the scientific experiment or the socio-political life of a people. Religion also, throughout the ages has proved its truth through practice i.e., the "pragmatic test," in the words of Doctor Muhammad Iqbal. How could religious communities exist till today, and their beliefs still inspire their individualist religion, being in accord with the true qualities of human nature, had not practically solved their various problems?

The fourth characteristic of a science is that it is a systematic knowledge organized on the basis of general principles about a particular section of natural phenomena as framed in the light of sense perception. Religious knowledge is also systematic, based on certain fundamental principles about the nature of man and universe and their relationship with God as revealed through religious experience. Not only is this knowledge systematic itself but, being revealed within, it has also the dialectical power to organise individuals and communities into well organised systems, which move from within creatively rather than mechanically. Man has not to apply religious knowledge like scientific theories, on external objects from outside but he applies it to himself from within; and the truth of religion is proved by its practical suitability for such an application to various aspects of man's life, individual, socio-political, economic, educational etc., etc.

Now let us examine unity and diversity of religions. All true religions have been proclaiming Oneness of God. From this viewpoint there is a basic unity in all true religions. They all have a common origin. Outwardly, there have been many differences in various religions, but inwardly they all have preached the same basic realities. Their names, details and rituals have varied over the ages but their essence has always remained unchanged.

There are only two basic religions in the world. The one is *Deen-e-Batil* (the False Religion) and the other is *Deen-e-Haq* (the True Religion). The false religion, in whatever form it may appear is man-made. The true religion has been revealed by God through His prophets in different ages and at different places. Right from Prophet Noah to Prophet Muhammad (peace be upon them all) all Apostles of God had preached this True Religion, which is characterised by two basic concepts: the Oneness of God and the Accountability of man for his actions in the life hereafter. Apparently one may ascribe different religions to the prophets who preached them. One may talk of the Religion of Abraham, of Moses, of Christianity, or of Muhammadanism, but in reality they are only different versions of the same True Religion.

Concept of Diversity : The concept of diversity of religions has been created by Western scholars. These people cannot think of various religions as creations of the prophets who preached them. They speak of prophets as 'founders' of their religions. Clearly, when one bases one's studies and observations upon superficial things, one loses sight of the common thread running through them all. This leads to the study of various religions as segregated from one another, with the result that when these scholars notice any point of similarity between two religions they hasten to conclude that the 'latter' religion has borrowed the idea from the 'former' religion. Naturally they notice similarities between the teachings of the Quran and the older Scriptures, and accuse the Prophet of Islam (peace be upon him) of having borrowed the various concepts from Christianity or Judaism or Zoroastrianism, and of composing the Holy Quran himself. They lose sight of the fact that all True Religions have basically preached the same two concepts: the Oneness of God and the Accountability of man for his actions. No prophet has ever declared to be 'founder' of his religion.

All have declared that they are 'Messengers' of God and have come to remind the people of the two basic concepts. The Prophet Noah preached "Worship Allah, fear Him and follow me" (71:3). But the people replied: "(O comrades) do not forsake your idols" (71:23). The Prophet Hud delivered this message to his nation, the Aadites: "O my nation, worship Allah besides Whom there is no God, you are only putting forth false claims" (11:50). His people replied, "We shall not forsake our idols simply because you say so and we are not going to believe you". (11:52). The Prophet Saleh said to his people the Thamud, "O my nation, worship Allah besides Whom there is no God" (11:61). They replied, "Do you forbid us from worshipping those (idols) whom our forefathers have been worshipping, we have doubts about what you are calling us to believe" (11:62).

Logical View

The Prophet Abraham said to his father and his nation, "In place of Allah do you worship these idols who can neither benefit nor harm you in any way. Damn you and those whom you worship besides Allah. Don't you see reason? (21:67). The people said, "Burn him down and support your idols" (21:68). This same true Religion was stressed by Abraham and Yaqub for their descendants, "O my children, this is the religion chosen by God for you, so do not die except as Muslims (sincere followers)" (2:1 32). The same lesson was taught by Prophet Joseph to his companions in prison, "O my co-prisoners, is it better to have so many gods or to have One All-Powerful God. Those besides Him whom you worship exist only in names coined by yourself or by your forefathers. God has not sent any authority for them. Power only belongs to Allah. He has ordered you not to worship anything except Him. This is the firm religion" (12:39-40). The Prophet Lot preached the same thing but was threatened by his people with banishment (26:167). Prophet Shoaib preached in Medina: "O my people, worship Allah besides Whom you have no god" (11:84). The people replied "O Shoaib, does your prayer order you to impel us to forsake our idols whom our ancestors have been worshipping" (11:87).

When Prophet Moses delivered his message to Pharaoh, he threatened, "If you talk of any god except me, I shall put you in prison" (26:29). Again when Jesus Christ came with explicit signs he said, "I have come to you with wisdom so that I may make clear to you the things in which you have been differing. So fear God and follow me. Allah is my Lord as well as yours, so worship Him only. This is the Right Path" (43:63-64). Last of all Prophet Muhammad (peace be upon him) was sent with the same message: "You (O Prophet) have been told the same things that Messengers before you were told" (41:43). And the teachings of Islam need no elaboration here. Islam is no man-made religion nor is it new. It has been in existence since the times of Noah. All prophets were Muslims (sincere servants of God). It is said of the *Shariah* of Muhammad (peace be upon him): "He has guided you to a *Shariah* (path) which was stressed by Noah; and what has been revealed to you, the same has been enjoined upon Abraham and Moses and Jesus, that uphold this religion and do not create differences in it" (42:13).

These were the prophets well-known to the Arabs. But the True Religion has been preached in all ages and all nations. "We sent a messenger to every nation that worship Allah and keep aloof from idols" (16:36). "And before you whosoever was sent as a Messenger was instructed with the same revelation that there is no god besides Me so worship Me only" (21:24-25).

This message was delivered to all nations by their prophets unamended because "No man has the authority that when God gives him the Book and the Decision and prophethood that he should say to the people 'leave Allah aside and worship me:' rather he would always say, Be sincere worshippers of God as you read and learn and teach the Scriptures; neither would he order you to take the angels and the prophets as your gods; would he order you to disbelieve after you have become believers" (3:79-80).

All True Religions, One : It is quite clear that all True Religions are basically one. They are, so to say, only different editions of the same 'Book'. The last and the most comprehensive edition is Islam. That is why Islam always enjoins upon its followers to keep this Unity of religions in view and to believe in all prophets and Sacred Scriptures. "Say, we believe in God and in the Book sent down upon us and in whatever was sent down upon Abraham and Ismail and Ishaq and Yaqub and their descendants, and in whatever was given by God to Moses and to Jesus and to other prophets, we do not discriminate one from the other, and we are sincere servants of God" (3:84).

Now compare this broad-mindedness of Islam with other religions. "The Jews say 'Christians have nothing' and the Christians say 'the Jews have nothing' whereas both these groups read the Scriptures" (2:213) Say: "We believe in God and the Book sent down upon us" (3:84) fully quoted above. And they say:

"None will enter paradise except those who are Jews or Christians" (2:111). In contrast with this narrow-mindedness Islam declares that every true religion ultimately leads to success. Indeed those who believe (in Islam) and those who turn Jews or Christians or Sabeans (etc.), among them whosoever believes in God and in the Hereafter and performs good acts, he shall find his reward with his Lord. These people will have nothing to fear, nor shall they feel sorrow" (2:62). Again, "Those who stick to their Scriptures and keep up prayers, so We shall not let the reward of the virtuous to go waste" (7:10). That is why Islam calls to itself and mankind, not because there is inherently any superiority of Islam over other religions but because Islam reminds the followers of other religions those basic teachings of all true religions which they have lost sight of—be it due to passage of time, or be it due to the fact that their clergy have passed on to them the Divine message in a distorted form.

"O People of the Book, come to a point common between you and us that we should not worship anything except God, that we should not make anything His partner, and that we should not take one another as our Lord except Allah, now if they turn away their faces, say: anyhow we are true believers" (3:64).

Final Settlement : The Prophet Muhammad (peace be upon him) was sent for this very purpose that he should settle down for ever the differences that had appeared in the True Religion over the centuries. "Call them to this very thing and be steadfast as you have been ordered. Do not go after the wishes of these people; rather say: I believe in the Book revealed by God. I have been ordered to do justice between you. Allah is our Lord as well as yours. We are responsible for our actions and you for yours. There is no dispute between you and us. Allah will bring us together one day and we have to return to Him" (42:15).

Islam, being the religion of all humanity, has been declared to be the only religion chosen by God (3:19). Here Islam is not just another name for Muhammedanism (as western scholars say), but it is the essence of all true religions. Its connotation is in its literal meaning of obedience and submission, and not as a technical term in the history of religions.

The Unity and continuity of the true religion is testified by the Holy Quran. "In the beginning people were one group. Then Allah sent the prophets as announcers of good tidings and as warners, and with them He sent True Book so that they may settle according to it those things in which people had created differences. These differences were created by none else than those very people who were given the Book and that too after they had received the clear orders, just out of mutual enmity. So Allah guided the believers towards that (Reality) about which the people had differences. Verily Allah guides to the right path whomsoever He desires" (2:213).

Let us now see the points of diversity in various religions. Verses 2:213, 2:253, 3:18, 10:19, 10:98, 11:119, 23:51-53, 41:45, 45:17 and 98:4, of the Holy Quran throw much light on the reasons and philosophy of diversity in religion. True religion, as has been shown above, is one, and has continued and has been revived by the Prophets throughout the ages. Whenever people lost sight of the teachings of the True Religion, God sent a prophet to remind them of the Truth. The differences were created by the people themselves and not by the prophets. The Diversity among religions relates only to the details of law and rituals as dictated by the exegencies of time and place. They are only different versions of the same Divine Message; different editions of the same book, so to say. All prophets delivered the same basic message. Those who accepted their message were called believers, others were disbelievers.

Thus, two basic groups were created. Later on, each group split up into various sects and creeds. Among Believers the rift was created by mutual prejudices and biases. Each group of scholars claimed to have the monopoly of understanding and teaching the Scriptures. Lust for popularity, power and material benefits led them to make changes in the World of God, omitting whatever was against their interests, adding whatever would add to their power over the people. Much the same happened among disbelievers. Various cults of worship sprang up. The number of gods kept on multiplying. Each tribe had its own set of idols. True religion—differences, reminders through prophets—the cycle was repeated throughout the centuries from the time of Noah to that of Muhammad (peace be upon him), when the Divine Message was preserved in its minutest details in the hearts of believers. Now that there was no longer any danger of change in the Divine Message there was no longer any need for sending a new prophet. The seal on prophethood was set with Muhammad (peace be upon him). The differences among the Muslim sects are only of a minor nature. There are no differences so far as basic teachings of Islam are concerned.

The root-cause of all diversity in religion has shown to be mutual enmity. Prejudices lead us away from the right path. We become prone to exaggerating defects of others and overlooking our own shortcomings. Distorted thinking leads us to revile others, leading to mutual enmity, hate, turmoil and even war. Any discrimination between the various forms of True Religion has been condemned by the Holy Quran. "Those who disbelieve in Allah and His Messengers and those who wish to create a gulf between Allah and His Apostles, and those who say: we believe in certain things and disbelieve others, and they seek to adopt a midway; in reality these people are disbelievers" (4: 150–152). This is because such people have fallen a prey to their biases, prejudices and self-interests. They accept what suits them, reject what does not suit them. The criterion for their acceptance or rejection of a religion is not based on principles but on personal likes and dislikes. They are led astray. Since all true religions seek to create in man healthy ways of thinking based on logical reasoning, therefore such rift-lovers have been called disbelievers.

Verse 11:19 of the Holy Quran says: "If your Lord had wished so He would have made all people one group; but they would go on creating differences except those on whom your Lord has shown mercy. He has created them for this". In another verse it is said: "The people were all one group in the beginning. Then they created differences, and if it had not been decreed by your Lord earlier, the matter in which they differ would have been settled once for all" (19:19). Now the question arises: if God hates discord why does He allow disputes to arise. He could nip the evil in the bud.

The reply to this objection is given in verse 5:48, "If God had wished He could have made all people one *Ummah,* but He desires to test you in what He has given you, so try to excel one another in doing good". Differences provide food for thought. If all people follow the same path it would become stereotyped. There will be no opportunities for thinking and judging. Differences provide men with the occasions to think, in order to discriminate between right and wrong. Use of these faculties is the wisdom behind disputes. A second advantage of disputes is that they provide righteous people with opportunities to call the wrong-doers to the right path (22:67). A third advantage is given in verse 10:19. If every time God comes to settle disputes the human faculties of thinking and deciding will rust. That is why settling down of religious disputes has been put off till the Day of Judgement. (22:17). God has made clear the right and the wrong. All human beings are required to use their discriminating faculties in choosing the right path.

Despite the philosophy behind diversity, human beings have been ordered to shun creating differences. The Muslim *Ummah* has been ordered emphatically: "And be not like disbelievers who created differences in their religion and divided into various sects" (30:31-32). "Be not like those who created differences and began to differ even after explicit orders have come to them" (3:105). Positively, we have been ordered to remain united. "Hold fast together the rope of Allah and get not scattered" (3:103).

3

Ideological Basis

The basic philosophy of Islam revolves round a set of beliefs and concepts. The Unity of God, Prophethood and the Hereafter are the irreducible fundamentals of this creed. These concepts are rooted in the basic awareness of man and the realities of human experience.

Human awareness springs from a sense of being which is inherent to man and his comtemplation of the physical universe. The Quran dwells on the reality of human consciousness generated by an interaction of the inner self of man and the outer world of nature. Sura Zariyat states:

> "On earth, and in yourselves, there are signs for firm believers. Can you not see? Heaven holds your sustenance and all that you are promised. I swear by the Lord of heaven and earth that this is true, as true as you are speaking now" (51:20-23).

The cardinal beliefs of Islam are not figments of imagination made sacrosanct by supernatural sanctions but emanate from deeper levels of human thought and experience.

As man delves into his own self and contemplates about his whereabouts he is irresistibly drawn towards four basic realisations which point to the reality of God. The universe is a vast mechanism of infinite complexity but it is perfectly ordered and regulated. Man has a limited vision and potentialities.

Perception of Faith

There are many areas of life and dimensions of the universe which defy his understanding. Man cannot comprehend the universe as a whole, much less control it. Sura Yunus states: "The unbelievers ask: Why has no sign been given him by his Lord? Say: Allah alone has knowledge of what is hidden. What if you will: I too am waiting. It is he who guides you by land and sea. You embark and as you set sail, rejoicing in a favourable wind, a raging tempest overtakes you. Billows surge upon you from every side and you fear that you are encompassed by death. You pray to Allah with all fervour. Deliver us from this peril and we will be truly thankful. Yet when he has delivered you, you commit evil in the land and act unjustly. Men, it is your own souls that you are corrupting" (10: 20-23).

Beneath the complex exterior of the universe lies a design, a pattern, a system. The Quran dilates on the impeccable order of the universe as a sign of divine being who presides over it. This is described being who presides over it. This is described as Hikmat Sura Yasin says:

> "Let the once-dead earth be a sign to them. We gave it life and from it produced grain for their sustenance. We planted it with the palm and the vine and watered it with gushing springs, so that men might feed on its fruit. It was not their hands which made all this. Should they not give thanks?

The night is another sign for men from the night We lifted the day—and they are plunged in darkness.

The sun hastens to its resting place: its course is laid for it by the Mighty One, the All-Knowing, We have ordained phases for the moon, which daily wanes and in the end appears like a bent and withered twig.

The Sun is not allowed to overtake the moon, nor does the night outpace the day. Each in its own orbits runs" (36: 36-43).

The Universe provides for man and caters to his purposes and requirements. This fact is epitomised by the Quranic term *Raboobiyat Sura Qaf* cogently states:

> "We spread out the earth and set upon it immovable mountains. We brought forth in it all kinds of delectable plants. A lesson and an admonition to penitent men. We send down blessed water from the sky with which We bring forth gardens and the harvest grain, and tall palm trees laden with clusters of dates, a sustenance for men; thereby giving new life to some dead land. Such shall be the Resurrection."
>
> (50: 7-11).

The universe holds out many benefits to man which are not accidental but form part of the cosmic design. This aspect of universal experience is embodied in the Quranic term *Naymat.* The mercy of God who has made the universe as the abode of man is not only unlimited but also continuous. The boundless mercy and munificence of God is described as *Rehman* while its continuity and timelessness as *Rahim. Sura Waqiah* states:

> You surely know of the first creation. Why, then do you not reflect? Consider the seeds you grow. Is it you that give them growth or We? If We pleased We could turn your harvest into chaff.

Consider the water that you drink. Was it you that poured it from the cloud or We? if We pleased We could turn it bitter. Why then do you not give thanks?

> Observe the fire which you light. Is it you that create its wood or We? We have made it a reminder for man
>
> (56: 58–74).

The awareness generated by human contemplation of the universe underpins the reality of God. Deep down the recesses of human psyche lies the evidence of a reality higher than man himself. The objective universe offers many hints and clues for the existence of a mighty power.

The concept of Prophethood flows from the concept of God with irresistible logic. God, who is the creator and sustainer of man enjoins upon him a certain way of life. The values and principles of life which God has framed for the salvation of man are communicated through revelation. The prophets are the messengers of God and teachers among men. They convey by word and deed the infallible message of God. The message of God was conveyed to man gradually. Islam marked the perfection of Divine communication and its apostle Muhammad (peace be upon him); embodied the finality of prophethood.

Although the fundamental beliefs of Islam are rooted in the introspective reaches of human personality and the many splendoured reality of physical universe, there are many queries and questions which agitate the mind and require a satisfactory answer. The prophets disabused the minds of men of erratic beliefs and mistaken notions. Apart from this, history bears proof of many societies which were so sunk in abysmal ignorance and superstition as to disallow any opportunities of contemplation. The prophets admonished such people to the right path and exposed their misconceptions.

The prophets drew the attention of ignorant and confused men to the reality of God and offered for human weal a full-fledged system of life. They were not day-dreamers but men of action who braved with courage and steadfastness the opposition of the uninformed. They were dynamic persons who changed the destiny of man by conviction and consistency. They were not closeted away from the ordeal and challenge which their environment posed. The prophets brought despairing men a message of hope and infused them with a noble purpose. Sura *Araf* states:

> Whenever, there come to you apostles from amongst you rehearsing my signs unto you. Those who follow them will be rewarded and those who reject them will be punished.

Sura Mujadala bears out the dignity and stature of the prophets:

> Believers, when you converse in private, do not speak with wickedness and enmity and disobedience towards the apostle, but with justice and piety. Have fear of Allah before whom you shall be brought together. Believers, when you confer with the apostle, give alms before such conference. That is best and purest for you. But if you lack the means, know that Allah is forgiving and merciful. (58:9-10).

How would the prophets be recognised? The Quran states that the first man on earth was a prophet, therefore, he needed no proof of himself. Thereafter, every prophet foretold the signs of his successor. Jesus told his people that he was the messenger of God as proclaimed to them by Moses. The Bible contained many hints and references about the advent of the Prophet (peace be upon him). The chapter of New Testament captioned Matthew makes many statements about the prophet who would follow Jesus. Prophesy reached its perfection and came to fulfilment in Muhammad (peace be upon him).

God's Supremacy

The Quran guarantees the triumph of good represented by Prophet (peace be upon him) over evil embodied in ignorant persons whom he confronts with the divine message. The prophets over-came by faith in God and personal resilience the storm of opposition raised by vested interest they sought to abolish. Those who persisted in evil despite the warning and admonition of apostle were exterminated from the face of earth by natural calamity. The Quran is unambiguous on this fact.

Those that oppose Allah and His Apostle shall be brought low as have been before them. We have sent down clear revelations. A shameful punishment awaits the unbelievers.

Do you see those that have befriended people with whom Allah is angry? They belong neither to you nor to them. They knowingly swear to falsehood. Allah has prepared for them a grievous scourage. Evil indeed is that which they have done. They use their faith as a disguise and debar others from the path of Allah. A shameful scourage awaits them (58.5: 14– 16).

Akhrat (Hereafter) is another cardinal concept of Islam. It has a basis in sound human experience. Man has limitless desires and aspiration. His self craves for the infinite. He has a natural urge to transcend the confines of time and space and rise above the transitoriness of life. The belief in *Akhrat* fulfils human promptings for and eternal life; it provides a point of certainty in flux and unending change.

Secondly, human beings live in communities. Social life entails a system of rights and responsibilities. No society exists in a perfect form. Here men are being deprived of fundamental rights and there responsibilities are being shrugged aside. Exploitation of man by man is a fact of life. The short span of life and human ways of doing things preclude the possibility of dispensing perfect justice. How can a person responsible for massacre be punished in this life? These facts provide a rational basis for belief in the Hereafter.

Bounty of God **:** Picking up threads from the concept of God discussed above, emphasis was laid on the bounty of God. If God has offered men certain benefits and previleges, why should man not be accountable for it? *Sura Naba* recounts the gardens of luxurious growth given to man and draws attention to the day of sorting out. The Quran dwells on the concept of *Akhrat* at great length:

About what are they asking?

About the fateful tidings—the theme of their disputes.

But they shall know the truth; before long they shall know it.

Did we not spread the earth like a bed and raise the mountains like pillars?

We created you in pairs and gave you rest in sleep.

We made the night a mantle, and ordained the day for work. We built above you seven mighty heavens and placed in them a shining lamp. We sent down abundant water from the clouds, bringing forth grain and varied plants, and gardens thick with foliage.

Fixed is the Day of Judgement. On that day the Trumpet shall be sounded and you shall come in multitudes. The gates of heaven shall swing open and the mountains shall pass away like vapour (78: 1-12).

The *al-Qiyamah* is variously described by the Quran as Day of Judgement, Day of Reckoning, Day of Sorting Out.

A rational interpretation of fundamental beliefs of Islam has been attempted. The Quran makes a cogent and convincing statement of how concepts like unity of God, Prophethood and the hereafter are rooted in human observation and experience. It rejects the view that religion is based on the instinct of fear latent in man and demonstrates that the roots of religious faith in positive aspects of human life.

Islam has made unique contributions to human civilisation; and among these is the concept of the dignity of man. According to the Holy Quran man is the noblest of God's creation, as it says; "Certainly, We created man in the best make". (95: 4). At another place the Holy Quran declares: "And surely We have honoured the children of Adam and We carry them in the land and the sea, and We provide them with good things, and We have made them to excel highly most of those whom We have created". (17: 70). Man was made Allah's vicegerent on earth, and he was destined to rule everything around him. The Holy Quran says: "And when thy Lord said to the angels, I am going to place in the earth one who shall rule in it". (2: 30).

The idea of man being the ruler of the universe is repeated in many verses of the Holy Book: "And He has made subservient to you whatsoever is in the heavens and whatsoever is in the earth, all, from Himself. (45: 13). "Allah is He Who made subservient to you the sea that the ships may glide therein by His Grace, and that you may give thanks". (45: 12). "He has made subservient to you the sun and the moon; each pursues its course till an appointed time". (31: 29). "And He has made subservient to you the night and the day and the sun and the moon. And the stars are made subservient by His command. Surely there are signs in this for a people who understand" (16:12).

According to Islam, man's position in nature was that of a conqueror. He was created to control all the forces of nature and to rule in the earth and not to bow before them. But man degraded himself to the utmost when started worshipping the earth, rivers, trees, fire, the sun and the moon and the stars, and all those objects of nature which were made subservient to him. He even worshipped unhewn stones, and sometimes carved out idols with his own hands and worshipped them as if they were Divine, or as if they controlled good or evil for him. As the Holy Quran says: "Do you worship that which you knew not? And Allah has created you and what you make" (37: 95-96). And as Abraham asked his Sire: "Why dost thou worship that which neither hears, nor sees, nor does it avail thee in the least" (19:42).

The gravest of sins, according to the Holy Quran is *Shirk* or associating others with Allah. This is not due to feeling of jealousy on the part of Allah, but because *Shirk* demoralises man, while Divine unity brings about his moral elevation. That is why Islam has laid so much emphasis on *Tauheed* or oneness of God, which is the most fundamental principle of the Islamic faith.

Man was endowed with vast capabilities for attaining knowledge. In the first place, he was given knowledge by Allah as the Holy Quran says: "And he gave Adam knowledge of all things" (2: 31). The Arabs were an illiterate people, and reading and writing was so rare among them that it may be said not to have existed at all. The Holy Prophet (peace be upon him), himself did not know reading and writing and is called Unlettered Prophet (peace be upon him), as stated in the Quran: "And thou didst not recite before it any book, nor didst thou transcribe one with thy right hand (29: 48). Yet the first Divine message received by him was about reading and writing. As the Quran says: Read in the name of thy Lord who created. Creates man from a clot. Read and thy Lord is most bounteous, Who taught to write with the pen. He taught man what he knew not". (96: 1-5).

Read and write, was thus His first message; and to these two means of gaining knowledge of things, the faculty of observation was also granted to man. The Holy Quran has repeatedly invited the attention of man to the creation of this universe and the various phenomena working around him. He asked to observe and reflect. To quote one instance from the Quran: "In the creation of the heavens and the earth and the alternation of the night and the day, there are surely signs for men of understanding. Those who remember Allah standing and sitting and (lying) on their sides and reflect on the creation of the heavens and the earth.

Our Lord, thou hast not created this in vain"; (3: 189-90). The process of observing and reflecting convinces man that every thing made by God is perfect. He sees no incongruity in Allah's creation, and this naturally leads him to His glorification. "Glorify the name of the Lord, the Most High; Who creates things, then makes them complete: And who makes things according to a measure then guides them to their goal". (87: 1-3).

Man, before Islam, was at the lowest ebb of human civilisation. He was just a slave of nature's forces. The Holy Prophet (peace be upon him) raised him to the dignity of the master and the ruler, and it was due to this realisation of man's position to the universe that the Muslims in their very early history took vigorous strides towards the expansion of knowledge and the advancement of the sciences. Reading and writing was within a few years spread throughout the whole of Arabia and other countries which came under the influence of Islam and the Muslim State so encouraged the pursuit of study and scientific research, that centres of learning and universities sprang up throughout the empire of Islam.

According to Islam, every child is born in a state of sinlessness; and it is afterwards in life, that a person becomes a Jew or a Christian or anything else by following the religion of his parents. The Holy Prophet (peace be upon him) said: "Every child that is born conforms to the true religion (Allah's *fitrat;* and it is his parents who make him a Jew or a Christian or a Magian" *(Bukhari,* 32: 79). Every child is, thus, recognised by birth to be a Muslim, and the purity of human nature is not affected by his being born of non-Muslim parents.

The Holy Prophet (peace be upon him) once related a vision in which he had seen the Prophet Abraham in paradise with children all around him, and he added that those children were all the children that had died in the state of nature, i.e. before they attained the age of discretion. Some of the companions of the Holy Prophet (peace be upon him) asked him if the children of the polytheists were also included? The Holy Prophet (peace be upon him) replied: "Yes, the children of those who set up gods with God *(mushrikeen)* as well" *(Bokhari,* 91:48). The doctrine of the sinlessness of man by birth is an aid to his leading a sinless life. If a man does good and avoids evil, he is true to his nature. It further strengthens him to overcome sin, because he knows that nature had fitted him for this task. And step by step he can further rise to very high spiritual levels.

Not only that no impurity is attached to man by birth, but he also partakes of the Divine nature, for it was the Divine Spirit that was breathed into man, into every human child. As the Holy Quran says: "Who made beautiful everything that He created, and He began the creation of man from dust. Then He made his progeny of an extract of worthless water. Then He made him complete and breathed into him of His spirit" (32: 7-9). The Divine Spirit spoken of here is something distinct from the animal soul. It shows a mystic relation of the spirit of man with the Divine Spirit, and refers to the higher life of man. The destiny of man, according to Islam, is thus higher than mere conquest of nature, it is to seek union with the Divine Spirit. The goal of life is "Liqa Allah", or the meeting of God. In the language of the Holy Quran: "O man; thou must strive hard striving (to attain) to thy Lord until thou meet Him" (84: 6).

Human Behaviour

Islam encompasses entire human conduct. Justice is the *sine qua non* of Islam. Like other religions Islam is not satisfied with just transformation of the moral viewpoint of the individual or society, leaving man to his own sweet whim of what to obey and what not to obey as per the dictates of his convenience.

Islam is concerned with all sides, all sectors and all levels. As such, it aims at making a compact, homogenous, steel-cast *'Millat'* with definite laws of do's and don'ts and, what is more important, with a sovereign enforcing authority backed by all powers of reward and punishment. It gives laws in all sectors of human conduct at levels of family, society and polity, trade, politics, social manners, citizenship, agriculture, industry, foreign relations, health, public finance, public works, education, civilisation and what not. And it gives justice to see that they are practically enforced.

After declaration of prophethood, for full 13 years in Makkah, the Prophet of Islam (peace be upon him) preached the best principles of individual and social conduct, presented the best logic and arguments, demonstrated the best powers of oratory and persuasion, gave the best specimens of personal virtues, quoted the commandments of the Holy Quran, discussed the life-after-death. More than 95 per cent of the inhabitants of Makkah and of the places around remained infidels showing intenser enmity towards the Holy Prophet (peace be upon him), his Companions and Islam. When, however, the scene changed to Medina with Islam becoming a state, a government, a political and military force, new people came within its fold and Islam could set up a model in all sectors for all times and climes.

At Medina, the Prophet (peace be upon him) blended the ever-warring tribes into one compact fraternity, changed hearts, values and viewpoints, reformed society and polity, created an atmosphere of dependable safety, peace and goodwill and overthrew the governments of oppression and tyranny whose game was to play one set of people against another.

The Holy Quran puts all emphasis on the suppression of oppression and enforcement of justice.

> "Verily Allah orders you to give the due to whomsoever it belongs and when you sit in judgement, be just and upright—" (4: 58).
>
> "O people of *Eimnan* (Faith) give all support and perseverance to the cause of justice in the way of Allah. And do not trespass for fear of this nation or that. And catch full hold of justice as it is close to

Taqwa. And fear none but Allah. Verily He knows every action of yours". (5: 8).

"Tell them, O Prophet, that your Allah has commanded justice."

"Sure, we have sent to you this Book of Rights so that you may pronounce judgements between peoples as per the commandments of Allah. And do not be among those who unjustly take sides" (4: 105).

Only 227 verses of the Holy Quran discuss laws and they pertain to no more than 11 sectors of human activity. Of course, this is the core and kernel, the nucleus. All the remaining parts of the structure of the Islamic polity have been furnished by the *Sunnah,* the sayings and doings of the Prophet (peace be upon him).

As regards the two evil courses of bribe and recommendations the Holy Prophet (peace be upon him) said that he who gives and he who takes bribe will both go to Hell. He has cursed the giver and taker of bribe.

True Judge : The Holy Prophet (peace be upon him) had to deal with hundreds of cases between persons belonging to erstwhile opposite camps. The least favour or disfavour on his part would have broken the oneness and unity of *Millat.* But it was his impartial justice that gave no loophole of criticism to anyone that kept the *Millat* intact, that is the model par excellence to all posterity.

He has prescribed the special qualifications of the judge, the *Qazi.* Once he said: "Judges are of three kinds-one of which will go to Paradise, recognises the right of one *vis-a-vis* another and pronounces judgements accordingly.

The other is one who recognises the rights but due to any worldly consideration does not act accordingly. And the third kind is one who does not care to recognise the rights and acts unjustly".

> "When a judge does his best to know the truth from untruth and finds the truth, he would get two rewards. But one who does not find the truth in spite of his best efforts would get one reward only."

As regards the court-procedure, he said: "None is to pronounce judgement if he is in wrath and anger."

> "Both the parties are to be present before the judge."
>
> "I am but a human being. I try legal disputes. It is possible that one of the party is more adept in presenting his side of the case and under the impression of his being rightful, I judge in his favour. So if a party secures such a favour by trampling the right of another party, the former is taking nothing but a piece of Hellish Fire. It is for him to take it or leave it."

He has ordered the judge to hear equally attentatively both the parties and to deliver judgement only when the truth comes out. Similarly, the Holy Prophet (peace be upon him) has laid down the essential qualifications of the court witness. He had refused to accept the evidence of (1) person guilty of breach of trust, (2) person guilty of immoral sex; (3) person who has previously been inflicted with court punishment; (4) person who harbours feelings of revenge or hate against his brother, including the party in question; (5) person who has been guilty of giving false evidence; (6) person who is related to or in service of one of the parties or is a flatterer to one of the parties.

He said that giving false evidence is equivalent to committing *Shirk*.

The Holy Prophet (peace be upon him) while awarding judgement took full notice of the condition of health, of finance and of other factors of the guilty and gave relaxations accordingly. He always pardoned whenever it could be. He always arranged for compromise and *Qasas* whenever it could be. He gave punishment only when it had to be.

Islam considers the whole humanity as one family and treats mankind as one community. The Holy Prophet (peace be upon him) was first to demolish narrow visions of geographical and political nationhood, and taught the lesson of broadmindedness and international brotherhood to the world at large.

Paying his tribute to the Holy Prophet (peace be upon him) the French poet Lamartine wrote: "Muhammad is the one great man without whom the world would appear incomplete. Truly, Muhammad stands to this day, and for all time to come, at the peak of humanity.

Every nation at sometime or other, in its history, had its superman, the luminary who gave it light, the reformer who inspired it with noble ideals, and the Prophet who raised it morally, intellectually and spiritually on a high pedestal. But no other prophet of any religion has exercised so deep and lasting an influence in the religious, historical and social history of mankind as the Prophet of Islam (peace be upon him).

As a prophet and reformer, entrusted with the noble mission of raising mankind from the depths of degradation and the dungeons of moral, political, social and religious bankruptcy and decadence into which it had fallen in the sixth century, Prophet Muhammad (peace be upon him) could not be otherwise than a revolutionary in the fullest sense of the term. The lofty ideals he preached not only brought about a complete change in the political situation but also had an equally important and a more enduring bearing on the social conditions of the people.

To consider that the advent of the Holy Prophet (peace be upon him) on the Arab horizon merely heralded the birth of a politically unified Arabia is to pay but poor tribute to him and confess shocking ignorance of the implications of the message and his dynamic personality which ushered in a revolution of considerable magnitude in the thought and actions not only of the Arabs but of mankind itself.

Islam, the religion the Holy Prophet (peace be upon him) preached, introduced the conception of the nation as a unit and a vital stage in the organisation of human society. It is lofty in the conception of the relationship of man to God and noble in its doctrine of duty of man to man to the lower creation. It was the first religion that preached and practised democracy in its true sense.

It was Islam which for the first time proclaimed liberty to mankind, and introduced universal brotherhood in humanity. It does not recognise differences of class, caste, race, nation, or geographical and political boundaries and territories of the world. No one in Islam is better because of creed or colour. "An Arab has no superiority over a non-Arab, nor a non-Arab over Arab except piety". Islam laid down the ideal that nobility depends not in belonging to a particular family or tribe but upon being noble in personal conduct and character. The Divine Message has come down to us in the form of the Holy Quran which is the basic source of guidance for humanity.

It is a great charter of the freedom of humanity. As a book of ethics, and a code of conduct, clear, concise and simple in terms, there is no other sacred book in the world to replace it. It is "a stupendous monument of solitary legislation", to quote the words of Washington Irving. No wonder it has exercised a most potent and powerful influence over mankind throughout the ages.

Islam's institutions are unique: they do not compromise with materialistic dogmas. They stand firm on individual piety and individual freedom a close-knit family devoted to the welfare of a classless, benevolent society.

The principle of equality and brotherhood, justice and freedom which the Holy Prophet (peace be upon him) defined as integral elements of faith have engendered a righteous character and a noble spirit in society.

Distinguishing the essence of piety from the mere form of ceremony of righteousness, the Holy Prophet (peace be upon him) made faith in Allah and benevolence towards man the essential features of religion. He brought to perfection the grand idea of unifying the whole human race and gathering it together under one banner.

His was "a life consecreted, from first to last, to the service of God and humanity". He preached that a true Muslim is one from the danger of whose tongue and hands all Muslims are immune and that the best occupation is service to mankind, that knowledge is a valuable legacy, manners and courtesy the various ornaments, and carefulness a clear and transparent mirror and that spiritual virtue consists in adoring Allah.

The Prophet of Islam (peace be upon him) denounced vehemently meanness and slander, hypocrisy and untruthfulness, superstition, gambling, drinking, oppression of the weak by the strong and other evils, and gave new light and guidance to mankind.

The supreme place he gave in the faith to the duty of alms-giving and charity to the poor is another praiseworthy feature of religion he preached. He told us that every good act is a charity, an exhortation to your fellowmen to do virtuous deeds is equal to alms-giving; guiding the wanderer to the right path is charity; assisting the blind in crossing the street is charity; removing stones and thorns and other obstructions from the road is charity; giving water to the thirsty is charity, and so on. There is hardly a religious duty which is more sacred and benevolent to the Muslims than that of charity to the poor. The Holy Prophet (peace be upon him) preached that true poverty is not merely lack of wealth but lack of desire for wealth.

The strict observance by the Muslims of the daily prayers for five times is another testimony to the value of a living faith and the spirit of universal brotherhood. One should also witness the congregational prayers offered by the faithful to see for himself the atmosphere of equality, brotherhood and love. In the presence of Allah, all stand shoulder to shoulder, the rich and the powerful with the poor and the lowly, the master and the servant offering prayers and bowing themselves before Allah in abject submission. Can there be any more levelling influence in the world?

Faith for All

The Holy Prophet (peace be upon him) upheld the dignity of women and gave them an honoured place in society. The economic and cultural position of women was raised to a high status, and recognition of women's right to property marked the beginning of a new era, which is now the recognised feature of every civilized society. With his far-sighted vision, the Holy Prophet (peace be upon him) laid down a complete social system containing minute regulations for man's conduct in all circumstances of life.

His love for, and human treatment of, animals are too well-known. According to a *Hadith,* the Holy Prophet (peace be upon him) is reported to have said: "If you behold three mounting an animal, stone them until one descends".

The Prophet of Islam (peace be upon him) will for ever remain the symbol of the most exemplary human conduct. All his efforts were aimed at elevating man's mind and soul, and giving him an exalted position. He preached righteousness and toleration, and in his own self presented the most accomplished model of his teachings. In his own lifetime he moulded the character of his fellowmen, reformed them, changed their thoughts, put new ideals before them, elevated them to a higher plane and let them onwards, towards the path of progress and to the fullness of a better and nobler life.

With the passage of time, Western writers, in spite of their ignorance and prejudice, began to assess the position of the

Holy Prophet (peace be upon him) and the revolution brought about by him. In the case of some honest and fair appraisal and objective considerations have been dominant. A case in illustration is that of Dozy where truth found to favour: "We see then that the Arab conquests of the seventh century have continued to play an important role in human history, down to present day. It is this unparalleled combination of secular and religious influence which I feel entitles Muhammad (peace be upon him) to be considered the most influential single figure in human history". (The 100: *A ranking of the Most Influential Persons in History*– Michael H. Hart). In this list the name of the Holy Prophet (peace be upon him) is on the top. Jesus Christ is number three.

Lamartine in his *"History* de *La Turquie"*, Vol. II, says about the Holy Prophet (peace be upon him):.

> "No person in the world had ever willingly or unwillingly, independently or under duress kept before him an object or goal higher than the goal of Muhammad (peace be upon him).

Higher Goal : This goal was much higher than general human level, much above human intellect. What was this goal? To do away one by one with the curtains of superstition that were hung between God and man to fill the heart of man by his presence and dye man in colours of God's attributes, to present in the crowd of false deities the sacred and reasonable concept of God free of any defect. Up to now no man has dared to undertake such a stupendous and grand task, which is beyond human reach and then its sources should be so limited. This is so because neither when he conceived the idea of this responsibility, nor when practical steps were taken to implement it, he had only his person or a few residents of a corner of the desert at his disposal.

There were no sources, no support, nor necessary arrangements. With this sort of paucity of resources, no man in the world, up to now, has brought about such a glorious and splendid revolution.

"A revolution of such dimensions that within two hundred years, Islam practically as a religion ruled over Arabia. In the name of God, it had conquered Iran, Khorasan, Western India, Syria, Egypt, Ethiopia, territory of North Africa known at that time, many islands of Mediterranean and Spain. If the loftiness of the goal, absence of resources and brilliancy of results is the criterion of human genius, then where is the man who can dare present any other human being to compete with Muhammad (peace be upon him). Great men in the world have piled arms, codified laws and ruled over extensive empires. At the most they created material powers and resources which in most cases were reduced to ashes. But this man did not shake only the armies and battalions, legislative assemblies, big empires, nations and families but also the hearts of millions of people living in one-third area of the known world of that time.

"And more than that. This personality shook places of sacrifices, deities, religions and rituals, conceptions and convictions and as a matter of fact shook the very souls of men. On the basis of a book, whose every word has a legal significance, he built up a community which in its turn fused different languages and races into one single nation. This everlasting nation, rebellion and hatred against false gods and overflowing love for one God are the legacies of this great personality. In the midst of a plethora of false gods the proclamation of conception about one God in itself was such a miracle that as soon as these words were uttered by him all places of worship of false gods were destroyed. One-third of the world was set on fire.

"His life, his devotion, his relentless efforts against superstition and the great courage to scoff at the fury and anger of false gods is known. His life at Makkah and thirteen years' tribulations and severe opposition were met with supreme fortitude and courage. He gladly bore the ridicule and denial of the opponents. All these troubles and then migration by him, his continuous preaching and invitation, his supreme efforts, his full confidence in the success of his mission and in unfavourable circumstances his supernatural calm and collected disposition at the time of victory and success, amnesty and forgiveness not for the sake of statecraft, but for the success of his divine goal and object. His wishes and hopes in the world of deep strance, his regular prayers, his supplications, secret contacts with his God, his life, his death and his popularity and influence after his demise, all these facts provide evidence for what kind of life? Do these facts show a life of a deceitful fabrication or the life of a person who had unshakable confidence and trust in his claims. It was his this very iron-clad confidence and faith generated in him a very strong current on power and strength by which he made his belief ever-living and everlasting. What was this belief?

"First Oneness of God and the second to explain what God is not. This *"illa"* and the other *"illa"*. One part to wipe away the false gods in the world (even use of sword if pressed by necessity) and the other part to lay out the carpet of one true God's majesty. A great thinker, orator of a high order, prophet law-giver, military leader, victor of beliefs and convictions, responsible for presenting correct ideology of life with reason and clarity of vision; the founder of a system, in which false gods cannot enter man's mind; twenty worldly states and above them the sovereignty of One God. This is Muhammad (peace be upon him).

> "Bring all of your criteria, all of your tests by which the greatness of human beings is checked and measured and then reply if the world has produced any man greater than him?"

The views of another Western author, viz., Pringle Kennedy should be taken into consideration. After dealing with the subject of social, religious and cultural condition of the world he says: "It is a matter of surprise that this new culture was born in Arabia at a time when it was urgently needed.

> "For those among us who think man is everything, Muhammad (peace be upon him) is a great example of what a man can do. Those who believe that changes and revolutions in history are not the result of one man's efforts but are more dependent on the peculiarities of environments and the ability of human mind to accept them cannot deny that if a revolution had to come (as it came in Arabia) it could not take place without Muhammad (peace be upon him) and would have remained pending for an indefinite period". (Pringle Kennedy—
> *"In Arabian Society at the Time of Muhammad").*

The Eclipse of Christianity in Islam by L. E. Brown bears testimony to the fact that: "Due to influence of Muhammad (peace be upon him), Arab clannish pride and exclusiveness came to an end. They became members of a brotherhood which they never knew. This link was the faith of Oneness of God. If brought them to a centre and conquests followed easily.

Hitti opines in his book *"History of the Arabs"* as under: "This was the first time that the Arabs were brought together not in the name of blood-relationship but in the name of religion. Allah was the supreme sovereign of this state. The Prophet (peace be upon him), throughout his life was His representative and ruler of the country. For this reason Muhammad (peace be upon him) in addition to his spiritual responsibilities, directed the affairs of the state like state officials. In his nation after forsaking all tribal preferences and old relationship became brothers."

The Reverend Stephenson is of the opinion: "It must be freely admitted at first that for his nation the personality of Muhammad (peace be upon him) was the source of many and great benefits. He was born in a country where political set-ups, reasonable beliefs and ethical behaviour were unknown. He brought about these three things. Through his mature intelligence, he reformed all these three simultaneously. In place of different tribes he made them one nation, similarly he preached the Unity of God in place of deities and gods. All the major unwholesome practices were done away with. As Islam flowed out of old Arabia, barbarians were gathered in its fold and they became the possessors of the benefits of Islam. Islam is an instrument to lead human beings from darkness to light and from *Satan* to God.

The Reverend Bosworth Smith observes: "On account of such a good fortune which has not parallel in history, Muhammad (peace be upon him) is the founder of three elements. One nation, one state and one religion. The founder himself was unlettered but he gave the world a Book which has poetic and musical stance in it as also complete code of conduct and law. This is the miracle of Muhammad (peace be upon him), permanent miracle and actually a miracle."

Revolutionary Role

They all write about an unprecedented revolution not only political but social, religious, moral, ethical and in short all matters covering life of man. They all pay tribute to Quran. At this stage it is necessary we should know what was there in the world at that time that was swept away to make room for higher and bright set up and a new world was created.

Pringle in his *"Arabian Society at the Time of Muhammad"* (peace be upon him) says that at that time it seemed that the grand edifice of civilisation which had been built during the last 4,000 years, was about to collapse and human beings were about to revert to the same barbaric state wherein every tribe was deadly enemy of the other and nobody had any knowledge or regard for institutions and regulated existence. Ancient tribal values had been lost, and on the lines of old methods kingship could no longer flourish. The institutions which Christianity introduced they did not inculcate spirit of discipline or unity but were being the cause of disunity estrangement and destruction. Time had come when all-round there was gross indiscipline, bloodshed and there was no horizon of man's life. It had gone down to the level of beasts of jungle.

The tall tree of civilisation whose green and flourishing branches provided shadow and comfort to the world and were laden with the golden fruits of art, science and literature was shaking about to fall. It no longer received the moisture of respect and attachment. Only the outer crust remained. The holocaust of wars and battles cut it down to pieces and these pieces were supported by old customs and ceremonies. It was feared that they would fall down any time. Was it possible under these conditions to create or introduce emotional culture which could bring round humanity to one central point and save civilisation. This culture had to be of a new pattern because all old customs and usages had finished and to resurrect them needed centuries.

Says Carlyle: "The humanity like a dry jungle was waiting for a spark. That spark of electricity appeared in the form of that great personality and ignited the universe."

This is the evaluation of great revolution brought about by the Holy Prophet (peace by upon him). They could not go further for two reasons. Firstly, the prejudice and opposition generated by Pope Urban II (1042—1099) who initiated the crusades. This prejudice still exists. Secondly, the West is devoting all its energy and deploying all scientific discoveries to destroy opponents besides exploiting the weak. Deadly arms are being manufactured and sold. Humanity today stands at the brink of mass destruction. For these reasons, the West has not been able to turn its attention towards higher values, and sanctity of human life.

Historic March : Islam has always faced challenges on its historical march. It faced its first crisis when the Holy Prophet (peace be upon him) passed away from this earthly scene. This was very close to the rise of Islam as a historical force. When the Holy Prophet (peace be upon him) died, the crucial point was whether there should be any Islamic history at all. Some of the then Muslims (e.g. the Beduins) felt that the affair was now over: they had taken a vow of fidelity to a leader, he was no more, and that was the end of the affairs. Others felt the need for restoring status quo and emphasising the recognition of urban and tribal realities. Besides, it was presumed that new religious faith should take its course on those basis. But this was rejected and it was decided that to keep the followers of the Holy Prophet (peace be upon him) united as a socio-political economic unit and as one that marches forward in the world to enforce and spread as unit the message of Islam. This decision was taken not without opposition which was finally crushed and silenced. This decision was of immense significance for the later history of Islam.

The decision to keep the community intact and choose a leader for itself in place of the Holy Prophet (peace be upon him) appeared to be more pertinent than the issue (which has received immeasurable attention) of who that leader should be. Then emerged the issue of the actual development of Islamic history on earth, having understood the significance of its last success and homogeneity. The early Muslims took the whole burden and opportunity of government as well as cultural creation in the widest sense. They completed this task significantly so that when they could presently look at this society that they had constructed, they felt satisfied that it led the world. God had enjoined upon men the way to live; those who followed the path were visibly receiving His blessings.

Great Debacle : History, however, has its own inner logic. Muslims feel it to be will of God on earth.

But this period of Islam's earthly glory did not last long. The early period of Islam primarily comprised Arab elements, it lost its vigour after spending its inherent force with the fall of Baghdad in 1258, the successful Arab rule came to its formal end. The Mughal invasion gave a death blow to the Arab ascendency of Islam. Many millions were massacred; whole cities were laid waste and political rules passed into the hands of infidel barbarians. This ended the classical period of Islamic history. This was a first great crisis of Islamic history. With the demise of the Arab Empire, Islamic history seemed to have lost its driving force. It appeared as if divine purpose as conceived by Islam was faltering, if it has not actually failed.

Great Survival : Despite this debacle, Islam on earth survived this crisis and it re-appeared in a new and rather different mould. With the drawing to a close of the European Middle Ages, Islam's mediaeval period—between its classical and modern eras—set in motion. Historians of Islam—whether Muslims or Westerns have taken much less interest in this mediaeval phase of Islam than that of the classical. In spite of it, there were new aspects which were not without significance. This phase of Islam produced constructive answers to the issues raised.

New Development : On the religious side, *Sufism* was a new major development. The *Sufi* or mystic interpretation of Islam has its germs even in the classical period. Yet at the time it was confined to an insignificant minority, comprising an elite of the pious withdrawn from the main stream of Islamic march. The mediaeval period bolstered its immensity throughout the Muslim world. The movement took an institutional form and gained popularity. There were additions also in interpretation; as for example, the *Masnavi* of Jalaluddin Roomi which was produced after the fall of Baghdad.

Besides, Islam converted the conquerors. After imposing on the Muslim alien rulers for 50 years, the Mughal dynasty which had subjugated the Muslim world, itself embraced Islam as a historical force soon asserted itself in Persian and Turkish forms. These forms were different from the preceding ones. New forms were different from the old in the government structure, social organisation and in cultural and aesthetic values. In this new era, Islam again began to march as a political force.

After its nadir in the Thirteenth Century, Islam began to touch a new zenith in the Sixteenth; which could be put forth as the Islam's greatest century uptil now. Then the Ottoman Empire was a most powerful state on earth; Europe shivered before its apparently unending series of conquests. At the same time, *Safuids* had established a family based on imperial power in Iran, the Mughals then had firmly entrenched themselves in India and constituted the greatest rule the subcontinent had seen for many a long time. This second revival of Islam was confined not only to the building of Empires, but it was a new expansion also in geographical and spiritual senses. The second great wave of military expansion and missionary fervour brought for Islam new converts: in the Northern Asia Minor and the Balkans and Central Asia, in the South Negro Africa and in the East Indonesia. Thus, classical Islam was doubled in area and numbers. Once again, it was evident that historical Islam was a power to be reckoned with.

However, the second flowering of Islam, with the possible exception of the Turkish, has not been generally regarded by the Muslims as fully consistent with the classical Islam. What the Muslims accomplished in it is not so keenly regarded as a complete example of Islam at work in the world, moulding into a divine pattern the flux, of historical development. But this tendency should not be overemphasised. The classical version of Islam has always remained official, and its social importance cannot be minimised. But even in this period Muslims never grudged to extol any individual who either successfully defended Islamic domain or extended it. Even then, there were many Muslims in the world who regarded conquest of Constantinople in 1453 as an example of God's power as well as Sultan Muhammad's effort. However, it is a fact that in the sixteenth century Muslim World was again a mighty force having wealth and splendour. Whatever opinion one may hold up of it, the Muslims of this period were victorious in a history expansive and successful.

But even this success did not last long. The second wave of Islamic Revival was more short-lived than the first. The advance of Muslim society ceased and by the eighteenth century it entered a period of decline. Its military and political power underwent serious reverses; its commercial and economic life enfeebled, its intellectual efforts stagnated, its artistic talent lost lustre and religious vitality ebbed. The writings of great masters were confined to commentaries and classical systems were used to congeal mental faculties rather than as an impetus for opening up new horizons of thought. On the *Sufi* side, the orders degenerated from mystic perception to exploitable superstition. Besides, it is a strange coincidence that this decay coincided with a new upsurge of Europe. At about the same time, Western civilisation set about its greatest venture of expansion that human history has ever seen. It accumulated vitality, skill, and power on a vast scale; with them the West was then refashioning its own life and soon the life of the globe.

Forces of West **:** The force of the West which was imbued with exploratory restlessness met the Muslim World in decline and subdued it. By 1800, the West subjugated such centres of Muslim power as remained on many areas and imposed its rule. During most of the nineteenth century many Muslim countries lost their freedom. The Dutch entrenched them in Indonesia; Iran and the Ottoman Empire, though formally independent, lost their freedom to act. Muslim society, once dignified was now everywhere despondent in spirit and prey to outside forces.

Muslims uphold that Islam essentially is a religion, and as such deeply personal and also conclusively surpassing all particularities and limits of this existence and all its affairs; despite this, it has the distinction of having a deep concern for these affairs. It was essential for a true Muslim to carry out in this world the divine obligation as to how mankind, individually and collectively, should live. If this is seen from another angle, it appears that Muslims should see how that ideal society is built. In short, Islamic history is the fulfilment, under divine guidance, of the purpose of human history.

It is a fact that actual Islamic history, for some centuries, approximated to this ideal. We have also observed that in actual fact, periods of decay and regeneration in Islamic history have alternated. Besides, we have also noticed that the mediaeval period of Islamic history has ended in disorder. Although, many Muslim countries had gained independence after World War II and their economic plight has considerably improved, yet the basic problem has persisted; and the issue of internal cohesion and fear of foreign interference remained. In this age of Super Power contention for the domination at the cost of the other, fears of foreign interference and internal disorder have not vanished and then a challenge to Islam's will to carve history according to its dynamism.

The basic malady of modern Islam lies in perception that something has gone wrong with Islamic history; hence the fundamental problem of meodern Muslim is how to restore that history; and set it working in full vigour again so that Islamic society may again be luxuriant as a divinely-guided society. In the twentieth century the basic spiritual crisis of Islam results from the realisation that something is discordant between God-ordained religion and the historical development of the world controlled by God. Muslims have failed to establish any tangible interconnection between these two factors—otherwise they would have long subjugated the contemporary historical situation to the requirements of their faith.

This is not to say that the Muslims have ignored this problem. Of course, men like Abdul Wahab Najdi (1703- 1887),

Jamaluddin Afghany (1839-1897), Shah Waliullah (1703-1762), and many others have tried to analyse and solve this problem. Their efforts in this direction have immense value. But the problem still persists and the Muslim world despite its area, numerical strength and potential wealth had failed to shake of fears of internal disruption and foreign interference.

This is not to say, that the Muslims did not try to adopt suitable devices for the transportation of its worldly condition. Many attempts have been made to solve the problem; firstly, liberalism was tried, but it failed. From the late nineteenth century to the First World War, European liberalism was in great vogue in many Muslim countries, but Muslims soon realised that this internal Westernising of the Islamic community constituted subtler and more dangerous version of the same threat; subversion from within. Its inherent threat to Islamic history and society was enough to alarm those who fervently cherish the realisation and embodiment of classical divine precepts as the goal of Muslim endeavour. This attitude to Westernisation has in recent decades reappeared with new vigour and vehemence.

Above all, there has been despair in the particular ties between Islam and Western liberalism itself. In the early stages of contact of Muslim world and the Western liberalism, Muslims hoped that Western liberalism could assist them in their basic enterprise of reconstructing the Islamic society, and thereby setting Islamic history on road to progress. The resulting disenchantment had led Muslims to seek new ways of fulfilling Islamic mission on earth as the Islamic Revolution in Iran, the shift in Pakistan to a new search for Islamic solution of problems and revival of Islam-oriented parties in many Muslim countries. But behind this new trend lurks the danger of an emerging new dogmatism which in its old form severely blocked the progress of Muslims for centuries. The need remains for reconciling Islam with rational modes of thought and behaviour to reconstruct Islamic society.

4

Universal Faith

Islam is an Arabic word and like many Arabic words, has no single word equivalent in the English or any other language. As for the meaning of the word, it connotes profoundest security and, therefore, peace obtained through submission. And since such peace and security can be derived only through submission to the Will of God, it implies total Submission of God.

Such being the literal meaning of Islam, man's awareness of submission to God must not be dated as commencing with any particular era, philosopher, prophet or scripture. The Holy Quran itself clarified this beyond a shadow of doubt. All the prophets from Noah to Muhammad (peace be upon them) are the Messengers of God and therefore the prophets of True Religion *(Deen-i-Haq)*. Obviously, the best of media for learning the ways of such submission is the education imparted by those inspired from the Divine Source.

Eternal Value

The reason why Orientalists and those we speak of as Muslims refer to Islam as the religion of the illustrious Prophet Muhammad (peace be upon him) is that he is the last in the lineage of the prophets, the Book revealed to him is the last revealed word of God, and his pattern of life is the only one worthy of being followed in practice, because far more is known about him than about any other prophet and therefore it can be said with authenticity that every act and deed of his is the matchless example of piety and righteousness. This finality, both of the Book and prophethood has established the fact beyond any shadow of doubt that Islam and Islam alone shows the Light of Allah to the entire humanity which has been groping in pitch darkness.

Some great Western thinkers, for instance Thomas Carlyle in his *"Hero and Hero Worship"* looks upon the Prophet of Islam (peace be upon him) as his idea! of a true prophet and Islam equated with submission to God as the ideal religion. Goethe believed the same, though it is not on record that he subscribed to the same estimate of the Holy Prophet (peace be upon him). To his question: "If this be Islam, do we not all live in Islam?" Carlyle answers, " yet we that have any moral faith, we all live so." So much for the literal meaning of the word Islam, and it is this sense that the Quran and its Prophet (peace be upon him) use the word.

Having established the meaning of Islam, we proceed to the implication of the word submission. Submission is obedience-in-action. There is no such thing as believing in submission but no submitting in action. Ignorance of this simple logic—or wilful evasion of it—underlies the tragedy of those who preter d to be Muslims but just as the implications of Islam are ignored so also are those of being Muslim. The general belief conveniently developed is that if you recite the words " There is no god save Allah and Muhammad is the messenger of Allah" you are a Muslim, and you need trouble yourself no more about deeds or misdeeds, the fire of hell being now forbidden on you. There could be no greater mistake.

Oath of Allegiance : During the Holy Prophet's (peace be upon him) lifetime and for at least some decades after him, the recital of these words was no more than an equivalent to an oath of allegiance, and it was understood by the convert that having conceded and acknowledged the Holy Prophet's (peace be upon him) Divine-messenger status, the convert would do as the messenger bade him do. For instance, as long as the authority of the messenger was not acknowledged he could not reasonably expect one to demolish one's idols, but once that authority was acknowledged, his orders and counsels were acted upon in word and spirit in all matters.

It was never taken for granted that having accepted the validity of his Messenger-of-Allah status there was no change required in deeds and practices. If it were otherwise his claim to prophethood would have been acknowledged by everyone the first day he made the announcement. On the contrary, we find that he is offered immense bribes of wealth, position, and beautiful women, if only he would let them continue to do as they wished to do. But this condition was not acceptable to him. The objective of his mission was not to get himself acknowledged but to get humanity do the right things.

But today, it is regrettable indeed, the Holy Quran, its arguments, words and spirit have all been modified to suit the conveniences of those having vested interests. The *'kalima'* has been given a technical significane, made a magical chanting and regard to the practice of the Holy Prophet's (peace be upon him) councils has been consigned to oblivion.

In not a single instance does the Holy Quran commend belief or acknowledgement of its Prophet (peace be upon him) without action. The words repeated again and again are:

> "Those who believe and do good work, for them are gardens below which rivers flow...." Paradise is never held out to those who merely believe or recite *'kalima'*.

"Forgiveness" says the Holy Quran is incumbent on Allah only towards those why do evil in ignorance and then turn quickly in repentence to Allah. These are the ones toward whom Allah relenteth. Allah is ever Knower, Wise. Forgiveness is not for those who do ill deeds until when death attends one of them, he says I repent (4:17-18). "He who does wrong will have the recompense thereof and he will not find against Allah any protecting friend or helper. And who does good works, whether male or female and is a believer, such will enter paradise" (4: 123-124). "For those who do good is the best reward and more thereto. Neither ignominy nor dust cometh near their faces. Such are rightful owners of the garden" (10:26).

That a believer is not necessarily a Muslim the Holy Quran clarifies:

> "O you who believe; observe your duty to Allah with right observance and do not die save as Muslims: (4: 102). Here the Holy Quran is directly addressing those who already believe, not disbelievers, in the Messenger-of-God status of the Holy Prophet (peace be upon him) telling them that such belief or acknowledgement is not necessarily to be equated with Islam. To be Islamic they shall have to be performers of submission to God even unto death; Again the Prophets Ibrahim and Yaqub (peace be upon them) are quoted as advising their sons not to die except as performers of submission (2: I 32). The sons of Ibrahim and grandson Yaqub and the latter's many sons were always believers in the unity of God and the messengership of their prophet-fathers, yet their belief or assumption was not enough. What was still required and would be constantly and always required was submission-in-action. The advice quoted was a reminder to them and is to all others.

Not Mere Belief : It is clear that mere belief is not looked upon by the Holy Quran as qualifying one to the status of being Muslim. There is a good reason for this. Belief unaccompanied by action can be very deceptive, a person may think quite sincerely that he believes while he really does not believe. True, genuine belief is a state of the mind that firmly grips the substrata and conscious levels of it. When belief comes into total possession, it becomes impossible for the mind so possessed to do anything but what the belief directs. The validity of belief can be tested only by deeds. If the deeds are not right, the belief too is not right. People who assume that though they are habitual sinners, they do have *Iman,* only victims of self-deception. Faith and deeds cannot contradict one another.

There are not a few people today who observe the five daily prayers, fast and even perform *Haj.* At the same time, if they are Government servants, they live on bribe-accumulated wealth, even after retirement. Or, if in business, they may be smugglers, or landlords, and in *every* case live in violation of the Quranic injunctions in respect of *Riba,* their excuse being that since they perform the elementary prescribed rituals and offer contributions to various *mazars* (shrines), salvation is assured to them. Not content with the sins of their own bribes they try to bribe the souls of dead saints.

The Holy Prophet (peace be upon him) like the Quran, does not offer any assurance to mere observer of ritualistic prayers, fasting or pilgrimage *(Haj)* but he does guarantee paradise for him from whose preserves his modesty. He commends giving water to a thirsty dog, and declares that the acquisition of learning or keeping a night's watch at the frontier is better than many a night of prayers. All this is not to say that prayers, fasting or the Annual Pilgrimage to Makkah are valueless. They are of immense value but like priceless pearls, are fragile and quickly demolished by the stroke of wrong deeds. Helped by good deeds they are polished imbued with lustre and become meaningful. Deeds and rituals act and react on one another. Wrong deeds indicate that the rituals are not being effective.

Of course, there are levels of submission, surrender. Human nature being what it is, weaknesses being inherently compulsive, it is not to be expected that one may never stray off the straight and narrow path. God does not expect the same calibre of devotion, say, from a man of humble capacity and means with modest ambitions, of common pursuits and little learning as He does from one capable of high thinking and commanding greater resources and leisure. The level of Islam or Submission differs from man to man. Thus, the Holy Quran tells certain Bedouins who came to the Holy Prophet (peace be upon him) declaring they had *Iman* (faith):

> "Do not say that you have faith *(Iman)* because faith has not entered your hearts yet: but say rather: We have acknowledged with preliminary submission. Yet if you act in obedience to Allah and His Messenger, He will not withhold from you the reward of your deeds. Allah is Forgiving, Merciful."

And the Book goes on to define faith:

> "The full of faith are those only who believe in God and His Messenger and afterwards do not waver but strive with their wealth and their lives for the cause of God. Such are the sincere." (49:14-15).

The test of true faith, that is striving with one's wealth and even life. Money is the anvil on which *'Iman'* is hammered out.

On one occasion, while sitting in the company of his companions the Holy Prophet (peace be upon him) exclaimed:

> "Who is it that will carry out four behests?"

Abu Huraira said, "I will, O Messenger of Allah". Then the Holy Prophet (peace be upon him) grasped his hand and said:

> "If you are content with what you have, you will be rich. If you do good to your neighbours, you will be a *momin* (truly imbued with faith); and if you wish for others what you wish for yourself, you will be a Muslim. And do not laugh much, for too much laughter dulls a man's intellect."

Test of a Muslim : The Supreme Being in one instance tells us that the test of a man being a true Muslim is that he spends his wealth and his life according to the revealed commandments, and in the other, the Holy Prophet (peace be upon him) defines a Muslim as one who makes no difference between what he desires for himself and what he desires for his fellowmen. Salvation is elevated to a superordinary level namely doing to others what one would have others do to him. The highest submission is that of the Prophets (peace be upon him).

Just as doing good has levels, so has doing evil. There is the evil that God forgives. This is what might be called a slip. A man going along the *sirat-i-mustaqim,* the straight path, strays off but realising his error, returns immediately to it. Misdeeds that are planned and persisted in do not fall in the category of forgivable sins.

Sins that are crimes which corrupt society victimise millions of human beings. A judge or police officer, for instance, who takes a bribe, primarily deprives someone of his right. This is the first wrong. But the fact that he sets an example for corruption, that he becomes an abettor in the economic inflation—to note but one result— thereby causing prices to rise and, consequently bringing hardship to the poor in short, becoming a corrupter of social conditions, the extent of his misdeed is surely not one that God overlooks.

Their professions have the sanctity of law behind them. But does the Holy Quran justify their activities? Does the Holy Quran justify or condemn profiteering? Does the Holy Prophet (peace be upon him) countenance the renting out of land or building property? Does the Holy Quran forbid turning any wealth into a commodity of circulation among the rich? It is permissible to market the free gifts of nature, pre-eminently land? Is exploiting labour Islamic? Is dividing humanity into wealth-based classes not against the words and spirit of the Holy Quran and the *Sunnah* of its Holy Prophet (peace be upon him)?

Finally, what then is our religion? The religion of wrong-doers is wrong-doing, not Islam. Such people take shelter behind the shield of the slogan that religion is a personal affair. In the present day world this has become the rule rather than the exception. You may claim to be a Muslim, well and good. But whether you offer your prayers or not, whether you observe fasting during *Ramazan* or not, whether you pay *Zakat* or not, whether you perform *Haj* or not, no one bothers. It is presumed to be your personal affair. None has a right to interfere in the personal affairs of others. This is the prevailing situation the world over. But has this the sanction of Islam? Nothing that the slogan: " Religion is a personal affair" is a creation of the anti-Islamic forces, let us examine this attitude in the light of Islamic teachings.

Progressive Faith

Contrary to the hostile propaganda Islam of all the religions of the world, is perhaps the most tolerant though not compromising religion. There is no compulsion in matters of faith is its basic proclamation of Human Rights. It not only proclaims the human right of freedom, but extends to all mankind the fullest freedom of thought, of action, of speech and expression. "Say, O people; Truth has reached you from your Lord, so whosoever seeks guidance, does so for his own benefit, and whosoever goes astray is himself responsible for it and I am not a supervisor on you" (10:108). Again, "Say, Truth is from your Lord, So whosoever wishes may believe and whosoever wishes may disbelieve." (18:29). Also, "Act as you please, verily Allah sees what you do" (41:40).

Islam preaches without being in the least coercive. It brings to light the inherent weak-spots in various systems of thought. It lays bare before our eyes the final outcome of the right or wrong ways of life. It distinguishes for us what is good and what is bad. It unfolds the mysteries of the universe and holds before our eyes a unified view of cosmos. It urges us to observe, to think to mediate to infer and to do justice to ourselves not deceiving ourselves by making false decisions knowingly not to be misled by biases, prejudices, self-interests.

Everything has been made as clear as day. Yet there is no compulsion. You choose the right path, well and good. You feel inclined to tread the wrong path? Well that is your own outlook and choice, Islam gives you the basic freedom. But please have the courage to declare your faith or your faithlessness. Be clear in your mind. Do not mix up things. Do not hesitate. Choose any system and stick to it. Own it boldly. Let there be no hypocrisy, no showing off, no lip-service, no contradiction in your thought and action.

But once you have exercised your option, your choice is automatically curtailed. You are bound to act in a specified way you have no option to claim to have certain faith and to disobey the injunctions of your faith. "Where God and His Apostle have decisively laid down (the course) in any matter, it does not behove a believer man or woman to act on their own sweet will in that matter" (33:36). This is for Muslims, for the Jews and the Christians a similar law has been laid down. "And whosoever does not decide (his affairs) according to what God has laid down, he is an unbeliever" (544: 5.47).

Here your choice is curtailed. Option is still there, but in one direction only. You may offer prayers night and day, but you cannot cut them down to less than five times a day. You may observe fasting for most of the year, but you cannot disregard fasting during the month of *Ramazan*. You may give away all your wealth to the poor and the needy, but you cannot withhold *Zakat*, if it is due from you. You may perform *Haj* as many times in your lifetimes as convenient, but you cannot forego it altogether if you are liable under *Shariah*. The option you see, is now on the positive constructive side only. There is no option on the negative, destructive or regressive side.

Practising your religion is no more your personal affair. It becomes a state affair as well. Now that practice of religion becomes partly a State affair, let us see how an Islamic State should deal with it. According to the Holy Quran, there are four classes of people to deal with by a State internally. First there are True Muslims, the *Mo'minin.* These are the people who have willingly accepted Islam as their religion and practice it faithfully out of a love for it. This class seldom causes any trouble to the State.

***True Muslim* :** Next come the Muslims—ordinary Muslims who profess Islam mainly through inheritance to some extent consciously. Before preoccupied with worldly affairs, they often neglect to observe the injunctions of Islam meticulously, mostly because of their preoccupations, lassitude or heedlessness or even ignorance, with no intention of repudiating such injunctions. How should the State deal with them? Islam's preferred course seems to be educative rather than coercive. Islam believes in inner self-discipline more than an outer imposed discipline through legal measures.

The Holy Prophet (peace be upon him) is said to have expressed his indignation at those who do not fast in *Ramazan* by saying, "Were it not for children and the sick ones, I have an urge to set fire to those houses from which smoke rises during daytime in *Ramazan*". Imam Abu Hanifa has labelled those who give up their prayers intentionally as expelled from Islam. Similar expressions of wrath, indignation and dislike are met with against those who show laxity in the observance of Islamic injunctions. However, if non-observance of Islamic injunctions become massive and widespread and poses a threat to true religious thinking by setting up bad example for the masses, the State may take suitable steps to ensure that religious injunctions are followed faithfully or at least not flouted publicly. No punishment has been prescribed by the Holy Quran for drinking, but Hazrat Omar prescribed 80 lashes for drinking perhaps with a view to nipping the evil in the bud.

Thirdly there are the Hypocrites. These are a dangerous class. They follow no rules except the dictates of their self-interest. They claim to be Muslims not out of any love for Islam, but because of a likelihood of sharing the benefits accruing to the Muslims. Should tables turn on Muslims, they will not hesitate to join anti-Islamic and anti-State forces. For these the course to be followed by the State has been laid down in the Holy Quran. "O Prophet; fight against the infidels and the hypocrites and be stern with them". (66:9). Muslim history provides examples of tackling these people.

In the days of Caliph Abu Bakr (God be pleased with him), for example, some tribes made an open attempt to make the practice of religion a personal affair by refusing to pay *Zakat.* Hazrat Abu Bakr's keen foresight saw in this attitude a danger for the State and decided to wage a war against them disregarding their observance of prayers and other injunctions of Islam. This example provides a hint for an Islamic State to interfere in the so-called personal affairs of the Muslims to ensure that Islam is followed by the Muslims in its entirety and not piecemeal. But State intervention is warranted only when non-observance of Islamic injunctions becomes massive and widespread and poses a threat to Islam or State. Short of that the preferred course is one of educating the masses in religious teachings and setting right patterns of behaviour at the top levels of society from where they shall automatically percolate to the levels of the masses.

Fourthly, there are the minorities. As hinted earlier, they too are expected to follow faithfully their own religious injunctions. Islamic State can provide them help by proper legal administrative and organisational measures.

Holy Quran, the Guide : Islamic polity in modern times will always be guided and inspired by the teachings of the Holy Quran and by the sayings and traditions, acts and deeds of the greatest benefactor mankind has known, the Holy Prophet

Muhammad (peace be upon him). Blessed by and chosen of God, his was a divine mission, one of lifting humanity from the depths of moral and spiritual degeneration and guiding its steps towards a new destiny, a new life of peace, equality and brotherhood. All world historians are agreed that there has been no revolution greater than the one the Holy Prophet (peace be upon him) brought about. If there has ever been a total revolution it was this.

Unlike so many incomplete ideologies of later ages, it at once gave its followers moral elevation, economic emancipation and political freedom. It brought peace; it brought equality; it banished racism, it ended exploitation; and it founded a society which by its orderliness, discipline and progress dazzled the entire world. There is for the modern man the beautifully worded but largely ignored U.N. Charter. But Islam gave a much more comprehensive charter of human freedom some 1400 years ago and, what is more, unlike the present day got it fully implemented wherever it held sway. Islam has played a pioneering role in the evolution of human civilisation in the sense that it was the first to rise above the considerations of race, colour, language and ationality—problems that still afflict humanity—and did not just give a call but actually established a world brotherhood, based on its lofty ideals.

Answer to Problems

It is no self-righteous claim that given its moderation and balanced approach, Islam provides an answer to the spiritual and material problems of 20th century society as well. Islam is not a static ideology. It is a dynamic force, forever evolving to meet the new demands of the times and guiding the faithful on the basis of its eternal, God-ordained principles. Nothing better illustrates the undiminished vitality of Islam than the creation of Pakistan itself and lately the revolution in Iran. Avoiding the extremes of the various isms in vogue today and steering a middle course, Islam alone can lead the world out of its present turmoils and act as a vehicle for the establishment of a new international order. This is acknowledged by some of the leading thinkers in the West too.

After the failure of both outdated Capitalism and repressive Communism a disillusioned world is increasingly turning towards Islam in search of salvation. Witness the reawakening in the length and breadth of the Muslim belt and a new interest in and respect for the message of the Holy Quran among non-Muslims. The revival has most significantly coincided with the advent of the 15th century of Hijra which, according to tradition, is the century that will see the final triumph of Islam. At this juncture in history, clearly a special responsibility devolves on us Muslims. We have to act as the vanguard of the coming revolution and it is only fit that we prepare ourselves suitably to play our ordained role.

No doubt, some preliminary measures towards uniting the Muslim *Ummah* and realising its hidden potential have been taken, but the fast changing times demand of us to make still greater efforts. There is need to bring together the disparate Muslim countries into an unbreakable bond of politico-economic unity; there is need to create a new machinery for the united defence of the Muslim lands; there is need to achieve greater diplomatic co-ordination for the attainment of common goals. Above all, there is need to hold fast to Islam and revert to its spiritual and moral basis, for recording our individual and collective lives, but once made Muslims an irresistible force in Africa, Asia and Europe. Needless to say, it is only by reviving the spirit of early Islam that Muslims can win back their lost glory and the leadership of mankind Almighty Allah has promised them. This we can do by bringing about a revolution in our minds, in our thinking and attitudes, in the light of the eternal teachings of Islam and the Holy Quran.

In modern times when territorial nationalism is the order of the day and material and economic considerations almost wholly shape people's outlook and policies, what is unique about the Islamic polity is the fact that it is the triumph of an ethical concept and a cultural ideal. In this context, it should be kept uppermost in the mind that Islam is not merely a religion in its narrow import. It is not a set of dogmas, mythological beliefs or mere rituals. It does not divide life into watertight compartments. There is no dichotomy in Islam between the temporal and spiritual; the structure of Islam is essentially religio-political.

In this system the state forms an integral part at the apex and as Allama Iqbal points out "is only an effort to realise the spiritual in human organisation". Lectures on *Reconstruction of Religious Thoughts in Islam,* (page 115). Thus, Islam presents the whole of reality to man and wants to give him guidance in every walk of life. It requires him to discriminate between the right and wrong and to accept a path because it is right and not because it is secular or non-secular. It attempts to bring the realities of this world in harmony with the ideals that provide security for this world and the Hereafter. It is a complete code of conduct. It is a way of life and a philosophy of life. It is a social, economic and political system.

It is with this background that the tradition of Islam is considered a better ideal for the entire mankind than any other way of life, religion or ideology. As Toynbee aptly puts it: "In a world in which distance has been annihilated by the progress of Western technology, or in which the Western way of life is having to compete with the Russian way of life for the allegiance of all mankind, the Islamic tradition of the brotherhood of man would seem to be a better ideal for meeting the social needs of the times than the Western tradition" (Arnold J Toynbee: The *World and the West,* section: Islam and the West).

5

Source of Inspiration

What is the consequence of abstracting the text and treating it symbolically? Our impression is that such an interpretative approach either becomes trivializing or fascist. The trivializing aspect comes about because truths are abstracted from their context and end up being recorded as bland statements, like 'Islam is peace', or 'Islam teaches us to be just', or 'Jihad means to struggle for peace'. In such a context, how important could careful adherence to the *ahkam* (legal properties) be? The fascist part comes about because the key interpreter gets to play games with symbols that are manipulated exclusively by him and his cohorts. In that context, external or outward or literal Islam, with its laws and regulations, is so much drivel for people not sufficiently elevated. (One could call the first approach *ibahiyyah* and the second *batiniyyah).*

Divine Book

In contrast, the consequence of closer readings of the revelation, of more grammatically aware and precise readings, of increased attention to the tiniest details of the revelation in its original language is, ironically, a discovery of a polysemantic and multifaceted text. The broadest, most varied and dynamic, vibrant and living understanding of the revelation comes from the closest, most careful, detailed, linguistic, and literally based reading. It happens too that the closest fidelity to the *ahkam* (such as those related to placing one's hands while standing during the *salah,* for example) opens up a range of authentic and true positions. Instead of denigrating the truth of following normative practices by trivializing them, this interpretation invests great significance and relevance to multiple true positions; instead of in-group fascism, this interpretation affirms other true positions, without denying any one of them.

In one passage we saw Ibn al-Arabi incorporating the peculiar linguistic fact that in the Arab language the word *khafiya is* its own antonym, such that, for those of the perception, the Hidden is the Manifest, the exposed is the concealed. When I mentioned this to a colleague of mine, she said that the secrets of the Quran are safely hidden away—in the outside, literal text! As with Poe's purloined letter, the best place to hide something is in the most exposed place. The *haqqiqah* is the *shariah.*

Let us examine the depths, details, and particularities of one portion of a verse to show what kind of polysemanticism comes about with a close; literal reading of the revelation. This portion of a verse in the chapter *al-Maidah* sets down the description of *wudu.* The portion reads, *O you who believe. When you go to the salah, wash your faces and your hands to the elbows and wipe your heads and your feet to the ankles [5:6].* The two operative imperatives are wash (gh.s.l) and wipe (m.s.h.). The question is which imperative governs the phrase 'your feet'.

Wiping is where wet hands brush over the bodily part in question, whether head or foot. Wiping the feet entails a brisk movement similar to the wiping over the shoes, and Sunni scholars have generally believed this movement of wiping over the bare feet to be negated by the *hadith* evidence in which the Prophet Muhammad admonished a group of Muslims to pay attention to their heels in *wudu,* saying, 'Woe to the heels in hell-fire'.

This particular line of argument unfolds as follows. The obvious and literal meaning of the verse in the Quranic Arabic indicates the feet, much as in English 'wipe your heads, and your feet', means 'wipe your heads, and wipe your feet'. But the *hadith* seems to indicate 'washing' the feet, so as to make sure the heels are covered in *wudu*. How should these two different indications be reconciled? We examine some of the major arguments which seek to do just that below, and then we examine Ibn alArabi's treatment of this issue.

Let us look first at three areas essential to this *fiqh* debate. First, the recitations involved for the verse; that is, the authentic, correct *(sahih)* recitations of the word 'your feet'. Second, the list of authorities and what method of *wudu* of the feet they practised, and why. Third, the arguments proffered by scholars over the ages to address this issue.

The raw citations and data are to give the reader a glimpse of the intricacies and fine points of the classical scholarly discourse, where the direction one moves toward truth is not out towards abstraction and generalization, but in towards detail and specificity. As with fractal geometries, Escher's drawings, Borges and Eco's writings, the 'truth' of things lies in the patterns one perceives as one peers closely and with a narrower field of view.

The weight of this massive debate should demonstrate the futility of the desire for conclusion and answers, and should begin to show us instead the value of searching for polysemanticism in randomness, complexities, and ambiguities.

Good Recitations : There are three recitations of 'your feet', namely *arjulakum* (with *nasb), arjulikum* (with *khafd),* and *arjulukum* (with *raft*) :

1. The first recitation is recited by Nafi ibn Abu Nuaym (169/785), Asim ibn Abu al-Nujud (127/744), and Ali ibn Hamzah al-Kasai (189/801).

2. The second recitation of *arjulikum* with *khafd* is that of Abd-Allah Ibn Kathir (120/737), Abu Amr ibn al-Ala (1455/771), and Hamzah ibn Habib (156/772).
3. For the third recitation, Nafi is reported, by Walid ibn Muslim, to have also recited *arjulukum* with *raft*, and it is the recitation of Hasan and al-Amash Sulayman?

Generally, but not necessarily, as we shall see, the recitation of *arjulakum* supports a reading that implies that the operative imperative here is 'wash'; the recitation of *arjulikum* supports a reading that implies that the operative imperative is the proximate verb 'wipe'; and the rare recitation *arjulukum* supports a reading that implies that either of the two imperatives are operative—wipe *and wash* your feet.

Effective Authorities : The following are authoritative positions of early Muslims.

Arjulakum—Washing

Urwah ibn Zubair *(nasb):* recorded in Ibn Mundhir.

Mujahid ibn Jabr *(nasb):* in Ibn Mundhir.

Nafi ibn Abd al-Rahman *(nasb):* reported from Abu Ubayd, in Ibn Mundhir.

Kisai *(nasb):* in Ibn Mundhir.

Abu Ubayd al-Qassim ibn Salam *(nasb):* in Ibn Mundhir.

Al-Shafii *(nasb):* in Ibn Mundhir.

Ali *(nasb):* al-Qurtubi records, 'Asim ibn Kalib reported from Abd al-Rahman that he said, Hasan and Hussayn, Allah's mercy on them, recited *wa arjulakum,* and Ali heard that, and was adjudicating between the people, and said *arjulakum.*' Ibn Mundhir confirms that Ali recited with *nasb.*

Arjulakum—Wiping

Ibn Masud : *(nasb :* wiping);

Ibn Abbas *(nasb :* wiping): al-Qurtubi records, 'It was

reported from Ibn Abbas that he said *wudu* is two washings [arms and face] and two wipings [head and feet]'. Ibn Qudamah records, 'It is related from Ibn Abbas that he said, I do not find in the Book of Allah anything but two washings and two wipings."

Ibn Kathir records that Ibn Abbas wiped the feet. He says, 'Ibn Abu Hatim said, *haddathana* my father *haddathana* Abu Mamar al-Mungari *haddathana* Abd al-Wahhab *Haddathana* Ali ibn Zayd from Yusuf ibn Mahran from Ibn Abbas about this verse that it is a wiping. '

Ibn Majah records in his *Sunan, 'haddathana* Abu Bakr ibn Abi Shaybah *haddathana* Ibn Ulayyah, from Ruhi ibn al-Qasim from AbdAllah ibn Muhammad ibn Aqil from Rubayya, who said, Ibn Abbas came to me and he asked me about this *hadith,* that is, the *hadith* in which it was mentioned that the messenger of Allah *(sallallahu alayhi wa sallam)* did *wudu* and washed his feet. Ibn Abbas said, "The people insist on nothing but washing, but I do not find in the Book of Allah anything but wiping"."

Arjulikum—Wiping

Al-Hasan al-Basri : in Ibn Mundhir.

Sulayman ibn Mahran al-Amash : in Ibn Mundhir.

Abu Jafar : al-Razi records, 'The people disagree about wiping the feet and washing them', and Ibn Abbas, Anas ibn Malik, Ikrimah, Shubi, and Abu Jafar Muhammad ibn Ali obligate wiping, and it is the position of the Imamiyyah among the Shiah.'

Ikrimah ibn Abd-Allah: al-Qurtubi records, 'Ikrimah used to wipe his feet. He said there is no washing for the feet: The Quran was sent down with wiping them.' He also records that Ibn Jarir said, *'haddathana* Yaqub *haddathana* Ibn Uliyah *haddathana* Ayub who said, "I saw Ikrimah wiping his feet, and he argued for it".'

Abu Dharr: Ibn Hajar (852) in *Fath al-Bari* records that to the *hadith* 'woe to the heels in hell-fire', Abu Dharr added, 'And he did not wipe his feet."

Al-Qatadah : al-Qurtubi records that al-Qatadah ibn Daamah (117/ 735) said, 'Allah made required two washings and two wipings.'

Arjulikum—Washing

Amr ibn Sharhbil al-Shubah : in Ibn Mundhir. He is recorded as saying, 'The Quran came down with wiping but the Sunna is for washing.'

Al-Thalab : Ibn Manzur in *Lisan al-Arab* cites Abu al-Abbas al-Thalab (291/903) as saying, 'The Quran came down revealing wiping but the Sunna is for washing."

Anas : al-Qurtubi records that Al-Hajjaj ibn Yusuf al-Thaqafi (95/ 714), governor of the eastern provinces, 'gave a *khutbah* in Ahwaz and mentioned *wudu*. He said, "Wash your faces and hands and wipe your heads and feet because there is nothing of the sons of Adam closer to filth than his feet, so wash them, their bottoms and their tops, and their tendons." Anas ibn Malik heard that and said, "Allah spoke the truth and Hajjaj spoke a lie, because Allah said, Wipe your heads *wa arjulikum*. When he wiped his feet, he (simply) moistened them".' Al-Qurtubi also records, 'It is also reported from Anas that he said the Quran was sent down with wiping but the Sunna is with washing.' Ibn Mundhir records the above from Ibn Umar and also records, '*haddathana* Ismail *haddathana* Abu Bakr *haddathana* Muhammad ibn Abi Adwi from his father that Anas used to wash his hands and feet until they dripped.'

Ibn Kathir records the same story about Hajjaj: 'Ibn Jarir said *haddathani* Yaqub ibn Ibrahim *haddathana* Ibn Uliyah *haddathana* Hamid who said Musa ibn Anas said to Anas, when we were with him, O Abu Hamzah, Hajjaj gave us a *khutbah* in Ahwaz, while we were with him and he mentioned purification. He said, "Wash your faces and wipe your heads and feet because there is nothing of the sons of Adam closer to filth than his feet, so wash them, their bottoms and their tops, and their tendons." Anas heard that and said, Hajjaj spoke a lie: Allah said, *Wipe your heads wa arjulikum.* When Anas wiped the feet, he moistened them. The chain is authentic.' Ibn Kathir also confirms: 'Ibn Jarir said *haddathana* Ali ibn Sahl *haddathana* Mumal *haddathana* Hammad *haddathana* Asim about the case of Anas, and he said. The Quran came down with wiping but the Sunna is for washing. This too has an authentic chain.'

Arjulukum—Wash and Wipe

Hasan (combine): al-Zamakhshari records that Hasan said, 'It is a combining of two matters.' He also records, 'Hasan recited *arjulukum* with *raf,* with the meaning *wa arjulukum,* washed or wiped to the ankles'.

Dawud (combine): al-Razi records that Dawud al-Isfahani al-Zahiri obligates combining the two; it is also the position of al-Nasir of the Zaydis.

Al-Nahhas (combine): al-Qurtubi records, 'al-Nahhas said one of the best things said about the issue is that wiping and the washing are both obligatory together, so the wiping is obligatory because of the recitation of one who recites *nasb,* and the two recitations have the status of two verses.'

Arjulikum or Arjulakum—Wash or Wipe

Al-Tabari (choice): al-Qurtubi records that 'Ibn Jarir al-Tabari (310/ 922) judged that required for the feet is to choose between the washing and the wiping.' Al-Razi adds that this was Hasan al-Basri's position too, recording, 'The position of Hasan al-Basri and Muhammad ibn Jarir al-Tabari is that the one responsible [for *wudu]* chooses between wiping and washing.'

Ibn al-Arabi al-Maliki records that Muhammad ibn Jarir al-Tabari ,reasoned that the recitation *is arjulikum* with *khafd* in conjunction with the head, so the head and feet are wiped, and the recitation with *nasb is* in conjunction with the face and arms, so they are washed; so in that way it functions in accordance with both recitations.

Al-Nawawi adds, 'Jubbai, the head of the Mutazilahs, chose between wiping and washing.'

Logical View

Arguments from Sunna : The conclusive argument for the classical Sunni scholars for washing is based on Sunna. A terse argument for washing is that given by Ibn alArabi al-Maliki, who says, 'Our proof is the continuous practice *[amal al-mutassil,* that is, from the time of the Prophet (PBUH) to today, of washing the feet] and the multiple unbroken chains of transmitted text *[naql al-mutawatir]'*. Related to this argument for washing is the consensus of the scholars, described by Al-Qurtubi as his last proof, namely,

Consensus *[ijma]*. They agree that the one who washed his feet has in fact fulfilled his obligation, but they disagree about one who has wiped his feet. Certainty is with what they have agreed about and not with what they have disagreed about. The transmitted tradition of all the vast majority *[jamhur]* is from their Prophet (PBUH) that he washed his feet in his *wudu*, once, twice, and thrice, until he had cleaned them.

But while the Sunna is to wash, this was not always the case. Ibn Qudamah reports, 'Said *haddathana* Hashim that *akhbarana* [it was told us in the form of a report] Ibn Ata from his father that he said *akhbarani* [it was told me in a report] Aws ibn Aws Abi al-Thaqafi that he saw the Prophet come to a *kizamah* of the people of Taif, and he did *wudu* and wiped his feet. Hashim said this was in the initial period of Islam.' Interestingly, the Sunna of washing is so established that when Ibn Manzur cites this *hadith* in order to explain *kizamah* in his dictionary, he says this: 'The *kizamah* is a pipe under the ground and water flows through it. It is mentioned in the *hadith* that the Prophet came to a *kizamah* of the people and did *wudu* with its water and wiped over his *shoes*."'

But besides the argument from Sunna, the classical Sunni scholars also provide numerous arguments for washing based on the Quran. Most of these arguments are linguistic, but some fall into other categories. Let us look at the other categories first.

Symbolic Arguments : Al-Zamakhshari (d.538) in his commentary *Kashshaf* records *wa arjulikum* and says, 'The majority recite *arjulakum* with *nasb,* thereby indicating that the feet are to be washed. If someone asked me why did you [O Zamakhshari] make it recite with *jarr* [that is, *khadf arjulikum]* and make the admission of a property of wiping [when you actually argue for washing the feet], I would say that the feet are among the three bodily parts washed with a pouring of water on them, so they are places of anticipated wastefulness—that is blameworthy, and actual wastefulness is forbidden—so the feet are placed in conjunction with the third part, which is wiped (i.e., the head), not so as to wipe them, but in order to remind one of the obligation of frugality in pouring water over them.'

So avoiding waste is a consideration which explains away the linguistic inclination toward wiping. This argument relies neither on the Sunna of *wudu* nor on other linguistic possibilities. This is al-Zamakhshari's major argument, and it is repeated by many of the great classical scholars.

Another argument which does not rely on the Sunna nor on linguistic evidence appeals to a sense of symmetry in *taharah.* The argument is recorded by Al-Qurtubi in this way:

Amr al-Shabi said Jibril sent down wiping: Do you not see that *tayammum* has wiping for what was washed [in *wudu*—hands and face] and eliminates what was wiped [in *wudu*—head and feet]?

Ibn Kathir uses this argument too, recording that:

> Ibn Jarir said *haddathana* Abu al-Sayb *haddathana* Ibn Idris from Dawud ibn Abu Hind from Shabi that he said, Jibril came down with wiping, then Shabi said, Do you not see that *tayammum* is wiping what was washed and it eliminates what was wiped?

Ibn Qudamah uses this argument as well.

Significance of Languages

Now let us turn to the linguistic arguments. I have collated six different linguistic arguments. These include attempts to show that it is possible in the Arab language (meaning the Arabs have used such a linguistic configuration in the period before and during the descent of the Quran) to have 'your feet' be governed by the initial verb 'wash'.

The first linguistic argument we consider is lexigraphic. Al-Qurtubi records, 'Abu Zayd al-Ansari [215 A. H./830 C. E.] said, wiping in the Arab language is washing and wiping. An example is that the Arab says about someone after *wudu* who has washed the limbs that *tamassaha* [he has wiped].' This argument accepts that 'your feet' is governed by the proximate verb 'wipe', but goes on to posit that `wipe' in effect means a light washing.

Al-Qurtubi also argues that the word 'wipe' may also apply to 'wash'. However, wipe is usually seen as a subset of wash. The argument of al-Qurtubi is that 'Abd al-Haqq ibn Atiyah (546 A. H./1151 C. E.) said, "There are people among those who recite with a *kasrah [khadf]* who judged that the wiping of the two feet is a washing. It is correct that the word wiping shares multiple meanings, applying to wiping and to washing".'

A second argument takes the instances of imperative verb plus a delineated or non-delineated object, as they occur in the verse for wudu and for *tayammum.* We have for *wudu* a clear 'wash the hands to the elbows'. When it comes to *tayammum,* we have a clear 'wipe your face and hands'. Based on these instances, the arguments goes, we see that objects governed by the imperative 'wipe' are not given delineations, and the object that is definitely governed by the imperative 'wash' is given delineation, that is, up to something. Therefore, when we come to 'your feet', and we note that they are delineated with 'up to the ankles', we can conclude that the governing verb must be 'wash'. Al-Qurtubi says, 'Allah bounded the area and said *to the ankles* as He said about the arms *to the elbows.* This proves the obligation of washing the feet, but Allah knows best.'

Ibn Hisham in his *Mughni al-Labib* and al-Zamakhshari in his commentary on 5:6 say, 'It was said *to the ankles,* so He mentioned the end-point, and that dismisses the supposition that the feet are wiped, because wiping is not given an end-point in the *shariah.*'

A third argument is based on the idea that the sequence of bodily parts purified in wudu-face, hands, head, feet-is given precedence over syntactical considerations. To illustrate this argument, suppose that the imperatives were given precedence. We would then have, 'Wash your face, hands, and feet, and wipe your head'. But because the head should be washed before the feet, we have, 'Wash face, hands, (but wipe) head, and feet', meaning 'and wash too your feet'.

Al-Qurtubi with this argument, juxtaposes the strong case for wiping based on the Quran and the strong case for washing based on the Surma. Given this tension he argues that there must be an overriding concern which motivates the inclination of the Quranic phrase towards wiping. That concern, he says, is the sequence.

Al-Qurtubi says:

> And it is said, Allah has *wiped* what you have when He has *washed* and purified you from your sins. *So* if it *is* from Arab tradition that the wiping may mean washing, then the statement which preponderates is

> this statement: *if* the consequences of the recitation with *khadf is* washing... and the many *hadiths* fix washing, and there is the warning not to neglect the washing *of* the feet in the numerous reports published by the Imams, then the wiping for the head *is* rather inserted between the things which are washed [arms and feet] for the sake of sequence, that the head should be wiped before the feet are washed, according to this syntax: so wash your faces and your arms to the elbows, and your feet to the ankles, and wipe your heads. But as the head is done before the feet, it precedes them in the recitation—Allah knows best—not because they share with the head in being wiped, but because the head precedes the feet in the process of purification.

Abu Thawr (d. 240) also explains that there must be some overriding concern which interrupts the list of bodily parts and their imperative verbs. He says that the reason your 'feet is placed' after 'your head' is not because it should take the imperative 'wipe', but because the verse is rather establishing the sequence of *wudu.* He says, 'The munificent verse mentioned something wiped [the head] among the things washed. The custom of the Arab when he mentioned like things and unlike things [e.g., wiped and washed bodily parts] is to gather the like things and then to put the other thing in conjunction to them [last], and that custom is not opposed except for a bounty, and the bounty, here, is the [teaching of the] sequence [of *wudu].*" Ramli [d. 1004] uses this argument too in his commentary to the *Minhaj* called *Nahayat al-Muhtaj.*

A fourth argument is that in the Arab language before the descent of the Quran, there is a kind of poetic sentence which puts two objects into conjunction, but where the second object is not governed by the same verb as the first object. This would explain how the Quranic phrase puts 'your heads' into conjunction with 'your feet', while the first object is governed by 'wipe' and the second is governed by something else, in this case 'wash'.

Ibn Manzur argues this way in *Lisan al-Arab*. He says, 'So one who recites it *arjulakum* does so for two reasons. First, in this there are things anterior and things posterior, as if He said, 'Then wash your faces and arms to the elbows, and your feet to the ankles, and wipe your heads', thereby putting things first and putting things last so that *wudu* would be a succession of things one after another. Then, it is as if He meant, 'Wash your feet to the ankles' because His statement *to the ankles* has already proven that is just as we described it [that is, the argument of delineation], so 'your feet' is arranged with washing, as the poet said:

If only your husband had come tomorrow!

Armed with sword, and lance

meaning 'armed with sword, and carrying a lance', where the verb `carrying' is supplied, as 'armed' is an inappropriate verb for 'lance'. Ibn al-Arabi al-Maliki uses the same verse to show that the noun of `feet' may be in conjunction with the word 'head' but not in conjunction with its meaning (that is, 'wipe'), like the poet's verse:

I saw your husband, clamoring

Armed with sword, and lance.

Al-Qurtubi multiplies the examples of this use of language. He says, 'The Arab puts something in conjunction with something with an act which applies to only one of them. The Arab says, "I ate bread, and milk", meaning, "I ate bread and I drank milk".' Another example is the statement of the poet:

I fed them straw, and cold water.

Another example is [from Labid ibn Rabiah]:

The two used the leaves of the cabbage plant, Giving birth

On the banks to her gazelle, and her brood.

Another example is:

I drank milk, and dates and cheese.

'The *taqdir* [the meaning of sentences with ambiguous syntactical elements] is as follows: I fed them straw, and gave them water to drink; the one giving birth on the banks to her gazelle; and the other brooding her ostrich (the ostrich does not 'give birth to' but rather 'broods' the egg); and finally, I'drank the milk, and I ate the dates. So, His phrase *Wipe your heads, and your feet* could be in conjunction with washing in spite of the conjunction with wiping, carrying the meaning and purport of washing. But Allah knows best.'

Al-Jurjani (d. *816)*, al-Zamakhshari's commentator, also uses the poet's verses:

Armed with sword, and lance

And feeding the animal straw, and cold water.

A fifth argument is based on the different instances of *jarr,* which means the vowel 'i' *(khafd)* given to a word because of proximity. Al-Qurtubi finds this in the Quran, where we have, *Sent down to you will be a flame of fire, and smoke (55:35),* where 'and smoke' *is muhasin* (in some recitations), which *is khafd* because of *jarr,* because 'the smoke' means 'fumes', so the meaning is 'sent down to you will be *smoke,* and a *flame* of fire', where *smoke* and *flame* are the direct objects of the sentence, even though *smoke* is in *khafd.*

Also, al-Qurtubi adds, 'He said, *No, it is a glorious Quran, in a tablet preserved' (85:21-2).* Here *preserved is mahfuz-in,* which *is khafd* because of *jarr.* In this sentence, *Quran-un, majid-un,* and preserved are all nominatives (raft so that one would say, 'It is a Quran, it is glorious, and it is preserved, in a tablet', but instead of *mahfuz-un,* we have *mahfuz-in,* which is explained as being from proximity to *fi lawh-in* (in a tablet).'

Al-Qurtubi also cites Imru al-Qays, who said: *kabir-u unas-in* fi *bijad-in muzammal-i* meaning, 'He is great among the people, in his striped garment, wrapped up.' Al-Qurtubi remarks, '*muzammal-i is* made *khafd* by proximity, because "wrapped up" refers to the man, not to the striped garment, so that its inflected termination would otherwise be *raf*".'

He also says, 'It is like the Arabs say, *hadha juhr-u dabb-in kharib-in* [this hole of a lizard, deserted]. The word *kharib-in* [deserted] is made *jarr* even though it would be raf.' That is, the sentence reads, 'this deserted hole of a lizard.' He says, 'This is the position of Akhfash and Abu Abidah, but al-Nahhas rejected it and said this statement is a great error, because it cannot be that the proximate be brought into relationship with something in such a sentence, but it is really an error, like changing the vowel to achieve a rhyme.'

Ibn Kathir remarks that the recitation with *khafd is* 'produced because of proximity and the relationship [to wipe your heads] in the sentence, as in the Arab's sentence *juhr-u dabb-in kharib-in,* and as in His statement, *They will have on them clothes of silk, green, and brocade [76:21]*. This is common in the language of the Arab.'

The grammarian Ibn Hisham says, 'A word gives governance to another word when it is in proximity to it, like the statement of some of them: *hadha juhr-u dabb-in kharib-in* with *jarr* but most of them make it *raf*.' That *is, kharib-un;* this is a hole *(juhr-u)*, deserted *(kharib-un)*, of a lizard *(dabb-in)*. He also cites Imru al-Qays's verse:

ka-anna abanan fi *afanini wadqihi*
kabir-u unas-in fi *bijad-in muzammali.*

Ibn Hisham al-Ansari also argues from a passage in 56:11-22, which reads in part, 'These will be nearest to Allah, in gardens of bliss .... Circling them will be ever fresh youth, with goblets, glasses, and cups ... and fruits ... and flesh of fowl ... and black/white eye'." One question in this passage is what governs the phrases. Ibn Hisham notes that some take 'black/white eye' as *jarr,* that *is, hur-in,* so that 'black/white eye' is governed by 'ever fresh youth'. The meaning is then 'ever fresh youth ... with black/white eye'. But the conjunction could go all the way back to 'gardens of bliss'. Then, we would have 'gardens of bliss', with 'many fruits', and 'flesh of fowl', and *hur-in ayn-in,* which is then read as a synecdoche, as in 'companions with *hur-in ayn-in'*. *'Cups'* would be in conjunction with 'ever fresh youth', so that it would be 'ever fresh youth, circling them with cups'. But Ibn Hisham ends his discussion with the comment, 'Actually, the *khafd* of proximity is rare.'

Ibn Qudamah quotes Imru al-Qays's verse which we saw and also:

fa-zalla tuhatu al-lahm min bayni mundij-in

safifa shiwa-in aw qidir-in mu ajjabi

The meat cooks erred between a well-cooked

grilled row and quick boil

where *qidir-an* (cooked in a pot) is made *jarr – qidir – in – by* being in conjunction with what is proximate, but referring back to *al-lahm* (the meat).

Ibn Qudamah also cites the Quran, where we have *inni akhafu alaykum adhaba yawm-in alim-in* (I fear for you the punishment of a grievous day) (11:26), saying that *alim-in is jarr* because of the proximity of 'day', while it is a description of the punishment, which is *nasb* (the direct object), because of its proximity to the proximate *yawm-in.*

But Ibn Manzur questions the occurrence of the *khafd* of proximity as proving 'washing' in this verse by citing Abu Ishaq, the grammarian, who said, 'Making a noun *khafd* because of proximity is not permitted in the Book of Allah, while it is permissible for poetical imagery.'

Al-Razi too, is doubtful about this argument. He says that the *jarr* of proximity means that the 'feet' are the conjunction with 'wipe your heads', and are governed by 'wipe'. He cites the arguments that this *jarr* is not conclusive, saying 'If it is said no, it is not possible to say that this vowel "i" is there just because of proximity [while "feet" is still in conjunction with "wash your faces"], as it is in the statement:

juhr-u dabb-in kharib-in

and the poet's verse:

kabir anas fi *bijad-in mazmal-i*

we say that is false.' Al-Razi says the above examples may be explained by poetical exigency.

Second, in the above examples, there is no question of ambiguity. In the statement *juhr-u dabb-in kharib-in* the word, 'deserted' cannot be describing the lizard but must be describing the hole. So, he concludes, 'in this verse certainty in the face of ambiguity is not produced.' For al-Razi, the linguistic argument of *jarr* is ultimately inconclusive.

Al-Shawkani cites the possibilities of an argument of *jarr*, but then acknowledges its weakness and sustains an argument from Sunna. He says:

> The ones who argue that washing the feet is not obligatory, argue from a recitation of *jarr* in His statement *arjulikum* being in conjunction with His statement *your heads.* They say *arjulikum is* one of the [three of the] seven recitations which are authentic. There is an argument for the conjunction being with washing the faces, even though it is recited with the *jarr* of the proximate; this has been related by the majority of the Arab 21 Imams, like Sibawayh and Akhfash, but it certainly *is* very rare; it differs from the obvious meaning and it cannot sustain the contested position. We argue instead that obligatory is carrying the argument with *his (sallallahu alayhi wa sallam)* consistent practice of washing the feet.

Finally, there is an argument that there is an ambiguity in washing or wiping the feet precisely so that the verse can bear two contexts: wash the feet in one context, and wipe the feet when they are shod.

Al-Qurtubi says, 'It has been said that if the *khafd* of the feet rather mentions restrictively wiping them, it could be for when the feet have shoes on. We learn this restriction from the messenger of Allah, as it is not correct about him that he wiped his feet, except when they were shod. So thereby the messenger of Allah explained with his action the context for washing the feet and the context for wiping them. This is a fine argument.'

Ibn al-Arabi al-Maliki also gives this argument, saying 'Or, the meaning of "wiping" could be for the context of wearing shoes, so the two recitations could be for both contexts [bare feet and shod feet], once *nasb* for the bared feet and once *khafd* for the covered feet.'

Ibn al-Arabi's Position : Ibn al-Arabi alludes to this argument when he discusses the *fiqh* disagreement about what to do when wiping over the shoe when there is a tear in the shoe. He says, 'We argue for wiping what emerges, because we were commanded in the Book of Allah to wipe the feet, so when something of the foot emerges, we wipe it. Thus, there should be no obstacle in wiping the torn shoe where some of the foot sticks out, because the verse's imperative of 'wipe' fits both cases of shod/bare foot.

Ibn al-Arabi reviews the various positions of the ulema, saying, 'The ulema concurred that the feet belong to the bodily parts of *wudu*, but they disagreed about a format of their *taharah*, whether that is through washing, wiping, or choosing between the two.' As we saw, the position of washing is the position of the majority of the classical Sunni scholars; the position of wiping is the position of many companions and successors, including Ibn Abbas, Anas, and Ikrimah; the position of choosing between the two is that of al-Tabari, Hasan al-Basri, Jubbai,

Nasir, and Dawud. It is appropriate here to emphasize that Ibn al-Arabi is neither part of the Zahiri school of jurisprudence associated with Dawud and Ibn Hazm, nor is he a part of the Shi'ite school.

Ibn al-Arabi says, 'Our position is choice' and goes on to say 'the combination is best'. This last phrase probably refers to al-Nahhas own position which is characterized by al-Nahhas as `one of the best things said about the issue'. We saw above that al-Qurtubi recorded, `al-Nahhas said one of the best things said about the issue is that the wiping and the washing are both obligatory together, so the wiping is obligatory because of the recitation of one who recites with *khafd* and the washing is obligatory because of the recitation of one who recites with *nasb,* and the two recitations have the status of two verses.'

There is an argument of Ibn Hisham found in his classical grammar *Mughni* which holds that the *wa* (and) could have the meaning of *aw (or).* In this case there is a linguistic argument for choice. The argument goes as follows.

The meaning of the *wa* here could be 'choice'. One of (the poets) said:

> They said, Go far away, choosing for her
>
> patience *'wa'* crying
>
> She said, Crying *is* healthier if I want revenge.

The meaning then is patience *or* crying if patience is not joined to crying (that is, patience *and* crying).

Ibn al-Arabi's position embraces two themes, ease and relief of difficulty, based on the verse *We did not make for you in the religion any constriction (22:78),* a verse which begins with *jahidu fi Allahi* (exert for Allah) and suggests the *ijtihad* of effortful exertion to understand the determined properties *(ahkam)* and the many consequences of a polysemantic text.

Wiping and washing are related as two forms of purification, the one being subsumed' in the other. Ibn al-Arabi says, 'Know that washing contains wiping from one perspective, so the one who washed has already subsumed wiping in it, just as star light is subsumed in the sun's light.' He acknowledges too that it is possible to see wiping simply as a synonym for washing, as we saw above, saying, 'The one who has wiped did not wash, except in a position of the one who believes, and quotes the Arabs, that "wiping" is a word for "washing", so they are synonymous.'

In Ibn al-Arabi's *fiqh,* each command which is operative in the outwardness is also operative in the inwardness. The command of this verse, therefore, has an inward dimension. He says:

> The correct meaning of the *hukm* for the inwardness is that wiping is used for whatever specific practices are necessitated and washing for whatever general practices are necessitated.

Because of this, we propounded choice commensurate with the moment, because perhaps you run to a philanthropist for a designated need, on behalf of an individual himself, then that is in a way station of wiping. And perhaps you run to the king for a need diffused over the entire population, or needs, so that that individual would be included in this general public, so this is in a way station of washing in which is subsumed wiping.

Now Ibn al-Arabi investigates the linguistic evidence of the verse. He notes, 'As for the reciting of His statement [Wash *your faces,* and *your hands to the elbows, wipe your head] wa arjulkum* [your feet] [5:6], with either *arjula,* or *arjuli*—on account of the letter *wa*—according to whether the *wa* is in conjunction with "wipe", through *khafd,* or in conjunction with "wash", with the vocalization *arjula*. Our position is that even the recitation *arjula* does not actually contraindicate wiping, because this wa may be the 'and of simultaneity', and the 'and of simultaneity' makes the word *arjula*.'

Even though the recitation of *arjulakum* which we noted above, was generally associated with the argument for taking the initial verb 'wash' as the operative imperative, the argument for wiping is still linguistically strong. Ibn al-Arabi then gives examples of the 'and of simultaneity'. He says:

> You say, *qama Zayd wa Umar-an;* and *wa stiwa-al-mau* was *l-khashabat*an; and *wa ma anta wa qasat-an min tharid;* and *wa marrartu bi-Zayd wa Umar-an*. You mean, (I passed Zayd) with Umar. And likewise for the one who recites [with *nasb*] *Wipe your heads and your arjula, with a.*

So,

The argumentation of the one who argues for wiping, in this verse, is stronger, because his argumentation shares with the proponent for washing in giving expression to the recitation arjula. But one who argues for washing does not share with the proponent for wiping in giving expression to the recitation *arjuli*.

From the verse 'wiping' is stronger, and the proponent for 'wiping' can point to either vocalization for proof.

Among 'our colleagues', Ibn al-Arabi says, there are those who 'preponderate the specific over the general, and among them there are those who would preponderate the general over the specific: all of that absolutely.' Using the metaphor developed above, some of our colleagues always go to a specific philanthropist, and others always go to the king. They are not sensitive to the context, but instead go fixedly and rigidly to one place.

Ibn al-Arabi then says:

> But our position is other than that. We walk with the Real according to a determined property *[hukm]* of the circumstance, so we generalize where He generalized, and we make specific where He makes specific.

We do not initiate a property, because one who initiated a property has already initiated in his self Lordship, and the one who has initiated in himself Lordship has already diminished his servanthood, to the extent of this issue. And if he has diminished his servanthood, to that extent, he shall diminish the divine self-disclosure of the Real in him. And if he has diminished the divine self-disclosure of the Real in him, he has diminished his knowledge through his Lord. And if he has diminished his knowledge through his Lord, he is ignorant about Him to the context he diminished it, because if there should appear to that one, the one who diminished it, a property in the world [the macrocosm] or in his world [the microcosm], he would not recognize it. Because of this, our position is that we do not initiate a property in one fell swoop.

Ibn al-Arabi is completely familiar with the range of arguments produced by the legal scholars of his time. Their arguments generally seek closure and finality—although without exception, the final theme among all the classical scholars is 'But Allah knows best.' That is, even though they desire closure and finality, the classical scholars leave the door open to continuing divine guidance.

The desire to achieve a single and monolithic understanding of Islam is a perennial problem. Every *qadi* who ever insisted on having the right to use *ijtihad* to settle cases, using any of the schools of jurisprudence which best applied for that particular case, was also fighting against the desire of the sultan and state to codify and impose a Procrustean vision of Islam.

So the sum consequence of the polysemantic text of washing/wiping the feet is 'that or perhaps that', or 'this and that'. The more one knows about this verse, the more one is aware of not knowing. For Ibn al-Arabi, the response to 'not knowing' is not *qiyas* or *ray* but *taqwa,* becoming protected by Allah through doing acts which will protect oneself from His punishment (which is its Arabic definition).

Interestingly enough, the conclusion or last word of Ibn al-Arabi for every issue, then, *is taqwa,* and this is a conclusion which is valid for every level of knowledge. Ibn al-Arabi's treatment of this particular issue is to multiply its polysemantic nature, to increase the possibilities, to deconstruct false closures and *taqayyid,* and the smugness of 'knowing'. He seeks to convince his audience that for this and every issue we must void ourselves of Lordship and exaltedness, becoming instead humbly receptive and alert to divine command.

In the mater of purity *(taharah)* in the same verse we have been considering (5:6), Allah says that He does not wish for us any constriction *ma yuridu Allahu li-ajala alaykum min haraj,* but instead, *He wishes to make you pure.* Then, following this verse He tells us to remember our covenant with Him,. when we said, 'We hear and obey'. One might gloss here we listen, we hear, and we obey. For Ibn al-Arabi, assumption of lordship on our part, whether openly or not, precludes our listening, hearing, and ultimately, obeying. And right after that, Allah says, *And have taqwa [fear] before Allah; Allah is aware of the bottom of the hearts! (5:8).*

God's Words : There is a great thirst for the direct word of Allah. Knowledge in the Quran is linked with water; rain comes down from the heavens, the parched earth drinks it, and vegetation is produced. Muhammad received the rain, which comes 'freshly from its Lord'. Rain is the direct knowledge which Allah gives to make us whole. River water is indirect knowledge—knowledge from our intellects—which gets mixed up with impurities and is subject to pollution. I used to joke that now we have acid rain: but, now I think that is our situation indeed. We no longer have the direct, clean, pure rainwater which Allah provides because the medium above us is itself polluted.

Clearing the Air : We have tried here to clear the air of the irritants and obstacles which come in the way of hearing the word directly. What Ibn al-Arabi does, above all, is to prepare his audience for the encounter and then to become transparent before the encounter. His intellect, his genius, and his skill pale in comparison with this gift: a way to hear in clear and clarifying language, the divine word.

And as therefore neither conclusions nor resolutions are appropriate, we take up three passages from Ibn al-Arabi's *fiqh.*

Three Passages from Al-Arabi

The First Passage : In the first passage, we hear Ibn al-Arabi's discussion on *awrah.* This word is not translatable, but it is describable. Classically, *awrah* meant the part of the body, men's and women's, which had to be covered. The classical *fiqh* books spent most of their time discussing the man's *awrah* and the man's clothing. Today of course, *awrah* means the shameful part of women, including their voices, smell, and very presence. In fact, in Urdu, woman herself is called shameful—aurat. In order to recover the direct knowledge of the Quran, let us take up Ibn al-Arabi's discussion here; I have first translated Ibn Manzur's descriptions of key words needed for this passage from Ibn al-Arabi's *Futuhat al-Makkivvah.*

Awrah ('w.r.): Ibn Manzur says, 'The *awrah* of the man and the woman is their private parts.' And 'the *awrah* is everything that causes embarrassment if it is exposed.' Also, 'The *awar* ['w.r.] has only one eye'. He also says, 'Covering the *awrah* during the *salah* and other than the *salah* is obligatory; about covering it when secluded there is a disagreement'. And 'in the Quran we have, Our *houses* are *awrah* (33:13), that is, they are open to the thief because the houses have been cleared of the men, but Allah caught them in their lie, saying, *But they* were *not awrah, they only, wanted to desert* [33:13]. It is said its meaning is. Our houses are *awrah,* that is, our houses are near the enemy and we were stolen from them. But Allah knew that their intent was deserting the battle.'

Ibn al-Arabi says, 'The ulema agree that covering the awrah is obligatory, with no disagreement, and absolutely, that is, during the salah I shall mention its boundary of the man and the woman.'

Mayl (m.y.l.): Ibn Manzur says, '*Mayl* is inclining toward something.'

Ibn al-Arabi says, 'The crossover for that in the inwardness. It is obligatory on every intelligent person to cover the divine secret which, if it were disclosed, would lead someone, who was neither knowledgeable nor intelligent, to a lack of a sense of taboo toward the Side of the divine, Exalted, Forbidden, because the reality of *awrah* is *mayl*. Because of this that person said *Our houses are awrah* [33:13], that is, inclined, bent on destruction, when they sought to desert; then Allah caught them in their lie, before His Prophet, with His word, *But they were not awrah; they* only *meant* to desert [33:13], that is, to desert what you [Muhammad] called them to. There is also the *awar* [one-eyed man], because his view inclines [m.y.l.] to a single perspective.

'Like that it is appropriate that the knowledgeable one cover from the ignorant one the secrets of the Real; secrets like His word, *There* are *no whisperings of three except He is the fourth [58:7];* His word, *We are closer to one than the jugular vein [50:16];* and His word, *1 become his ear, and his eye, and his tongue,* because when the ignorant one hears that, it leads him to forbidden conceptualizations like divine incarnation or bounded divinity. Therefore, it is appropriate that with which the Real turns and inclines to the hearts of the knowledgeable ones—Exalted is He and Holy—with His address, be covered up with whatever His Majesty necessitates of Independence absolutely from the worlds; in addition to His word on the tongue of His messenger, *I was hungry and you fed me not, I was sick and you visited me not, I was thirsty and you did not give me to drink.*

'So he covers up the knowledge of this secret from the ignorant one and he does not add to what He said as a commentary to it [that is, I *was hungry]* at all. He covers up as the Real does with His word, *So and so was sick, and if you had visited him, you would have found Me with him.* This is more ambiguous than the first statement, but He gives in this commentary to the ones who know Allah, another knowledge about Him which they did not have.

That is that in the first He made Himself the very same sick and hungry one but in His commentary He made Himself the Helper of the sick one, as He is *with him,* because whoever helps the sick one is with him. How far away is this from the One who made Himself the sick one himself! Each statement in that way is real, and to every real *[Haqq]* is a Reality *[Haqqiqah].*'

Ammi (' m.m.): (This is one of the most loaded classical words, usually full of the absolute class distinctions of the elite and the mass. Ibn al-Arabi's use of the word is, however, quite different and is tied into one of the descriptions used by Ibn Manzur). Ibn Manzur says, 'A *ummayy ['m.m.]* man and a *qusriyy [q.s.r.,* utmost] man. The *ummay* is the *amm* and the *qusriyy* is the *khass.* In the *hadith:* When he used to go home, he gave upon entrance three *juz'*: a *juz* to Allah, a *juz* for his family, and a *juz* for himself. Then he apportioned *juz* for him and the people and he correlated that portion to the *ammah* through the *khassah,* meaning that the *ammah* were not with him at that moment, so the *khassah* communicated to the *ammah* what they heard from him; it is as if the benefits were transferred to the *ammah* from the *khassah.*'

According to Ibn al-Arabi, 'As for the covering up of that before the *ammi,* it is that one say to him about His statement, You *would have found Me with him* that the condition of the sick one is certainly that of dependency and need of the one in whose hand is the cure—and that is no one but Allah, so mostly what we need is to remember *[dhikr]* Allah with each instant to repel what befell him, which is different from the healthy one: He said, I *Myself am seated with the one who remembers [dhikr] Me.* This is the healthy condition. The *ammi* is satisfied with it and the knowledgeable one stays with what He taught him about that upon his knowledge; this is the cover up of the divine *mayl* from the gaze of the *ammi.*

'The ulema then disagree about whether covering the *awrah* during the *salah* is a precondition for the validity of the *salah* or not. There is one who says that covering the *awrah* is one of the Sunnas [voluntary but customary practices] of the *salah,* and there is one who says that it is one of the obligations of the *salah.*

'As for the crossover for that spiritually, we have already taught you the concept of *awrah* above. About this issue, as it is established [by an authentic *hadith]* that the one praying is in intimate conversation with his Lord and that the *salah* has been divided in two between Allah and His worshipper, so the one who sees predominate [in this issue] that the Real is the One praying through the acts of His worshipper, that is, the outward practices of the worshipper in the *salah,* as it is established that *Verily Allah said on the tongue of His worshipper during the salah, Allah hears the one who praises Him [sami Allahu li-man hamidah],* when one rises after *ruku,* and the worshipper is the speaker, certainly; and He said:

> *Give him [asylum] so that he may hear the Word of Allah [9:6],* while it is the messenger (PBUH) of Allah, who is reciting, certainly; [that one who takes this position says] the covering of the *awrah* is one of the obligations of the *salah,* that is, the likes of this should not be made manifest before the *ammi,* meaning its supra-sensory meaning and its secret, which is known by the knowledgeable one; rather, the *ammi* should believe in it [without understanding it], as is mentioned, *Only the knowledgeable ones will understand it [29:43].*

'And the one who sees that there is no gradation in this issue between the knowledgeable one and the *ammi,* and that there is nothing but what the text relates, and if it causes to lead, before the hearer, towards what it leads to—if he does not go outside of what the language requires for that—even though their degrees are granted preference [one over another], then the covering of the *awrah* in his view is one of the Sunnas of the *salah,* not one of its obligations. *Allah says what is real, and He is the guide of the way [33:4].*

'About the boundary of the *awrah,* there is one who says that the *awrah,* for the man, is the two private parts and there is one who says that it is, for the man, from the navel to the knee. It is, according to us, only the private parts.

'The crossover for that spiritually: whatever is blameworthy, hated, and filthy of humankind is the *awrah* according to Reality. The two private parts are a place for what we mentioned. It is at the location of the unlawful; and in addition to the private parts is what encroaches on the private parts, the navel on the upper and the knee on the lower; the encroaching area is at the location of the Doubtful, and it is appropriate that one protect oneself [w.q.y., cf. *taqwa]* [from the Doubtful], because *The herder going around the enclosed precinct may almost get into it* [and so should stay well away from the boundary of the Unlawful].

'About the boundary of the *awrah* for the woman, there is one who says that all of her *is awrah* except the face and palms and there is one who argues for that and adds that her feet are not *awrah.* And there is one who says that all of her is *awrah.* As for our position, there is nothing *awrah* of the woman, in fact, except the private parts, just as He said, (*their sawah {two private parts) became visible to them, and they [Adam and Eve] started weaving for themselves the leaves of the Garden [7:22],* so He treated Adam and Eve the same in the covering of the private parts; they are the two *awrahs.* Even though the woman is commanded [in the last shariah, of Muhammad] to cover [more], and that is our position, yet this is not because of it being *awrah.* That [covering of the leaves of the private parts] is a legal property set down by shariah mentioning covering; but it is not necessary that anything else be covered as *awrah.*'

The Second Passage : To understand this second passage, we need to understand Ibn al-Arabi's Arabic conception of *sawm.* It will become immediately clear why this word can not be translated, either by 'fasting' or by any conventional Arabic phrase.

Ibn al-Arabi begins his large chapter on the *sawm* with its definition. He says, 'You should know—may Allah strengthen you!—that the *sawm is imsak* [abstention] and *rifah* [elevation].' As usual, we turn to the description of the word in *Lisan al-Arrab* and find the same: Ibn Manzur says, 'The word *sawm* in the language is *imsak* [abstention] from something and *tark* [leaving] it.' This is the first description. For the second, Ibn Manzur says, 'There is *sama* [from the same three letter root s.w.m. from which the word *sawm* is derived] the day when it draws up and rises to the zenith of mid-way. Imru al-Qays (one of the pre-Islamic poets whose Arabic usage is authoritative) said, *idha sama an-nahar wa hajjara* (the day rose up and became mid-way).'

To demonstrate the second description, Ibn al-Arabi says, 'One says, *sama an-nahar* when the day elevates. Imru al-Qays said, *idha sama annahar wa hajjra,* that is, became elevated. Because the *sawm* has been elevated above the rest of the worships [the pillars of Islam, such as *salah* and *zakah]* by a degree, it is called *sawm.* He—Exalted beyond—elevated the *sawm by* refusing any similarity with it to the worships, as we shall explain. He takes the *sawm* away from His worshippers even though they are doing it as a worship and attaches it to *Himself-subhana-hu* [He is exalted beyond]-and gives with His hand the reward to the one with the attribute of *sawm* who does it. He links the *sawm* to Himself by refusing any similarity [of it to the other worships].'

Ibn al-Arabi will explain below why the *sawm* is elevated above the other worships using the same evidence which Ibn Manzur uses. Ibn Manzur says, 'There is a *hadith* where the Prophet (PBUH) said, Allah said, *Every act of the offspring of Adam is theirs, except the sawm, because it is for Me.* Abu Ubayd said, Allah has made the *sawm* special with it being His and as being something which He rewards.'

In fact, the conception of elevation *(rifah)* and abstention *(tark)* both point to the particular description of *sawm.* Ibn al-Arabi says, 'The *sawm* is in reality a *tark,* not a practice, and the refusing of similarity is a negative attribute which intensifies the relationship of the *sawm* to Allah. He said about Himself, *Laysa ka mithlihi shayun* [There is nothing like Me] [42:11], so He refused that there should be to Him a *mithl* [similar], because *He—subhana-hu—has* no *mithl,* according to intellectual and *shariah* proofs. And al-Nasai [one of the authoritative collectors of *hadith]* published from Abu Umamah that he said, "I came to the messenger of Allah and I asked him, Command me with a command which I can take from you. He said, On you is the *sawm,* because it has no *mithl* [there is nothing like it]." Thus, he refused that any of the worships which are made *shariah* for the worshippers be made similar to it.'

In order to pursue this particular conception, Ibn al-Arabi continues with the usual evidence for this worship. He says, 'And Muslim published in his authentic collection from Abu Hurayrah that he said, The messenger of Allah said, *Every act of this offspring of Adam is theirs, except the sawm; I reward it.* And *siyam (sawm) is* a shield; when there is a *sawm* day for one of you, do, not be loud and noisy on that day. If someone insults you or fights you, say, I am one with the matter of *sawm [saim], I am a saim* [one fasting]. And by the one in whose Hand the soul of Muhammad is, the breath of the one with *sawm is* better, according to Allah, on the day of judgement, than the scent of musk. And the one with *sawm* has two joys which he enjoys: when he breaks [fast] with his *iftar* there is a joy and when he meets his Lord there is a joy in his *sawm*.'

The last phrase is awkward and not an expected turn of phrase. This should be a signal to us that something quite particular is happening. Indeed, taking the conception of *sawm* which Ibn al-Arabi has developed gives an explanation why we have this strange turn of phrase. He says, 'Know that as he refused any similarity with the *sawm*, as was established in what preceded with the *hadith* of al-Nasai and the reality that *Laysa ka mithlihi shayun* [there is nothing like h/Him, 42:11], the *saim* meets with his Lord by the attribute of *Laysa ka mithlihi shayun* and sees Him by it, so He is the Seer who is Seen. Because of this, he said, There is a joy in his *sawm*, and he did not say, There is a joy in meeting his Lord, because the joy is not a joy enjoyed by himself but is a joy enjoyed in *it*. And the one about whom the Real is his eyes with which he sees and witnesses, he himself does not see except by His seeing.'

This last phrase is the thematic *hadith qudsi* which is as follows: 'My *abd* draws near to Me by means of nothing dearer to Me than that which I have established as a duty for him. And My *abd* continues drawing nearer to Me through supererogatory acts until I love him; and when I love him, I become his ear with which he hears, his eye with which he sees, his hand with which he grasps, and his foot with which he walks.'

Concluding, he says, 'So the joy of the *saim* is his meeting at the degree of refusal of similarity. His joy in the *iftar* [breaking of the fast] is in the world, in respect to giving due to the physical self which needs nourishment for itself. As the *abd* is described in this *hadith* as having *sawm*, and deserving the name *saim* because of this description, so after the affirmation of his *sawm* the Real negates it and attaches it to Himself, saying, [Every act of the offspring of Adam is theirs] except the *sawm;* it is Mine [or, it is for Me], that is, an attribute of *samadani* [cf. *Allah ussamad] [* 112:2], which is being beyond needing nourishment. "It is Mine only; even though I may describe you with *sawm, I* so describe you by some delimiting metaphor of *tanzih* [being beyond an attribute], not by the absolute *tanzih* which is appropriate to My Majesty.

So I say, And I reward it." So the Real rewards the *sawm* for the *saim* when he turns to his Lord and he is cast to his Lord by the attribute of "He has no *mithl*" – which is the *sawm,* as the one to Whom "There is nothing like unto" cannot see anything but one whom "There is nothing like unto." Abu Talib al-Makki-he was one of the masters of the folk of tasting determined the text *jaza-u-hu man wujida fi rahl-ihi fa-huwa jaza-u-hu* [12:75] — for what this verse requires for this circumstance.'

Now we can turn to the passage in question. 'The most surplusing and balanced *sawm is* "fasting" one day for yourself and fasting one day for your Lord and between them a day breaking fast .... But when some of them saw that the right-claim of Allah is more right, they did not see treating equally the right of Allah and the right of the worshipper, so they fasted for two days and broke fast for one day. This was the fasting of Mary, because she saw that *men have a degree over women* [2:228], so she said, Perhaps I shall make this second day of fasting one to counter this degree. And that was how it was, because the Prophet *testified* that *she* was complete [perfect], just as he testified to the completion of the Men.'

And when she saw that the testimony of two women was balanced with the testimony of one man, she said, "Two days fasting for me is at the level of one day fasting of the Man." Thus, she got the station of the Man for that, and she equalled David in surplus in the fast. So because of this, the one who overcomes in himself his *nafs* has overcome in himself his [tendency to] divinization; then it is appropriate that he treats his *nafs* as Mary treated her *nafs* in this context, lest her *nafs* overtake her *aql*; this is a fine allusion for the one who understands it.'

Dahr: Ibn Manzur says, '*dahr is* an extremely long time'. And 'there is the *hadith,* Do not revile *the dahr because Allah is dahr.'*

Qayyum (q.w.m.): Ibn Manzur says, 'The *Qayyum,* one of Allah's names; Allah is Standing up by Himself absolutely, not by [the help of] anyone.'

Ibn al-Arabi continues, 'When completion became hers, she caught up to the Men, and the most completion was hers in her catching up to her Lord. It was like Jesus son of Mary, her son, because he used to fast *dahr* and not break the fast, and he used to stay up (q.w.m.) at night and not sleep. Outwardly, in the world he was with the name *dahr* in the day and with the name Qayyum—the one whom *sleep does* not *seize,* nor *slumber* (2:225) at night. So divinity was claimed for him, and it was said, Allah is the Christ, son of Mary (5:72), and that was not said about any prophet before him, because the most that was said about Uzayr was that he was the son *of Allah* (9:30). It was not said, He is Allah.'

Kufr: Ibn Manzur says the word *kufr* is derived from *satr* (veil, cover). *Kanaf:* Ibn Manzur says, In the *hadith* of Ibn Umar, we have about salvation, The believer draws closer to his Lord on the day of judgement until He places over him His *kanaf.* Ibn Mubarak said, He meant, He covers (s.t.r.) him.

'So look at what effect this [divine] attribute had,' Ibn al-Arabi says, 'from behind the veil of the unseen, on the hearts of the veiled ones of the folk of disclosure such that they said, *Allah is the Christ, son of Mary* [5:72]; *kufr* is related to them for that, set up as an excuse for them, because they did not commit *shirk;* rather they said, He is Allah, and the one who commits *shirk* is the one who makes with Allah another god. So this is one doing *kufr,* not *shirk.* Therefore, He said, They have done *kufr* who say, Allah is the *Christ, son of Mary,* thereby attributing to them a sitr [a cover, that is, *kufr*]; they took the humanity of Jesus to be a locus of divine manifestation [*majalla*]. Jesus warned him [self] about this station, in what Allah reported, as a confirmation for them concerning what they said:

> Christ said, O *Bani Israil, worship Allah, my Lord and Your Lord.* They said, That is what we are doing! So they worshipped Allah through him. Then He said to them, *The one who commits shirk with Allah, Allah has made forbidden to him the Garden [5:72]*, that is, Allah has made forbidden His *kanaf* with which He covers [s.t.r.] him; but Allah already described them with being covered [s.t.r.] in that He described them with *kufr*. This is a verse whose literal meaning gives exactly that which the matter itself gives of that. The *tawil* [allegorical interpretation] of the verse is caught up in blameworthiness; if you comprehend what we have mentioned about it, you will fall into the great ocean and you will not be saved from drowning in it at all, because it is the endless ocean. There is no deeper' word of Allah for the one who sees it and has eyes to see it and is from Allah concerning it *upon insight [12:108].'*

The Third Passage : Ibn al-Arabi says, 'Abu Ahmad mentioned in a *hadith* of Abd-Allah ibn Buayl ibn Waraqa al-Makki from Amr ibn Dinar from Ibn Umar from Umar that he vowed to sit ('k.f.) in the sacred mosque, and the messenger of Allah (PBUH) said to him, Sit in *itikaf* and do *sawm.'*

Awliya: Ibn Manzur says, 'The *waliy [singular of awliya]* of the right hand is the one who is in charge of one's command and executes his tasks.'

'Its connecting crossover: Rasululah, the messenger of Allah commanded the one desiring to stand [q.w.m.] with Allah that they should stand with him by the attribute which is Allah's, and that attribute is the *sawm*, so that one should be with Allah, by Allah, for Allah, so nothing of them would be seen except Allah. This is the circumstance of the folk of Allah. It was asked of the Rasululah, Who are the *awliya* of Allah? He said, *Those who, when they are seen, Allah is remembered [dh.k.r,* cf. *dhikr]*, that is, in order to be made real by Allah they disappear in him from them and from the eyes of creation, so when the people see them, they see nothing but Allah, so their remembering of Allah is their seeing the *awliya*. It is like the above-mentioned verses. This is the station which the Rasululah asked for in his prayer, *And make me nur [n.w.r.]*, and Allah answered his prayer, as we were told that he was sent to people *as one of good tidings, warning, calling to Allah by His leave, and an illumined lamp [siraj munir, n.w.r.]* 33-45-6; so He made him *nur* as he asked.

'His word to his Lord, *And make me nur*, was, So that I would be in my essence the very divine name itself *al-nur*, and the one whom the Real is *his ear, his eye, his tongue, his hand, and his foot;* and one who *would not speak from caprice [53:3]*. So he is not he, and nothing remains for the one who sees him, who sees him, except Allah, that being known by the one who sees or not; this is the way the folk of knowledge of Allah witness him.

'Among the believers there are the *khulafa [kh.l.f.,* ones representing someone behind them, singular *khalifah]* who manifest in the world and among the masses with the attributes of the one who is behind [kh.l.f.] them. Bilqis [the queen of Sheba] said about her throne, *ka'anna-hu huwa,*" but it was nothing but *huwa [it/Him]!* But her veil was the extreme distance [between her palace and Solomon's] and the force of convention [which says thrones do not transport themselves across large distances instantly], and she was unaware of Solomon's power with his Lord, so this veiled her from saying, *huwa huwa* [it is It; he is He; etc.]. So she said, *ka'anna-hu huwa.*

And what distance could be greater than one to whom *there is no mithl* [like] compared to one whose *mithl is* things? The complete one [Muhammad] said, *Indeed I myself am a human being who is your mithl* [like yourselves]-this based on a command of Allah. It was said to him, *Say,* and he said, *Say: indeed I myself am a human being who is your mithl [41:7],* and by this we know that it is based on a command of Allah, because he conveyed the command to us just as he conveyed what was commanded.

'This statement is a remedy for the sickness which arose in the one who worshipped Jesus in his commentary; they said, *Indeed Allah is the Christ, son of Mary [5:72],* missing a great knowledge in that they said *son of Mary* and they did not realize. Because of this, Allah said in raising proof against the one with this description [the *mushrik*], *Say: Name them* [that is, name the partners of Allah, 13:33], but they could not name him [e.g., *Allah, the Christ, son of Mary*] except by one of the names they knew him by, in order that he understand from them what they meant, because when they gave them [the partners] names, it became clear, in the name itself *[Allah, the Christ, son of Mary],* that he was not one of the messengers who were sent demanded that they worship.

'But we rather said, *huwa huwa* [h/He is He] based on what sound disclosure gives the *khass* and what clear faith gives the *amm,* just as the prophetic report from the divine relates, that Allah, when He loves His worshipper, He becomes his ear, his eye; and He mentions his faculties and limbs. And humankind is nothing but these faculties and limbs which the Real makes his he-ness itself.' So if you are a believer, do you know what you believe in? And even if you are one with a sound vision, do you know what you saw? Most of this prophetic explanation about Allah is concerned with the human faculty so that the believer would be one with a state of seeing, so that one would know by that the One who is the entity itself of the things and the entities.'

6

Eternal Religion

Like other divine religions, Islam also keeps the reform of man's self as the first item in its programme of reforms. It makes the human self as the first target of its efforts and sows the seeds of the Islamic teachings in its depths, so that self and training become inseparable.

The teachings of the Prophets lasted till the Doomsday and around them gathered the group of faithful people. Its secret was this that the self of man was the objective of all its work and it was the axis of all its activities. Their teachings were not like something externally pasted that they could be separated from men in the movements of their daily life. These were not like the paint or varnish that could be worn out by the passage of time. They had imbibed their principles and teachings into the depths of man's hearts, which had turned into a very strong power that could keep it safe from the wickedness of men's nature and could rule over their decisions.

Many times some divine religions raised objections against the society and its culture and governments and its nature, and also presented remedies for the ills which had appeared in these quarters. In spite of this, the nature of all the divine religions has been this that they kept righteous self as the basis of all their programmes of reform, and considered firm and strong moral character as a permanent guarantee for the establishment and upkeep of every civilization.

But this does not mean that the importance of those who are striving for the construction of a better government and society is being reduced, or that their efforts are considered to be less important. No. Not at all. Here an attempt is being made to make the people realize the value of the reform of man's self for the safety of life and for the security of healthy and virtuous living.

The self that has become wicked can only spread disruption and disorder in the system of government, and can make use of the enforcement of the laws of that system for meeting its mean and wicked objectives. But a purified and noble self will perform the responsible task of stitching the tears in the garment of the environment and repairing it. It will try to enhance society's greatness and decency. It will consider it its responsibility to bring in regularity in the use of power, and to remove all kinds of defects from the government.

It is like a judge. If he is well trained and decent, he can reform the defects of the law by his selfless decisions and just orders. But a cruel and unkind judge can show indifference to the correct commands and authorities. Same is the condition of the self, when it is confronted with my ideas and views about world, and personal likes and interests.

That is why the reform of the self is the first foundation pillar of the supremacy of virtue in this life.

If no attention is paid to the reform of the individuals (selves), this world becomes the dominion of the dark forces, men's present and future will be ruled by corruption. That is why Allah says:

> "Verily, Allah will never change the condition of a people until they change it themselves. But when

Allah wills a people's punishment, there can be no turning it back, nor will they find, beside Him any to protect." —(Raad : 11)

Stating the cause of the corrupt communities, Allah says:

"Like (the deeds of) the people of Pharaoh and of those before them ; they rejected the signs of Allah and Allah punished them for their crimes ; for Allah is Strong and Strict in punishment; because Allah will never change the Grace which He has bestowed on a people until they change what is in their (own) souls." —(Anfal: 52-53)

From the viewpoint of reform and training, Islam considers this matter in its two aspects:

The first aspect is this : Every self has a decent and pure nature in itself which rushes towards righteousness and good, and feels happy on getting it. It hates wickedness and evil. It becomes sad and sorry on committing it. It sees the extension and development of its existence and the health of its life in truth and justice.

With this there is its second aspect also. Every self is in its exciting emotions and Satanic inclinations, which turn away from the right path. The present harm is in a glamorous way and throw it into the pit of meanness and lowliness. We are not interested in talking a survey of the principles and elementaries of these harmu inclination from a historical point of view so that it may be ascertained whether these emotions or desires enter the human nature from outside or whether they are ingrained in the nature itself. We are concerned with the fact that both these conditions are found in men, which are locked in mutual struggle for attaining leadership for guiding man's life. And whatever kind of leadership man accepts decides his final destination.

Allah says:

> 'By the soul, and the proportion and the order given to it; and its enlightenment as to its wrong and its right; truly he succeeds who purges it, and he fails who corrupts it." —(Shams: 7-10)

The achievement of Islam is this that it helps man fully, so that he may be able to make his nature strong and firm, he may make its rays more bright and more illuminating, and in its guidance and leadership may successfully complete his long journey of life.

Similarly it also prepares man to be free from the ways of wickedness and the inciting of the devil, because these try to mislead him and turn him away from the right path, and finally cause him to fall from his high rank.

The True Faith

Islam has called itself a 'Natural Religion' which is free from all these impurities

> "So (O Prophet !) set your face steadily and truly to the faith. (Establish) Allah's nature on which He has framed mankind. There is no change in what Allah has created; that is the standard religion ; but most among mankind do not understand."
> —(Rum : 30)

The function of the eye is to see until there is some disturbance in it. The ear hears the sound till it becomes deaf. The function of the nature is to follow the right path, and to rush towards it with such alacrity as the water rushes down from a height, unless it is overcome by corruption and wickedness, which may take its reins in hands and turn it away from the path of righteousness and blessings.

The disturbing things which corrupt nature are sometimes the result of the past centuries or sometimes they are the creation of the lowly environment and habits and customs, or both these things together are responsible for the disturbances. These things are a great danger for the nature of man. They cause a variety of diseases in it. The real Jihad of a reformer is to fight these inhibitions and customs and to weaken their strength. He tries to relieve Nature of these dangers in order that its original purity may be regained and it may be able to fulfil its real responsibility. Islam has given a full clarification of this method.

After explaining the natural religion in the above quoted verses, the holy Quran says immediately thereafter:

> "Turn back in repentance to Him, and fear Him ; Establish regular prayers, and be not you among those who join gods with Allah, those who split up and become sects, each party rejoicing in that which is with itself."
>
> —(Rum : 31-32)

To encourage faith in place of disbelief, righteousness in place of wickedness, to adopt the policy of fearing God, in place of disturbed thoughts in respect of Allah the righteous people's unity of thought and action-these are the manifestations that show that man has remained on the righteous nature.

This has been clarified in the following verse of the Quran:

> "We indeed created man in the best of moulds, then we have abased him to be the lowest of the low, except such as believe and do righteous deeds."
>
> —(At-Teen : 4-6)

What is the best mould or form of man? The understanding of Truth and adopting it, fulfilment of its requirements and meeting of its demands. This is called the attachment to virtuousness and decency, and consideration of these two good qualities in man's individual and collective life is the real achievement. And attempts to make them operative in all the departments of life is the real mould and form.

But there is a very large number of people who do not reach this high level. They remain attached to the earth only. They follow their own desires, and express disobedience of God's commands. In this way they fall to the lowest level. Quran has called this "Asfala safileen (lowest of the low), to which Allah has thrown such people.

To throw the men of such nature to the lowest level is according to the divine law regarding guidance and transgression. And these laws are true and based on justice. The holy Quran mentions them as under :

> "And Allah will not mislead a people after He has guided them, to order that He may make clear to them what to fear (and avoid) for Allah has knowledge of all things." (Tauba : 115)

In Surah Araf this law of guidance and transgression has been mentioned thus

> "Those who behave arrogantly on the earth in deterrence of right-them I will turn away from My signs; even if they see all the signs, they will not believe in them ; And If they see the way of right conduct, they will not adopt it as the way of error is the way they will adopt ; for they rejected Our signs, and 'failed to take warning from them."
>
> (Aaraf : 146)

Who is it then that remains on the 'best mould' and keeps himself away from the indignities of the world ? In the verses of the Surah At-Teen occurring immediately after those quoted above the answer is given

> "Except such as believe and do the righteous deeds."
>
> (At-Teen)

In the foregoing pages we have seen that the outcome of Faith and the Righteous Deeds is the excellence of moral character.

Answer to Evils : Islam's stand vis-a-vis man's pure nature and its strength and firmness has been discussed. As regards its dealings with the devil-like natures, that has also been made clear. Islam warns mischievous-natured people. It entrusts its reins in the hands of the healthy intellect ; it encourages it to bow down to the pure nature and to surrender itself to Allah.

The prophet has hinted at some of these kinds of natures:

> "The son of Adam reaches the old age and two of his habits do not leave him. One is greed and the second is the unending succession of hopes."
>
> —(Muslim)

> "The worst evil found in man is the frightening cowardice and the undignifying miserliness."
>
> —(Abu Daud)

> "If the son of Adam is given a valley of gold, he will desire to have another one. And if the other is also given, he will be greedy to have the third one. The hunger of Adam's son will not be satisfied except when his remains are mixed with the dust. And the one who turns to Allah, Allah accepts his repentance."
>
> (Bukhari)

The holy Quran has mentioned some of the habits in the Surah Ale Imran:

> "Fair in the eyes of men is the love of things they covet, women and sons ; heaped up hoards of gold and silver ; horses branded (for blood and excellence) ; and (wealth of) cattle and well-tilled land. Such are the possessions of this world's life ; but in the nearness to Allah is the best of the goals (to return to)."
>
> —(Al-e-Imran : 14)

The first thing Islam wants man to pay attention to is this that to run after the carnal desires of the self and to follow its unending demands will never satisfy self and make it contented. Truth and right path will not be acceptable to it.

The condition of the self is that when its one desire is satisfied, it immediately demands to have some other desire satisfied. It is always busy in eating, drinking, and having a good time, and greedy with desire to have more and more of everything. It has no hesitation in committing sin and acts of aggression and cruelty. Therefore, Quran has forbidden men to follow the desires that have been considered Haram

> "Nor follow you the lusts (of your heart), for they will mislead you from the path of Allah; for those who wander astray from the path of Allah, is a penalty grievous, for that they forget the Day of Account."
> —(Saad: 26)

The policy of the infidels and the necessity of opposing it and its importance have been mentioned in these words:

> "If the Truth had been in accord with their desires, truly the heavens and the earth and all beings therein would have been in confusion and corruption! Nay, We have sent them their admonition, but they turn away from their admonition." (Minimum: 71)

It is necessary that a distinction be made between the forbidden desires of myself and the lawful desires, because some so-called religious people have mixed up these two very dangerously.

If man wants to enjoy the goods of the world, then there is nothing wrong in it, but it is a very serious error that this kind of lawful demands and desires have also been included in the list of forbidden, wicked acts.

Its consequence is this that man satisfies his lawful and respectable desires, but his conscience becomes like the conscience of those people who accept crimes as lawful and adopt them willingly. In this way their conscience becomes a victim of a great error.

When he realises that he has committed a mistake, and that

sin is an inevitable part of his life, then he commits more serious sins and indulges in the strictly forbidden acts. In other words this time he becomes a criminal and a sinner in the real sense of the word.

The holy Quran has paid special attention to this aspect and has very clearly declared the pure desires of the self and the lawful wishes as proper and lawful, and provided it with a chance to use halal and clean things. It declared any interference of narrowness and inhibition in this respectable and lawful sphere by way of any checks on the self as bad and obscene, because it opens the gate for obscene acts and sinning.

> "O you people I Eat on earth what is lawful (halal) and clean (tayyib) and do not follow the footsteps of Satan. Indeed, he is an open enemy for yours. He will command you (to do) what is evil and indecent and induce you to say about Allah that which you do not know."
>
> —(Al-Baqarh : 168-169)

It is a fact that to put restrictions on the consumptions of what is lawful (halal) and clean (tayyib) is nothing but levelling false charges against Allah, and this thing amounts to evil and indecency which Satan commands men to do.

Islam does not like to repress such natures and inclinations with force and punishment, nor does it want to placate or flatter them, but Islam follows a balanced method which is free of any kind of excess.

Morality Holds the Reins : As the rules and regulations of the healthy nature are secure in faith and reform and they have no connection with heresy and agnosticism, similar is the case of the rebellious natures and habits.

In both the cases only a strong and firm moral character can control it. Where the holy Quran has mentioned man's weakness, his anxiety, his richness and indifference, there it has also made it clear that the remedy of these indignities lies in following the path of religion.

> "Truly man was created very impatient ; fretful when evil touches him ; and niggardly when good reaches him ; not so those devoted to prayer, those who remain steadfast to their prayer ; and those in whose wealth is recognised right for (the needy) who asks him and who is prevented (for some reason from asking) ; and those who hold to the Truth of the Day of Judgement ; and those who fear the displeasure of their Lord, for the Lord's displeasure is the opposite of peace and tranquillity ; and those who guard their chastity.
>
> —(Al-Maarij : 19-19)

It is common knowledge that good moral character does not develop suddenly. Nor does it become strong and firm in the beginning. It requires consistency and gradualness. And in strengthening it there come many stages.

That is the reason why in its nourishment and growth it is required to perform such acts that have to be repeated. The quality that is developed should have consistency, e.g. prayer, fasting, Hajj, Zakat, and the performance of other forms of worship, confirmation of the Day of the Judgement, and to be fearful of its punishment, etc.

When the rebellious natures insist on their acts and are steadfast on their wrong stance, and continue to attempt to traverse the wrong path from time to time, then to check and prevent it no fixed and temporary remedy can be found.

Their transgression and intensity can be brought to the normal level only by such an activist who is more strong and powerful than they and who may be able to bring them to a balanced level.

The long and short of the discussion is that Islam respects the human nature and considers its teachings as the voice of that nature. It warns the rebellious natures and reforms their point of view. Those forms of worship which have been made compulsory in Islam are such as strengthen the human nature and turn the wind of desires to the right direction. And these forms of worship do not perform their duties satisfactorily and the desired objective cannot be obtained from them unless they generate the excellent moral character and the tendency to exemplary treatment of others.

The Restrictions

To generate goodness in someone by coercion and to call him a man of good moral character is not possible. Similarly no faith can be developed in any person by means of force or terrorism. Only personal and intellectual freedom is the sole basis of responsibility and accountability.

Islam understands this reality and respects it. It builds up its edifice on the foundation of the excellent moral character.

Where is the need for Islam to use force and coercion to bring man to the right path and to make him run towards righteousness, when it has full confidence in the human nature and is certain that if the obstructions before man are removed then the best generation can be developed ?

Goodness is ingrained in the human nature. It does not mean that it cannot do anything except good, but it means that only good can coordinate with his original nature and offer resistance. The nature wants to attach itself to good only and wants to function in its light, like the bird that after getting free from the cage flies round and round in the sky in ecstasy in accordance with its foremost wish.

According to Islam the right method is to break nature's checks and chains. After this when man falls down to the ground, and has no strength to rise and walk, then he should be considered as sick and efforts should be made to treat him.

Islam does not order such kind of sick persons to be thrown out of society, provided his existence is not harmful and damaging to others.

Within the limits of this sphere, Islam fights against moral crimes. At first it imagines that every man wants to lead a decent life and wants to live by the sweat of his brow and enjoy luxuries on what he earns from his own labours, that is he does not depend on thefts and looting.

Then what thing compels him to take to thieving? In order to provide him for the necessities of life, therefore, Islam says that the necessities and the means should be in such abundant quantities that they may make him indifferent and above taking wrong steps.

This is the responsibility of the society. If it is deficient and compels the individual to steal, then the responsibility for this crime falls on the deficient society, and not on the head of the wrong-committing individual.

But if the society provides his requirements, and after this the individual advances in the wrong direction, then the actual condition of the individual should be ascertained before inflicting any penalty (Hudd) on him. Probably there may be such extenuating circumstances that may save him from the punishment. As it is, Islam desires delay in inflicting punishment. The Messenger of Allah his reported to have said : "It is better if the Imam pardons somebody by error than he penalises him by error."

Fixation of Penalties : When after examining the conditions and problems it is ascertained that the individual's nature is bent on rebellion, and that the society which has brought him up and had provided for him is being subjected to his depredations and he wants to repay its kindness with disturbance of peace, then if that society inflicts some penalty on this kind of an individual and wants to cut away that harmful limb, it cannot be criticised or blamed.

The holy Quran has termed a theft deserving the penalty of cutting the hand as the theft of tyranny and corruption, and about such a thief it has stated as under

> "But if the thief repent after his crime, and amend his conduct, Allah turns to him in forgiveness ; for Allah is Oft-Forgiving, Most Merciful." —(Maids : 42)

The penalty which Islam inflicts is in reality for saving the reformist, welfare, and just society from the damage that a harmful member may cause it. A criminal who repays justice with cruelty and reform with corruption — who would like to consider him deserving of mercy ?

Appeals to the Hearts : I have mentioned this example merely to show that the penalties for moral crimes have not been fixed with a view to generating forcefully goodness in society, nor does it amount to coerce people to follow the right path.

For Islam the better way is to appeal to the hearts of men, to awaken their sleeping nature, to stir their repressed inclination and desire towards progress and perfection, to return them to the presence of God, and to adopt such a method that would have convincing arguments and the sweetness of love and brotherhood. The moral values should be explained and clarified in such a way that the heart may be convinced that it is necessary to adopt them for attaining the good and the righteous qualities.

In such an environment the rule of that law is necessary which helps in nourishing the human capabilities and in developing excellent habits and good moral character.

There is nothing wrong if this useless and profitless limb is cut and thrown away, because in the society we are undertaking farming of various kinds of produce. The purpose is growth and nourishment, whether it may involve the clearance of the wild plants or the thorn bearing shrubs.

The security of the interests of common man and their

safety is not a thing of less importance, Therefore, there is no reason for being critical of these penalties which are inflicted by Islam. This thing has been mentioned in the Torah, and all the divine religions have placed emphasis on this.

Responsibility of the Society: According to Islam the society itself plays a very important role in the spread of good or evil that spreads in that society. It (Islam) wants to attain power because it wants, with other things, to form a society in such a way that it may be helpful in encouraging chastity, righteousness, aversion from wickedness, proliferation of good acts, indifference to love for world, steadfastness for the right path and consistency.

The Prophet has told the story of a murderer who wanted to repent for his crimes. He inquired of the address of the greatest learned man of the land. His name was given to him, whom he saw and said

> "I have committed hundred murders. Is there any chance of repentance for me?" He was told: "What thing can come between you and repentance. Go to a particular place, where some good slaves of Allah reside and are always found worshipping Him. You also join them in worshipping, and do not return to your village, because it is a bad place."
>
> —(Bukhari)

In another version, it is narrated that he went to a monk and related his whole story and placed his difficulty before him. The monk told him

> "You have committed a big mistake. How am I concerned with this ? However, there are two villages. One of them is named 'Nasrah' that is supporter of Allah and the other one is named 'Kaffarah' that is rejector of God. The people of Nasrah perform the

deeds of the people of the paradise. Any person who follows other methods cannot stay there. The citizens of Kaffarah perform the deeds of the people of the hell. If you stayed there and worked like those people, then there would be no doubt about the acceptance of your repentance." —(Tibrani)

For this reason Islam says that for the safety of the healthy nature and for the training and reform of the rebellious tendencies the care and vigilance of the environment is necessary, and in the formation of the good moral character it plays a very important role.

We are sure that if all these aspects are taken care of, then a clean and tidy society can be brought into existence, in which pure qualities and chaste character may be nourished.

Treatment of the Minorities : Every religion has its characteristic symbols, which make it distinct from every other religion.

Undoubtedly there are certain fixed forms of worship in Islam which have been made compulsory for its followers. Besides there are certain values prevalent among the followers which have no relation with the Non-Muslims.

But the moral teachings do not come under this category or within the sphere of this principle. Every Muslim has been made responsible to employ good manners in dealing with all the citizens of the land unhesitatingly. For every Muslim it is necessary that he should be truthful in dealing with the Non-Muslims. Similarly good qualities like charity, keeping one's promise, tolerance, decency, generosity, cooperation, etc. are to be brought into play while dealing with Muslims and Non-Muslims alike.

The holy Quran has commanded us not to indulge in such debates with the Jews and the Christians that may encourage mutual enmity, clashes and quarrels. It says:

> "And do not indulge in disputation with the people of the Book except in a refined way, unless it be with those of them who inflict wrong, and say: 'We believe in the Revelation which came down to us and in that which came down to you: Our Allah and your Allah is one; and it is to Him we bow'.
>
> (Ankabut : 46)
>
> And the followers of Moosa and Isa (Moses and Jesus) were asked, expressing wonder, whether they were indulging in this kind of argumentation and polemics? "Say: `Do you argue with us about Allah when He is our Lord as well as your Lord ? We are accountable for our deeds and you for yours ; so we are sincerely (dedicated) to Him'." (Baqarah : 139)

It is a famous incident of the biography of the Prophet that he owed something to a Jew. The Jew demanded repayment and in a very harsh tone said : "O Son of Abdul Muttalib ! You people unnecessarily delay the repayment of your loans." At that place Hadrat Umar bin Al-Khattab was also present. He decided to teach the Jew, who insulted the Prophet, good manners, and drew his sword from the scabbard. But the Messenger of Allah silenced Umar saying : "I and he deserve better treatment. Teach him to demand his money in a better way and advise me to repay it in a refined manner."

Islam has commanded to deal justly and fairly even if the opponent may be a wrong-doer or an infidel. ,Allah's Messenger has said:

> "The prayer of the oppressed is answered. If he is wicked and wrong-doer, his ill effects will go against him." (Ahmad)

In another Hadith it is stated : "Even if the oppressed person is an infidel, there is no obstruction between his prayer and its answer. Give up doubtful things and adopt those matters in which there may be no doubt."

In the light of these authorities and the commands, Islam has advised its followers not to maltreat their ideological and religious opponents.

In connection with the insistence on treating the followers of the other religion kindly, there is one more *Hadith*:

> Hadrat Ibn Umar says that a goat was slaughtered in his house. When he came home he inquired whether the gift was sent to the neighbouring Jew or not? He further says : "I have heard the Messenger of Allah as saying 'Jibbrail' had been regularly insisting on me to treat kindly my neighbours, so much so that I surmised that the neighbour would be made a recipient of the inheritance." (Bukhari)

Similarly Islam has ordered that its followers should be kind to their relatives, even though they may have rejected this religion which they have made their own. Therefore, following the Truth does not mean that the rights of the relatives may be usurped

> "And bear them company in this life with justice (and consideration), and follow the way of those who turn to Me (in love); in the end the return of I meaning) of all that you did." (Luqman : 15)

Need of Morality for the Nation and the Country : This discussion was on the importance of morality at the level of individuals. As regards the importance and need of morality at the public and collective level, Islam says that the progress and the survival of the nations, the nourishment and the development of their civilization and culture, and the consolidation of their power and strength depend on morality. If the people have good and excellent moral character, then all these good qualities will be found in them, but if their moral character is a lower level, then kingdom and rule will soon end.

"Nations live till their morality lives. When their moral character declines, they also decline." This reality is fully explained in a Hadith in which the Prophet says to the people of his nation that although they have control over the whole of Arabia, and are in a position to decide the fate of the people of the country, as they hold an important position, their power can be maintained on the pillar of morality only.

Anas bin Malik says: "We were sitting in a house where some members of the Ansar and Muhajir were present. The Messenger of Allah came into the room and everybody tried to make room for him near his own seat. Then he proceeded towards the door and stood taking support of the door and said:

> "The leaders will be from the Quraish, and I have great right on you and they have also a right on you as they would do. When they would be requested to show mercy, they would show mercy. When they would give a judgment, it would be based on justice. And when they would make a covenant, they would honour it. He who does not do like this, there would be on him the curse of Allah, of the angels and of all the people." —(Tibrani)

This *Hadith* unambiguously shows that any person, community, nation or government would be deserving of as much honour and respect as they would be the representatives of the best qualities in this world and would be striving to achieve high objectives.

If a government flaunts the label of Islam and Quran but the people are not satisfied with it, if it does not decide their matters justly, if it is not kind to the needy and does not honour its covenants, then it should be understood that in this government Islam and Quran are merely names, and this government is bereft of Islam's basic values and it deserves to be cursed from every corner of the earth and the skies.

Hadrat Hussain narrates that the Messenger of Allah has said :

> "When Allah wants to deal kindly with a nation, He entrusts its reins in the hands of the wise men, gives wealth to its generous people ; and when He wants to deal with a nation harshly, he entrusts its wealth to its miserly men." —(Abu Daud)

It is a famous saying of Imam Ibn Taimiyah : "Allah guards the justice-loving government, even if it is the government of the infidels, and destroys the tyrant government, even if it is the government of Muslims."

In the light of the holy Book and the Sunnah, morality is the perfect religion and also the perfect world. If any nation loses its honour in the eyes of Allah or commands no respect among the people, it so happens because of its losing good moral character and becoming deprived of decent and honourable traits.

Celebrating the Feasts : Feasts in Islam are confined to two occasions: Eid-ul-Fitr (Feast at end of Fast) which immediately follows the month of Ramadan, and Eid-ul-Adha (Feast of Sacrifice) which falls on the tenth day of the month of pilgrimage (Dhul-Hijja). Both are occasions to thank God for having allowed individual and community to fulfil their religious duty.

Observing the Feasts

- Taking a bath on the occasion of the two Feasts is recommended. This can be done any time after midnight preceding the Feast day.
- A Muslim should dress well and wear a pleasant perfume before leaving for the Feast prayers.
- Before going to pray in the morning on the day of Eid-ul-Fitr, eating some dates, or sweets, is recommended.

- It is preferable not to eat anything on the day of Eid-ul-Adha until performing the Feast prayer in the morning; then one should return home, slaughter an animal, and prepare the Feast meal.
- Walking to the place of the Feast prayer is recommended unless it is too far away to do so.
- The Feast congregational prayer is usually not performed in the mosque, unless it is raining. To perform it in an open square is recommended.
- It is recommended that the whole Muslim community, with the exception of invalids and the disabled, should gather in the open square for the Feast prayer. This includes menstruating women, who may be present at the occasion but who may not participate in the prayer.
- It is strongly recommended to wait and listen to the Feast khutbah given by the imam.
- When going back to his home after the prayer a Muslim should return by a different road from the one he took when going to the prayer. This will provide him with an opportunity to meet a larger number of Muslims than would otherwise be the case.
- One should take the initiative and congratulate Muslims on this occasion by saying: Taqabbal Allah minna wa minkum (May God accept the work we have done for His sake).
- The rules of conduct and behaviour in the mosque, must be followed here as well.
- Fasting on the day of Eid-ul-Fitr or during the three days following the day of Eid-ul-Adha is forbidden.
- A Muslim should dress his children beautifully, buy them sweets, and help them to celebrate and experience the occasion. This is necessary to help them identify with their Islamic culture.

- A Muslim must avoid doing anything that would annoy his family or dampen their good spirits and spoil their good humour on this occasion.
- Fathers and responsible persons should ensure on such occasions that Islamic law is adhered to, as these Feasts are to thank God and not to indulge in disobedience to Him. Thus, such things as mixing of the sexes, etc. should not occur, although such happy occasions could easily give rise to the wish to do so.

Behaviour on Eid-ul-Adha : Eid-ul-Adha lasts two days after the day of sacrifice, which falls on the tenth day of the lunar Islamic month of Dhul-Hijja.

- It is recommended, whether one is a pilgrim or not, that every family offer a sacrifice on this occasion. By sacrifice is meant the slaughtering of certain kinds of animals.
- The sacrificial animal should be chosen from healthy stock. An animal whose ear or tongue has been clipped, whose horns have been broken, or who is crippled, should not be selected; the animal should be more than one year old; if sheep, goat, cow or ox, more than two years; and if camel or she-camel, more than five years.
- The sacrificial animal is replaceable by alms equal to the cost of the animal.
- The sacrifice may be a sheep, a goat, a cow, or a camel. A cow or a camel serves for seven people, who share with one another the sacrifice.
- The correct time for slaughtering is upon return from the Feast prayer. Therefore, slaughtering should be avoided before that time, since that will not be considered a sacrifice. If one sacrifice is made before the prayer, another sacrifice may be made after the prayer.

- If a person can slaughter well, then it is recommended that he performs the slaughtering himself, otherwise he should entrust someone to slaughter on his behalf.
- When slaughtering the sacrifice the knife must be sharp, the animal must face towards the Kaaba and God's name must be mentioned, saying: Bismillah, Allah Akbar (In the name of Allah, Allah is most Great).
- A sacrifice may be slaughtered at home, though it is preferable, if possible, to perform the slaughtering in the open square where the prayer was performed.
- Parts of the animal may be eaten or kept by the person making the sacrifice. A large part of it, however, should be given to the poor. Something may also be given to the relatives of the person making the sacrifice.
- The time of slaughtering sacrifices lasts three days including the first day of the feast.
- Selling any part of the sacrificial animal or giving any part of it, including the hide, to the butcher or person who slaughtered it, in payment, is forbidden.

Special Instructions for Eid-ul-Fitr

- Zakat or Sadaqah al-Fitr must be given by every financially able Muslim on the occasion of breaking the fast of the month of Ramadan.
- Zakat al-Fitr should also be given for those who are supported by a Muslim, such as his wife and children.
- Giving the above-mentioned alms to the poor must be done before the Muslims go out to pray the Feast prayer. This will enable the poor to participate in the festival. However, if one forgets to pay Zakat al-Fitr before the prayer, it must be paid as soon as possible afterwards.

Attitude towards Animals

Mercy and Kindness

- Mercy and kindness should characterize all aspects of the treatment of animals.
- Animals should carry loads according to their strength and capability.
- Slaughtering animals should be carried out skilfully and perfectly, so that an animal is not tortured in the process.
- As mentioned in the rules of travelling, when passing with a beast through an area where there is grass and water, a traveller should proceed slowly. When, on the other hand, he is passing through a barren, or desert area, he should proceed quickly.
- Killing non-useful but nevertheless unharmful animals or insects, such as moths or small birds, should be avoided.
- Slaughtering animals who produce milk, eggs, etc. should be postponed for as long as possible.
- Castrating (emasculating) animals or spaying the female is forbidden in Islam.
- Killing some types of creatures should be avoided, unless they become harmful, such as bees, ants, hoopoes and frogs.
- One should not hesitate to kill the following four types of creatures: scorpions, mice, snakes and geckos.
- To refrain from killing snakes out of superstition indicates a weak faith.
- To cross a horse and a donkey in order to produce a mule should be avoided.
- To use gold or silver in an animal's saddle or bridle,

or in a dog's line, or to bedeck an animal with silk, is forbidden, for it is a waste of money and betrays arrogance and pride.

- To brand an animal on the face is forbidden. Branding an animal on any other part of its body is allowed, provided no harm is done to it, and branding is confined to necessary limits.
- When beating an animal, striking its face must be avoided.
- To set animals against each other, such as cocks, oxen or sheep, for the sake of fun or for any other reason, is completely forbidden in Islam and considered an act of cruelty.
- It is not allowed to sell or buy an animal which is still in need of its mother. If such a transaction has already been carried out, it must be annulled.
- When hunting birds or animals, hunting young animals still in need of their mothers should be avoided; likewise killing a mother who has young ones should be avoided, as the young ones would then die.
- Hunting animals during hajj or Umrah is forbidden. If it should happen that a Muslim does hunt or kill an animal or bird while performing hajj or Umrah, then it is his duty to make special atonement.
- Animals which feed on filth should be avoided for meat and for riding. Neither should their milk be used until the animals have been confined to clean fodder for a sufficient period.
- If a Muslim owns livestock, birds or animals, then it is his responsibility before God to feed them and to take care of them.
- Using an animal as a target for shooting practise with a gun or bow is forbidden.

- To seek refuge in God from the devil whenever one hears a donkey braying is a recommended act.
- A Muslim should ask God to bless him whenever he hears a rooster crow.
- Every animal is created for a certain purpose such as milking, riding, etc. Therefore, animals should be used according to their purpose.
- Dismembering a dead animal is forbidden.
- One should never curse an animal.
- Animals are of two kinds, clean and unclean. Unclean animals are dogs and pigs. When a dog drinks out of a vessel, it must be washed seven times, using earth once.
- A dog may not be owned by a Muslim except for two reasons: (a) as a watch-dog; (b) as a hunting dog. The place for such dogs, however, is outside the house, not inside.

7

Preaching Faith

And who is better in speech than him who calleth towards Allah, And Doeth Right and sayeth.

Lo! I am of those who surrender (unto Him).

(41: 33)

Basic Philosophy

1. Develop full appreciation of the position conferred upon you. You are the successor to the mission of the Holy Prophet [S.A.W.] and you have to discharge the same duty of communicating the message of Allah, testifying the truth through your practical life and propagating the teachings of Islam which the Holy Prophet [S.A.W.] performed all through his holy life. Try to develop the same degree of zeal and fervour for the propagation of Islam which was the unique and distinctive characteristic of the Holy Prophet [S.A.W.].

The Holy Quran affirms:

"He hath chosen you and hath not put you in any hardship in the matter of faith; follow the faith of your father Ibrahim. He hath given you the nomenclature of Muslim long ago and in this (Scripture) too, that the Prophet of Allah [S.A.W.] may testify the truth before you and that you may stand witness to the whole of Mankind."

In other words, the Muslims are the successors to the mission of the Holy Prophet of Allah [S.A.W.] and required, therefore, to discharge the same duty which the Apostle of Allah performed during his auspicious life. In the same manner as the final Prophet of Allah [S.A.W.] struggled day and night by his words and action and made the way of total submission to Allah clear to the people, the adherents to Islam have also to preach Islam, the religion of Allah, to all the people of the world and what is more, they have to practise it in their every day life and testify.

Call to Religion and prove it the religion of truth with the same high sense of duty and missionary zeal.

2. Always keep in view your real position in this world and constantly endeavour to order your life accordingly. You are not like the other people of the world. Allah has conferred on you a distinction and a privilege. You have been vested with the honour of leading the affairs of the world. You don't believe in extremes and are expected to keep yourself firm on the straight path of Allah with moderation.

The Holy Quran affirms:

"Thus we have appointed you a middle nation that ye may be witnesses against mankind and that the Messenger may be a witness against you."

(2: 143)

3. Seek knowledge of the real purpose and aim of your life and try to achieve it with confidence and conviction. The real mission and task before the Muslims is to establish and enforce the religion as a whole which the Holy Prophet Muhammad [S.A.W.] communicated to

the mankind-a religion which contains divine guidance and injunctions in each and every aspect of life such as beliefs and worship, morality, and social, economic and political spheres etc. The Holy Prophet [S.A.W.] during his auspicious days enforced Islam with all its details. The Holy Prophet [S.A.W.] taught beliefs, principles of morality and the modes of worship; he [S.A.W.] established and organised a society on the principles of Islam and brought about countless favours and blessings to the people.

Allah has affirmed:

"He hath ordained for you that religion which He commended unto Nuh,and that which We inspire in Thee (Muhammad), and that which We commended unto Ibrahim and Moses and Jesus saying: Establish the religion and be not divided therein."

(42: 13)

4. Always remain determined to eliminate evil and establish good. This is an obligation you owe to your faith to justify your existence as upholders of the truth. Live to achieve this aim and idea serving this mission. Allah has named you as the best people on earth only because you live to uphold the truth and sacrifice even your life for this noble cause.

"Ye are the best Community that hath been raised up for mankind. Ye enjoin right conduct and forbid indecency and ye believe in Allah." (3: 110)

The Holy Prophet [S.A.W.] has affirmed:

"I swear by Him Who has power over my life you must enforce virtue and curb evil, otherwise Allah shall send very soon such calamity over you that you will cry and seek mercy from Allah but you will get no response." (Tirmidhi)

5. Develop, missionary zeal and exemplary fervour and enthusiasm for the propagation of the message of Allah and to save the people of Allah from the fearful torment of Hell. The Holy Quran has acknowledged the unique fervour and abounding zeal of the Holy Prophet [S.A.W.] in the following words:

> "Yet it may be, if they believer not in this statement, that thou wilt torment thy soul with grief for them."
> (18: 6)

The Holy Prophet [S.A.W.] has himself described his feeling in these words:

> "I am like a person who lit a fire and when the surrounding area became bright with light, the moths and insects began to drop in fire. The person is now trying with all the force at his command to stop these moths and insects from dropping in the fire, but the moths and insects are rushing towards the fire rendering all his efforts ineffective. Likewise, I am trying my level best to draw you back and keep you away from the fire, yet you are bent upon falling in it." (Mishkat)

One day Hadrat 'Aishah [R.A.A.] submitted to the Holy Prophet [S.A.W.]: "O Prophet of Allah [S.A.W.]! Have you passed a harder day than the day of Uhud in your life?" The Holy Prophet [S.A.W.] observed: "Yes, 'Aishah! The day of *'Aqabah* was the hardest in my life." This was the day when, dismayed with the people of Mecca, the Holy Prophet [S.A.W.] had visited Taif to convey the message of Allah to the people there. Their chief 'Abd Yalil set ruffians after the Prophet [S.A.W.] who hurled stones at him in response to his message of blessing and salvation. The Prophet of Allah [S.A.W.] sustained serious injuries. His whole body was stained with blood and he fainted. Deeply grieved and frustrated, the Holy Prophet. [S.A.W.] returned to Mecca. When the Prophet [S.A.W.]

arrived at Qarn Aththaalib, he had overcome his grief. Allah sent the angel of calamity to the Prophet [S.A.W.]. The angel of torture submitted: "O Prophet of Allah [S.A.W.]! If you wish I shall collide Abu Qubais with Jabal Ahmar and crush all the wicked between the two mountains. The benefactor of the world [S.A.W.] observed:

> "No, no, let me warn my people of the torments of Allah. May Allah open their hearts to accept the truth and concede to the Divine Guidance or else their succeeding generation may submit to the truth."
>
> (Bukhari, Muslim)

The Meccans were constantly busy conspiring against the Holy Prophet [S.A.W.]. Some said that the Prophet [S.A.W.] should be exiled from the city while others counselled that he should be assassinated. In the mean time a famine struck Mecca. It was such a terrible calamity that the Quraish were constrained to eat leaves and bark of the trees. The children suffered from the terrible agony of hunger and the elder felt restless but helpless over the affliction of their children.

The benefactor of the mankind [S.A.W.] was deeply moved by the heart rending distress of the people. His devoted companions [R.A.A.] could not bear the grief and uneasiness of the Holy Prophet [S.A.W.]. The Holy Prophet [S.A.W.] conveyed his heartfelt sympathy to his deadly foes who had always been after him to harm and tease him and its unhappy memories were still fresh in his mind. The Holy Prophet [S.A.W.] sent a sum of five hundred dinars to Abu Sufyan and an equal amount to Safwan with the instruction that the money should be distributed among the famine-stricken people.

Truly speaking, to be sorry for the misguided, to feel disturbed over their wickedness and distress, to be anxious to save them from the wrath of Allah, to be distressed at their affliction and to have an extraordinary craving for their right guidance-such are the attributes of a missionary of truth which create irresistible attraction in his life and an impression uncommon in history.

6. Serve your people with selfless devotion and do not ask for any recompense for your devotion from anybody. Do whatever good you can only to win the favour of Allah and expect reward and blessings from Him only. The desire to earn the favour of Allah and to demand reward and blessings from Him alone lends weight to a man's word and makes him dynamic. Allah has always been-and will remain for ever. He neither sleeps, nor dozes off. No move or activity of man is hidden from Him. He never lets the reward of any of His devotees go waste. He pays more than ones labour and never deprives any one of His blessings. The Prophets (peace be upon them) repeatedly observed to their people:

"I demand not any reward or recompense from you. My reward lies with the Lord of the worlds."

Do acquire a deep understanding of Islam and be sure that Islam is the only true religion in the eyes of Allah. No mode of worship, except the one enjoined by this true religion has any worth before Allah. Allah holds only that religion as true and valid which He has revealed in the Holy Quran and which the Holy Prophet [S.A.W.] translated into practice during his auspicious life. The Holy Quran enjoins upon the Prophet of Allah [S.A.W.] to make it clear to the people that he had adopted his path with careful deliberation and full awareness.

> "Say, this is my way. I call on Allah with sure knowledge, I and whosoever followeth me-Glory be to Allah! and I am not of the idolators."
>
> (12: 108)

Allah makes clear affirmation:

"And whosoever seeketh as religion other than the

surrender (to Allan) it will not be accepted from him and he will be a loser in the Hereafter." (3: 85)

"The only religion unto Allah is the surrender (unto Him)." (3:19)

And beware it is for the performance of this grand task that Allah had sent Prophets (peace be upon them) one after another—and be convinced in your own heart that this wealth of religion which the Almighty has vouchsafed to you is the key to attain excellence and honour in the world and Hereafter. The worldly pomp and show which is transitory and short-lived can not be compared with the eternal and inestimable wealth of religion! The holy Quran affirms:

"And We have bestowed upon you seven oft-repented verses and a great book, the Quran. Hence care not for this mundane wealth Allah, have conferred on others." Addressing the believers of other Revealed Books before Quran, the Holy Quran says:

"Say: O People of the scripture! I guidance till ye observe the Torah and the Gospel and that which was revealed unto you from your Allah." (5: 68)

9. Make constant efforts to grasp the real spirit of religion and the wisdom it contains. The Holy Prophet [S.A.W.] has observed.

"Allah endows, whomsoever He wishes to bless with good the real understanding and deep insight into religion." (Bukhari, Muslim)

As a matter of fact, it is tire real knowledge of religion and insight into the spirit of religion which is the fountain-head of all goodness and the man who is deprived of this goodness is deprived of the blessings of this world as well as of the world Hereafter. Such a man can never achieve balance and consistency in life, nor can he truly represent religion in any walk of life.

10. Whatever you wish to proclaim to the world, address it to your self first. Tell yourself first what you wish to tell others and perform in your won life what you preach to others. The distinction of a missionary of true religion is that he tries to project in himself the true model of his preachings. His deeds and character stand testimony to his words. He himself yearns for the truths he propagates to other as a source of goodness. Whenever the Prophets (peace be upon them) rose to call the people to surrender themselves before Allah they proclaimed Ana awwalul muslimin (I am the first to surrender before Allah).

Testify by spoken as well as written word that truth is what you represent. Make it evident through your individual life, family relations, social dealings and through your national and political activities that piety can only be developed by adopting the way of life as enunciated by Islam. This system guarantees stability of homes, emergence of a morally oriented society and a culture and civilisation based on justice and equity. Those who ignore the duty of reforming and training their own character and ruminate over the reformation and training of others are completely devoid of common-sense. Their own house is on fire, yet they are carrying about buckets of water looking for a blaze anywhere else to extinguish.

Such people are losers not only in this world but in the Hereafter also. Their inaction in this world will render all their preachings ineffective and weightless and in the next world they shall undergo the most deterrent punishment. It is most hateful in the sight of Allah that they do not practise what they preach and tell others to do what they themselves do not do. The Holy Prophet [S.A.W.] has warned such missionaries of Islam who do not do what they preach, of the most fearful punishment. The Holy Prophet [S.A.W.] observed:

"A man shall be brought on the Day of Judgement

and will be thrown into the Fire. His intestines will spill out due to the Fire. He will then carry around his intestines as a donkey goes round the mill. On seeing him the denizens of hell will gather around him and enquire: "O man, what has become of you! Are you not the one who preached to us in the world to perform virtuous deeds? Are you not the one who dissuaded us from the performance of evil acts? How did you come into this place despite having performed such pious deeds?" The man will answer: " I did teach you piety, but never cared for it myself. I forbade you to do evil, but performed evil deeds myself."

(Muslim, Bukhari)

The portentous account of the night of Ascension which the Holy Prophet [S.A.W.] related to the people contains a warning for the misguided to reform themselves. The Holy Prophet [S.A.W.] observed:

"I beheld some people in the night of Ascension whose lips were being clipped with scissors of fire. I enquired from Jibbrail [A.S.]: "Who are these people?" Jibbrail [A.S.] replied: "They are the orators of your Ummah. They preached piety and fear of Allah to people, but forgot to follow these teachings in their personal lives."

(Mishkat)

The illustrious companions [R.A.A.] also used to issue stern warnings to such misguided and hypocritical people who did not follow what they preached. On one occasion, a person said to Hadrat 'Abdullah b. 'Abbas [R.A.A.]: "Hadrat I desire to instruct people in piety and forbid them to commit evil deeds. I wish to propagate religion among the people." Hadrat 'Abdullah enquired: "Have you acquired the proper qualifications for becoming a preacher?" The person submitted: "Yes, I believe I am capable of performing the task of a missionary." Hadrat ibn 'Abbas [R.A.A.] observed: "If you do not apprehend any condemnation in the light of three verses of the Holy Quran, do preach Islam." The person enquired: "Which three verses do you mean?" Hadrat ibn 'Abbas [R.A.A.] answered:

The first verse is:

'Enjoin ye righteousness upon mankind while ye yourselves forget to practise it.?" (2: 44)

Ibn 'Abbas [R.A.A.] then enquired: Do you follow this verse in your practical life fully?" The man replied: "No." Ibn Abbas [R.A.A.] then recited the second verse:

"O ye who believe! Why say ye that which ye do not do? (61:2)

Hadrat ibn 'Abbas [R.A.A.] then asked: "Are you sure you are following this verse" The man replied: "No." Hadrat ibn 'Abbas [R.A.A.] observed: The third verse is:

"I desire not to do behind your backs that which I ask you not to do." (11 . 88)

"Tell me now, have you fully carried out the instruction contained in this verse. The man submitted: "No." Whereupon Hadrat Abdullah observed: "Go then and instruct yourself in piety first and forbid your own self from evil."

11. Perform your prayers with full devotion keeping in view its rules, regulations and conditions. In addition to them also offer supererogatory prayers.

No one can propagate religion without establishing a close communion with Allah. Prayer is the sure means-a means prescribed by Allah Himself-of establishing a deep connection with Allah. Allah affirmed through a revelation to the Holy Prophet [S.A.W.].

"O thou wrapped up in the raiment! Keep vigil the

night long, save a little-a half thereof, or abate a little thereof, or add (a little) thereto and chant the Quran in measure, for We shall charge thee with a word of weight."7 (74: 1-5)

'Charge thee with a word of weight' implies 'Propagation of the Religion of Truth' and truly this responsibility is the most burdensome and heavy of all duties in the world. In order to be able to discharge this duty, it is important for you to derive strength from prayer and establish a firm connection with Allah.

12. Develop a fondness for and interest in the study of the Holy Quran and recite the Book regularly. Recite the Quran slowly and with deep concentration during the prayers as well as during the period other than prayers. When the Quran is recited with a interest and concentration, it becomes easy to understand and reflect upon the meanings of the Holy Quran. As soon as one starts appreciating the charms of the word of Allah, his interest and inquisitiveness increases and he goes deeper and deeper in the Book of Allah. The Holy Quran is the only source of guidance and warning. It has been revealed to make the people ponder over its contents and derive benefit from its guidance and warnings, so ponder over the meanings of the Holy Quran and learn wisdom from it. Recite the Quran with a firm determination to mould your own self as well as your society as a whole according to the injunctions of the Holy Quran. Only those can establish the rule of Allah who mould their own thought and action according to the teachings of Quran. He, who forsakes Quran, can no longer maintain his allegiance to the faith, nor can he contribute any way in the struggle to establish Islamic system of life. Readers of the Quran have been advised:

"(This is) a Scripture that We have revealed unto thee,

full of blessing-that they may ponder its revelations and that men of understanding may reflect."

(38: 30)

Moreover, the readers have been instructed: "Read the Quran slowly with pauses." (73: 4)

The Holy Prophet [S.A.W.] affirmed:

"These hearts get rusted as the iron rusts when water is poured over it." The people submitted: "O Holy Prophet [S.A.W.]! Tell us then what cleanses the rust of the hearts?" The Holy Prophet [S.A.W.] observed: "The rust of the hearts is cleansed when one remembers death frequently and secondly studies the Quran often." (Mishkat)

13. Be grateful to Allah under all circumstances. Look towards those who are below you in terms of material prosperity and social status. It will help you develop a sense of gratitude to Allah.

The Holy Prophet [S.A.W.] observed:

"Look at those who are below you in terms of material prosperity and social status. (You will then feel grateful to Allah). Do not look at those who surpass you in material riches, lest you depreciate the bounties and blessings that Allah has conferred upon you (as it may foster ingratitude to Allah)."

14. Abstain from pleasure-seeking and luxurious living. Be a watchdog of truth who is always on guard and never drops vigil.

The Holy Prophet [S.A.W.] observed:

"How can I live at ease or seek pleasure in life when I know that Israfil stands ready with the trumpet close to his mouth, to sound the call for Doomsday to descend as soon as he receives the Command of

Allah." Addressing the Believers, Allah affirms in the Holy Quran:

"Make ready for them all thou canst of (armed) force and of horses tethered that thereby ye may dismay the enemy of Allah and your enemy, and others beside them whom ye know not. Allah knoweth them whatsoever ye spend in the way of Allah. It will be repaid to you in full and ye will not be wronged." (8: 60)

15. Be prepared to sacrifice everything for the sake of religion and if needed, be prepared even to migrate from your homeland. Check up yourself off and on as to what extent you have developed this devotion. Giving an account of the emigration of Hadrat Ibrahim [A.S.], the Holy Quran has urged believers to be prepared to emigrate and offer sacrifices in the following verses:

"And make mention (O Muhammad) in the scripture of Ibrahim, Lo! he was a saint, a Prophet. When he said unto his father: O my father! Why worshippest thou that which heareth not nor seeth, nor can in aught avail thee? O my father! Lo! there hath come unto me the knowledge that which came not unto thee. So follow me, and I will lead thee on a right path. O my father! Serve not the devil. Lo, the devil is a rebel unto the Beneficent. O my father! Lo! I fear lest a punishment from the Beneficent overtake thee so that thou become a comrade of the devil. He said: Rejectest thou my gods, O Ibrahim! if thou cease not I shall surely stone thee. Depart from me a long while! He said: Peace be unto thee! I shall ask forgiveness of my Allah for thee. Lo! He was ever gracious unto me, I shall withdraw from you and that unto which ye pray beside Allah and I shall pray unto my Allah. It may be that, in prayer unto my Lord, I shall not be unblest." (19: 41-48)

16. Develop a burning zeal striving in the way of Allah, a spirit of fighting with all your means and soul and a pious desire to attain martyrdom in the cause of Allah. Truly speaking, 'Jihad' is the test of faith and the heart which is devoid of the spirit of Jihad is devoid of faith and right guidance and may be compared to a desolate ruin in the wilderness. It is really a great privilege to be able to reach the field of Jihad and to gain an opportunity of sacrificing one's life and property in the way of Allah. In case, the circumstances prevent you from availing of the opportunity to participate in the Jihad; if you lack means or wherewithal to prove your conviction in the field of Jihad, even then you may be counted among those soldiers in the eyes of Allah, who either attained martyrdom while fighting for His cause or returned from the field as the winners provided your heart is filled with the zeal of setting out in the way of Allah, you always take into account the feelings and sentiments which stir a man to perform heroic deeds in the way of Allah. On his return from the battle of Tabuk, the Holy Prophet [S.A.W.] addressed his illustrious companions [R.A.A.] on the way and observed:

> "There are some people left behind in Medina who did set out with you and traversed the valley and remained with you throughout the battle." The companions [R.A.A.] were astonished end submitted: "Did they do all this while staying behind in Medina all the time!" The Holy Prophet [S.A.W.] observed: "Yes, they did all this even while staying behind in Medina all the time, for circumstances forced them to stay back, otherwise they would not have held themselves back of their own accord."

In the Holy Quran, Allah has also praised those people who could not take part in Jihad, despite their burning zeal and were ever afterwards smitten with sorrow over this deprivation.

"Nor unto those whom, when they came to thee (asking that thou shouldst mount them thou didst tell) I cannot find whereupon to mount you. They turned back with eyes flowing with tears, for sorrow that they could not find means to spend."

(9: 92)

The Holy Prophet [S.A.W.] observed: "The man who died without waging a struggle in the way of Allah or had no yearning in his heart to wage such a struggle, has died in a state of hypocrisy." (Muslim)

In fact anybody whose heart is devoid of the spirit of fighting in the way of Allah and of sacrificing his life and resources for the cause of the Almighty is not a true believer.

Spread of Religion

1. Observe prefect decorum and propriety while preaching and propagating Islam. Adopt such an appropriate, dignified, and calculated technique to communicate your message as to generate fervour and zeal in the listener.

The Holy Quran affirms:

"Call to the way of thy Lord with wisdom and fair exhortation and reason with them in the better way."

(16: 125)

This comprehensive verse of the Holy Quran contains instructions regarding three principles:

(i) The call must be made in the most appropriate manner.

(ii) The instruction and guidance must be provided in the best possible way.

(iii) Discussion and reasoning should be fair and courteous.

Calling in a wise manner means to communicate your message according to the situation and circumstances aptitude of the people, their intellect and understanding and their social environments and status. Do not waste this precious treasure of knowledge and wisdom in a haphazard way. Address each class, group or individual according to their ability, capacity, and their mental level. Always start your discussion from such universal truths as are mutually conceded to and pave the way for mutual understanding and agreement.

Arouse one's best sentiments with sincerity and devotion. Create and develop in him an urge and desire to know the truth. Thus he will not only achieve peace of mind but adopt and accept the faith as his own inner urge. It will serve as a source of nourishment for his soul and a tranquiliser for his passions and sentiments.

To be courteous in criticism, and discussion means that you should offer constructive criticism. Your criticism should reflect your earnestness and sincerity. Your style should be so convincing and simple that the intransigence, hate, obstinacy, prejudice or pride may get no inlet. Your approach should be so rational and impressive and your discussion so charming and thought provoking as to make the listener think over your arguments and to feel an irresistible attraction towards the truth. Whenever you feel intransigence in attitude and reasoning, stop discussion and take leave.

Propagate religion as a whole and do not add to or expunge anything from its teachings or principles of your own accord. The preacher of Islam has no discretion to project what he thinks fit and to withhold what he does not think fit to project.

Allah affirms:

> "And when Our clear revelations are recited unto them they who look not for the meeting with us say: Bring a lecture other than this, or change it. Say (O Muhammad): It is not for me to change it of my own accord. I only follow that which is inspired in me: Lo'

> if I disobey my Lord I fair the retribution of an awful day. Say: If Allah had so willed I should not have recited it to you nor would He have made it known to you. I dwelt among you a whole lifetime before it (came to me). Have ye then no sense? Who doeth greater wrong than he who inventeth a lie concerning Allah and denieth His revelations? Lo! the guilty never are successful. (10: 15-17)

However unfavourable the circumstances may be, the preacher must propagate religion in its true and whole form. It is a hideous crime to introduce innovations into or to make alterations in the principles and teachings ordained by Allah to suit the prevailing trends. The people who are guilty of such alterations are the losers in this world as well as in the world Hereafter. Islam is a religion ordained by Allah who is All Knowing and Omnipotent. His knowledge is eternal and there is nothing beyond His knowledge of whole of this universe right from beginning to the end.

Whatever be the human conquests in the field of science and technology, discoveries and explanations, all are subject to the supreme Will of Allah. Nobody has got any right to make any addition or alteration in the Code of life ordained by Him. So much so that the Holy Prophet [S.A.W.], through whom this code of life has been conveyed to us, has been introduced to us as the most ideal servant of Allah who follows what is ordained to him in letter and spirit and dares not overrule His mandate.

3. Convey the message of Islam in a natural way, so that it may not be taken as an unnatural burden. The people may take it as a remedy for all their ills and sufferings instead of feeling scared and developing hatred against it. You should be so polite and rational in conveying the message of Islam to the people that they may feel an irresistible attraction towards Islam. Hadrat

Muawiyyah ibn Hakam [R.A.A.] states: "Once I was saying prayers behind the Holy Prophet [S.A.W.] when a man sneezed. I responded to the sneeze by saying in the course of the prayer. The people began to star at me. I said: "May Allah bless you! Why are you staring at me? The People indicated to me by gestures to keep quiet. I kept quiet. When the prayer was over, the Holy Prophet (peace and blessings of Allah be upon him) and may my father and mother be sacrificed for him, never did I see a better guide and teacher before or after him) neither reproached me, nor beat me, nor blamed me. He only said to me "Look. This is prayer and it is not admissible to talk during the prayer. Prayer is meant to acknowledge the purity, supremacy and exaltedness of Allah to recite the Holy Quran."

4. Be moderate in your writing, speech and conversation while conveying the message and call of Islam so that the listeners may feel hopeful as well as seized with awe. Neither overstress the terrifying aspects of the punishment for sins, lest the people should lose all hopes of mercy from Allah and consider salvation not only difficult but impossible; nor should you present such a rosy and one-sided picture of the kindness and forgiveness of Allah that people become fearless and irresponsible in their actions and feel free to transgress the divine commands trusting upon the Munificence and Forgiving Nature of Allah.

Hadrat 'Ali [R.A.A.] observed:

"The best scholar is he who invites the people to obey and submit before Allah in such a manner that people do not lose hope in Allah; he neither gives them allowances to commit transgressions against the Law of Allah nor makes them fearless of Divine punishment."

5. Observe perseverance and constancy in missionary activities. Continue implementing your programme with fortitude and a high sense of responsibility. Avoid the habit of abandoning your programmes half way and chalking out new schemes. Do little, but do it steadily.

The Holy Prophet [S.A.W.] has observed:

> "The best deed is the one which, however little it may be, is done constantly and regularly."

6. Meet all hardships and trials that confront you while preaching and propagating Islam cheerfully and with patience and fortitude:

The Holy Quran affirms:

> "And enjoin kindness and forbid iniquity and persevere whatever may befall thee." (31:17)

Hardships and difficulties do come in the way of truth and submission to Allah. These trials and hardships strengthen faith in Allah and season one's character and morals. This is why Allah puts those to trial who claim to be His servants and the trial gets harder and harder for those who are better seasoned in faith and devotion.

Allah affirms:

> "And most certainly shall We try you by means of same fear, and hunger and loss of worldly goods, lives and fruits, and glad tidings to the patient who, when adversity overtakes them, say: Surely Allah's we are, and unto Him we are to return. It is they, upon whom there are blessings of their Lord and (His) mercy and it is they alone who are guided aright" (2: 155-57)

'Hadrat Saad [R.A.A.] submitted to the Holy Prophet [S.A.W.]: "O Prophet of Allah [S.A.W.]! Which person is put to the severest trial?" The Holy Prophet [S.A.W.] observed:

"The persons who are put to the severest trials are firstly the Prophets of Allah [A.S.], then those who are nearest to the prophets in conviction and devotion, and then those who are next to them in their faith and submission. In fact one is tried according to his conviction and devotion. Whoever is firm in his conviction and devotion is put to a hard test and whoever is weak in faith and submission is confronted with a mild trial and these trials continue till a man is purged of all traces of sin." (Mishkat)

Recounting his own experience, the Holy Prophet [S.A.W.] observed:

"Never was a man more persecuted in the way of Allah than I was and never was a man more threatened in the way of Allah as I was. We spent thirty days and thirty nights in such state that Bilal [R.A.A.] and I had nothing that a living being could eat, save some little provisions in the small pack which Bilal [R.A.A.] kept under his arm." (Tirmidhi)

The Holy Prophet [S.A.W.] also affirmed:

"And person who will make an effort to be patient shall be granted patience by Allah. And there is no blessing which encompasses more good than patience." (Bukhari, Muslim)

In fact, trials are essential for strengthening and carrying forward the movement. No movement can achieve success without passing through periods of trial, especially a movement which calls for a universal revolution in human society and plans to raise the social structure of human life on entirely new foundations.

Reminiscing about the days when the stone-hearted Meccans were perpetrating endless tortures on the Holy Prophet [S.A.W.] and his illustrious Companions [R.A.A.], Hadrat Khabbab ibn al-Arat [R.A.A.] related:

"The Holy Prophet [S.A.W.] was resting with a sheet placed under his sacred head in the shade of Bait-Allah (House of Allah) when we reached his presence with the complaint: "O Prophet of Allah [S.A.W.]! Don't you seek aid for us from Allah! Don't you pray for an end to this oppression! (How long will this period of trial continue and when will it come to an end!) The Holy Prophet [S.A.W.] heard our complaint and observed: There had been people before you who faced unprecedented trials and oppressions. Often one of them was made to stand in a pit, half buried in the ground, and his body was sliced into two parts with a saw like a log of wood, yet the man refused to renounce his faith. Their flesh was pierced through with steel combs till the iron nails reached the bones and the fibres, yet the devotees of Allah did not resign from truth. By Allah, Islam shall prevail and you will see (such a state of peace and security) that a man riding from Sanaa (the Capital of Yemen) to Hadramut will have nothing to fear on the way except Allah. The shepherds will only fear the wolves lest they should carry off their goats. But, alas, you show impatience."

(Bukhari)

Hadrat Muawiyyah [R.A.A.] relates: "I have heard the Holy Prophet [S.A.W.] observing, "There shall always remain a group among my Ummah who will defend Islam and their faith. Those who do not support them or oppose them shall never be able to destroy or eliminate them till the final word from Allah. These defenders of Faith shall remain firm in their conviction.

(Bukhari, Muslim)

7. Do not show undue toleration, or shower undeserved praise on any one, nor sacrifice principles under any circumstances. In affirmation of a virtue of the believers, the Holy Quran says:

"They deal strictly with the non-believers."

In other words, the believers are extremely strict about matters of religion and principle and under no circumstances do they compromise their principles or tolerate wrongdoing. They can bear anything, but cannot sacrifice their religion or principles. Allah has transmitted through the Holy Prophet [S.A.W.] the following to the Muslims:

"Unto this then summon (O Muhammad). And be thou upright as thou art commanded, and follow not their lusts."

Accommodation for wrongdoing, undue toleration and compromise with falsehood are the weaknesses that destroy one's faith and religion.

The Holy Prophet [S.A.W.] has observed:

"When the tribe of Israel began to transgress the commands of Allah, their learned men checked them, but they did not refrain from their wicked deeds. Their learned men instead of boycotting their society, continued to attend their company and ate and drank with them. Consequently Allah equated these pious Ulamas with the transgressors and cursed them through His Prophets, Hadrat Daud and Hadrat 'Isa [A.S.]. Allah cursed the Israelites because they followed the path of disobedience to Allah and went too far on this way." The reporter of this Tradition 'Abdullah b. Masud [R.A.A.] relates: "The Holy Prophet [S.A.W.] changed his reclining posture and sat erect and observed: No, I swear by Him Who hath power over my life, you will certainly continue to enforce virtue and curb evil and you will hold the hand of the oppressor and bend the tyrant before truth. If you do not act as you must, you too shall assimilate with them and Allah shall withhold all His blessings and guidance from you and forsake you completely, just as He deprived the Israelites of His clemency.

8. To train and reform your children and to prepare them for the duty of establishing religion is not only your foremost obligation, but a logical sphere of your activity. On the other hand, it is unwise and unnatural to ignore your children and get yourself busy in missionary activities outside. It is a gross negligence and an escape from duty. It is as if you leave your own family writhing in agony of hunger and thirst during famine and go out in search of the needy to distribute grain among them to display your munificence. It shows that you are quite incapable of perceiving the suffering of hunger and thirst and are devoid of the sense of kinship and love; nor can you appreciate the wisdom that lies behind the act of distributing grain. The Holy Quran enjoins upon the believers:

"O Believers! Save yourselves and your families from the fire of Hell."

The Holy Prophet [S.A.W.] has elucidated the same verse as follows:

"Each one of you is a guardian and is charged with a respon- sibility, and each one of you shall be held accountable for those who have been placed under your care. The ruler is a guardian and he shall be held to account for the affairs of his subjects. The husband is the guardian of his family; the woman is the guardian of her husband's home and children. So each one of you is a guardian and charged with a responsibility and each one of you shall be called to account for the affairs of those who have been placed under your care." (Bukhari, Muslim)

9. Expend some care upon reforming and cultivating your neighbours and the people living around you and consider this task as a part of your duty.

The Holy Prophet [S.A.W.] delivered a sermon one day and in the course of his sermon praised some Muslims and then observed: "Why is it so that some people do not impart religious knowledge to their neighbours and do not season them in religion, neither do they warn them of the fearful consequences of their ignorance of religion, nor restrain them from committing evil deeds? And why is it so that some of you do not care to learn religion from their neighbours and do not acquire an understanding of its purpose and spirit, nor do they try to ascertain the fearful consequences of remaining ignorant of religion. By Allah!

The people must teach religion to their neighbours and inculcate an understanding of religion in them. The people should guide their neighbours, give them good counsel and restrain them from wrong and evil. Besides, it is the duty of people to learn religion and accept their counsels or else I shall punch them soon." The Holy Prophet [S.A.W.] then descended from the pulpit concluding his sermon.

Those who were present there enquired from each other: Against whom the Holy Prophet [S.A.W.] delivered this warning?" The others said, "The Holy Prophet [S.A.W.] was alluding in his speech to the people of the tribe of Ashar. These people are well-versed in religion, but their neighbours, who live in the Oasis, are ignorant yokels." When the people of the tribe of Ashar came to know of the sermon delivered by the Holy Prophet [S.A.W.] they presented themselves before the Holy Prophet [S.A.W.] and submitted: "O Prophet of Allah [S.A.W.]! You were pleased to shower praise on some people and expressed your displeasure towards us. Kindly let us know what is wrong with us?" The Holy Prophet [S.A.W.] observed: "It is the duty of the people to teach religion to their neighbours;

they ought to preach to them, educate them and restrain them from wrong and evil. Likewise it is the duty of the people to learn religion from their neighbours and to accept their counsels.

They should also cultivate an understanding of religion, otherwise I shall punish them soon in this world." The people of the tribe of Ashar again submitted: "O Prophet of Allah [S.A.W.]! Should we inculcate the spirit of religion among others?" The Holy Prophet [S.A.W.] observed: "Yes, indeed, it is your duty." Thereupon the people submitted: "O Holy Prophet [S.A.W.]! Allow us a grace period of one year." The Holy Prophet [S.A.W.] granted them a grace period of one year within which they were to teach religion to their neighbours and inculcate an understanding of religion in them. The Holy Prophet [S.A.W.] then recited the following verses:

> "Those of the children of Israel who went astray were cursed by the tongue of David, and of Jesus son of Mary. That was because they rebelled and used to transgress. They restrained not one another from the wickedness they did. Verily evil was they used to do." (5: 78,79)

10. Respect and give due regard to the religious beliefs and sentiments of the people among whom you are performing your pleasant duty of preaching and propagating religion. Do not desecrate the names of their forbears or leaders; neither attack their beliefs, nor denounce their religious doctrines. You should preach your religion in a positive manner with sense and wisdom. Your criticism, instead of provoking the listeners, shall be earnestly aimed at driving home your preachings to them. Impassioned criticism and disparaging speech never succeeds in bringing about the desired change in the addressee. On the other land, there is an ever present danger in this case that feelings of pride in ignorance and prejudice may be ignited in

the listener and under their influence he may pass impudent remarks upon Allah and religion and instead of drawing near to religion may go farther astray.

The Holy Quran affirms:

"(O Believers!) Do not revile those whom they call besides Allah lest they should unknowingly take to reviling Allah out of enmity."

11. When you become a missionary for spreading the message of Allah, you should confine your activities to calling people towards Allah and nothing else. Do not call the people of Allah towards anything other than Allah; do not issue your call in the name of a country, people, race, or language; nor call them on behalf of a party. The objective of the believer is to obey the Will of Allah. Call people towards total submission to Allah and cultivate an assurance among them that the slave's duty is to worship his Creator and Master, be it in the sphere of his individual or family life or in social and political affairs. The slave should obey in all spheres of his life the order of his Lord and Creator and submit to His Law with sincerity and devotion. A Muslim can have no objective before him other than this. He should, therefore call others also to achieve this objective. Whenever a believer should dare turn his back upon the Commands of Allah and set up anything else than obedience to the Will of Allah as his objective, he shall be condemned and rejected in both the worlds.

"Who is better in speech than he who calls people towards Allah, acts righteously and says 'I am surely of those who submit."

The Organisation

1. Form a strong organisation for propagating religion and make a concentrated and collective struggle to establish Islamic order.

And there must exist at least a group among you which should call people towards goodness enjoining good and prohibit the evils.

"*Al-Khair*" denotes all that is naturally good and which has always been regarded as good by human nature and which has been attested as good by the revealed Books. A comprehensive and systematic form of all that is good and virtuous is the religion of Allah which the Apostles (peace be upon them) have been transmitting to the world in every successive epoch and whose final, complete, authentic and fully preserved form is the Quran and Sunnah which the Holy Prophet Muhammad [S.A.W.] bequeathed to the Ummah. To call people towards this good and to enrich the world with virtue it is imperative that Muslims should form a party and perform this duty in an organised manner. They should forge strong and well-knit front and launch a well-organised and concentrated struggle to eliminate the wrong and evil from every sphere of life. Allah describes this unity and strength of the Muslims with appreciation and praise and lauds their collective and concentrated struggle.

> "Verily Allah loves those who fight in His cause arrayed in ranks as though they were a structure cemented with molten lead."

Stressing the importance of collective struggle and advising Muslims to live as an organised body, the Holy Prophet [S.A.W.] observed:

> "Three men who live in a jungle are forbidden to live together save they choose one from among themselves as their Amir (Chief)." (Muntaqa)

Further the Holy Prophet [S.A.W.] observed:

> "The person who wishes to secure a dwelling place in the centre of Paradise ought to remain firmly attached to the "Aljamaat" for the devil haunts a

single person, but if two persons join together, the devil runs away as far as possible."

"Al-Jamaat" implies a well-organised society of Muslims which is governed by the rule of Shariah under a Muslim Caliph and the Muslims as a whole agree and concede to his authority and leadership. In such a situation there is no justification, whatsoever, for any Muslim to keep himself away and aloof from such a society. In case such a society and such an organisation does not exist make an all-out concentrated and collective effort to bring about such a society which is called Al-Jamaat in Islamic terminology.

2. Make Islam the foundation of your unity and organisation as the distinguishing feature of an Islamic organisation is nothing but total submission to Allah. Any organisation, unity or alliance based on any thing other than total submission to Allah shall not be termed as Islamic, as it is not based on the foundation of Islam. The real base of brotherhood and bond of unity is Islam and Islam only. Anything other than Islam cannot cement relations of brotherhood and unison. It will rather disperse and disintegrate the people and instead of forming a powerful and well-knit unit and organisation with singularity of purpose and procedure, they will be divided into several sects and factions.

Call to Religion if you form a party, the only objective before you should be to establish the rule of Allah and all your struggle and efforts should be devoted to achieve this goal only.

The Holy Quran affirms:

"And hold fast all of you together to this rope of Allah and do not separate. And remember Allah's favour unto you how ye were enemies and He made friendship between your hearts so that ye became as brothers by His grace." (3: 103)

"The rope of Allah' means Islam, the 'Religion of Allah'. According to the Holy Quran, it is Islam which forms the basis of the unity and organisation for Muslims. Anything else will only divide them into a number of factions instead of uniting and unifying them.

3. Love those working for the cause of Islam from the core of your heart and consider this connection as the most important and the most inestimable of all connections.

Describing the characteristics of the believers, the Holy Quran affirms:

> "They will not find folk who believe in Allah and the Last Day loving those who oppose Allah and His Messenger even though they be their fathers or their sons or their brothers or their clan." (58: 22)

4. Extend support and counsel to your colleagues in the party and keep alive the spirit of mutual guidance and advice in your party life, for this is the real key to success.

"By the time, surely man is ever in a state of loss except those who believe and do righteous deeds and exhort one another to preach Truth and exhort one another to be steadfast."

5. Observe party discipline with full care, and do not consider it only a means of strengthening your party, but deem it as a religious duty.

Allah affirms:

> "They only are true believers who believe in Allah and His Messenger and when they are with him on some common errand go not away until they have asked leave of him. Lo! those who ask leave of thee, those are they who believe in Allah and His Messenger." (24: 62)

Party discipline and loyalty and devotion to the leader is not only a legal point, but an important issue. The Holy Quran has affirmed the true faith of those who are loyal to party discipline and in no case abandon their party duty without leave of their leader.

6. Extend sincere cooperation in all the good works that are being carried out by the party and exert yourself to the maximum in this effort. Do not stain the purity of your moral character by entertaining any evil sentiments such as selfishness, or personal motives and self-glorification.

The Holy Quran enjoins upon the believers:

"And cooperate with each other in good works of piety and Allah-fearing."

7. Maintain cordial relations with your colleagues. If at times a difference of opinion arises, resolve the dispute at once and keep your heart clear of any feelings of grudge.

"So fear Allah and maintain cordial relations among yourselves."

8. Obey the Amir of the Islamic Party with all sincerity and in good spirit and remain loyal and devoted to him.

The Holy Prophet (S.A.W.) has observed:

"It is the duty of the Muslims to listen to and obey the order of their leader, regardless of the consideration whether such an order is agreeable or disagreeable to them, provided such an order does not constitute a transgression of Allah's law. In case no such order is issued as is repugnant to Allah's law, it should not be listened to, nor obeyed. (Bukhari, Muslim)

Hadrat Tamim Dari reports that the Holy Prophet [S.A.W.] observed:

> "Religion means devotion and loyalty." The Holy Prophet [S.A.W.] repeated this observation three times. Thereupon we submitted: "Devotion and loyalty to whom?" The Holy Prophet [S.A.W.] observed: "Devotion and loyalty to Allah, His Messenger, His Book, the leaders of Muslims and the mass of Muslims." (Muslim)

9. Avoid party chauvinism, bigotry and factionalism. Cooperate with everyone with an open heart and in good cheer. Esteem those who are working for the cause of religion. Deal with them in good faith and sincerity and consider them as your colleagues and comrades. All those who work for the cause of religion are in reality supporters and helpers of one another. The goal of everyone of them is the glory of religion and all of them wish to serve religion according to their lights. It is auspicious and fruitful to point out each other's faults in a spirit of friendship and understanding and to focus attention on correct mode of thought and action. On the other hand, it is below the dignity and office of the preachers of religion to indulge in such despicable conduct as hatred, friction, envy, grudge, confrontation and hostile propaganda against each other. The character of the preachers must be clear of all these blemishes who sincerely and truly wish to expend their energies and talents in the way of Allah and to render some service to the cause of Islam during their lifetime.

Significant Elements

1. To lead and guide the Islamic party choose a person who excels others in piety and fear of Allah. Heritage nor wealth is the basis of leadership or eminence in

Islam. The best person in Islam is he who fears Allah most.

The Holy Quran affirms:

"O mankind! Lo! We have created you male and female, and have made you nations and tribes so that ye may know one another. Lo! the noblest of you in the sight of Allah, is the best in conduct."

(49: 13)

2. Regard the election of a leader as a sacred duty and use your vote as a trust from Allah only in favour of person who in your view is best qualified to discharge the onerous responsibility of leadership.

Allah affirms:

"Lo! Allah Commandeth you that you restore deposits to their owners," (4: 58)

This is a precise principle which encompasses all kinds of trusts. In the context of this Chapter 'trusts denote the responsibilities of an Islamic Party i.e. the duty of leadership should be vested by open choice in such a person who is the best qualified among you to discharge the onerous responsibility of leadership. To cast your vote in this case in a partisan spirit or to show undue favour or to act under the influence of other extraneous factors is a breach of trust. The character of a believer must be free from the taint of breach of trust.

3. If you are to lead an Islamic Party, you should be fully conscious of your responsibilities and should discharge your duty with complete honesty, diligence, sense of responsibility and energy.

The Holy Prophet [S.A.W.] observed:

"Allah shall ban the entry of that person into Paradise who is entrusted the duty of administering the affairs of Muslim society and he betrays their trust."

(Bukhari, Muslim)

The Holy Prophet [S.A.W.] also observed:

> "The person who accepts the charge of administering the affairs of Muslims and then does not serve their interests and does not tire himself out in their service to the same extent that he tires himself out to fulfil his own personal needs, Allah shall throw such a man headlong into the fire of Hell." (Tibrani)

4. Treat your subordinates with tenderness, affection, fairness and large heartedness so that they may cooperate with you willingly and Allah may grant your Party the favour of rendering some service to Islam. Describing the virtues of the Holy Prophet [S.A.W.] the Holy Quran says:

> "It was by the mercy of Allah that thou west lenient with them (O, Muhammad). for if thou hadst been stern and fierce of heart they would have dispersed from round about thee." (3: 159)

Moreover, Allah has urged the Holy Prophet [S.A.W.]:

> "And lower thy wing (in tenderness) unto these believers who follow thee." (26: 215)

In the course of a speech, Hadrat 'Umar b. Khattab [R.A.A.] remarked:

> "O people! You owe us a duty to support us sincerely in our absence and assist us in performing deeds of piety."

Furthermore he observed:

> "Officers of the government! No tenderness is greater before Allah and more profitable than the tenderness and leniency shown by the head of the executive. Similarly, no lack of wisdom and ineptness is more damaging, dangerous and despicable than the indiscretion, whimsical nature and haphazard actions of the executive head."

5. Realise the importance of your colleagues. Respect their sentiments and pay due regard to their needs. Treat them in such a fraternal way that they should look upon you as their greatest well-wisher.

Hadrat Malik ibn Hawarith relates: "Once some of us young men who were of the same age group went to stay with the Holy Prophet [S.A.W.] and lived in his auspicious company for twenty days. The Holy Apostle of Allah was no doubt extremely kind and tenderhearted.

When the Holy Prophet [S.A.W.] felt that we were homesick, he [S.A.W.] enquired from us: "What relations have you left behind at home?" We submitted details, whereupon the Holy Prophet [S.A.W.] advised us: "You should now return home and live with them and teach them what you have learnt and propagate good deeds among them. Tell them the exact hours of prayers and when the time of prayer approaches, one of you should announce the call and he who excels all others in learning and character among you should lead the prayers."

6. Appreciate the worth and importance of your colleagues and considering them your real assets, take pains to train them in right earnest. Do not underrate them as poor and destitute nor covet those upon whom Allah has bestowed worldly pomp, grandeur and wealth.

> "Restrain thyself along with those who cry unto their Lord at morning and evening, seeking His countenances and let nor thine eyes overlook them desiring the pomp of the life of the world."
>
> (18:29)

In fact the people who have devoted their lives and resources to the propagation and preaching of religion are the veritable assets of a religious party. The duty of the party leader is to realise the value of these people and concentrate all his attention on their education and training.

7. Settle and execute all party matters in consultation with your colleagues. Try to develop their interest in the party and consolidate their support for the activities of the party. Allah, in praise of the believers, also affirms that they settle their affairs by mutual consultation.

"And their affairs are (settled) by mutual consultation."

Allah has urged the Holy Prophet [S.A.W.] to consult his companions in matters of special importance.

"And consult them in (important) matters."

8. Display generosity and selflessness in party matters. Do not seek to advance your own or your family's interests in any party matter. On the other hand, show a liberal and unselfish conduct so that your colleagues may always be prepared to make all sacrifices with a willing heart and may not feel disillusioned with the party or severe their connection with it or may not be moved to act with selfish and interested motives. Hadrat Abu Bakr [R.A.A.] once observed to Hadrat 'Umar [R.A.A.]:

"O son of Khattab! I have chosen you and appointed you over Muslims so that you may deal with them with kindness. You have been a companion of the Holy Prophet [S.A.W.]. You know how the Holy Prophet [S.A.W.] used to prefer our interests to his own interest and that of our family to his family, so much so that we often returned as a gift to the Prophet's family whatever we received from him in excess of our needs and requirements." (Kitab ul-Khard)

9. Always avoid partiality and nepotism and never show undue regard and toleration. Hadrat Yazid b. Sufyan [R.A.A.] relates: "When Hadrat Abu Bakr [R.A.A.] appointed me chief of the army and sent me towards Syria, he gave me the following instructions:

'O Yazid! You have some kinsmen and relations. It is possible that you may feel tempted to prefer them to others for appointment to offices of trust. This is what I fear most about you."

The Holy Prophet [S.A.W.] observed: "Allah will accept no compensation or consideration from a person who is responsible for the affairs of the Muslims and appoints a man to an office of authority over Muslims merely on the basis of kinship or friendship, so much so that Allah shall consign the guilty person to Hell."

(Kitab ul-Khard)

10. Maintain strict party discipline as far as is possible and do not show weakness or leniency in matters of discipline.

Allah affirms:

"So, if they ask thy leave for some affair of theirs, give leave to whom thou wilt of them, and ask for them forgiveness of Allah." (24: 62)

In other words, when the members of the party assemble to attend to some party business and later some members begin to seek permission to leave on account of their personal needs or disabilities, it behoves the leader of the party to accept the requests of those people only whose personal needs are really more pressing than the matters confronting them in the meeting or of those whose disabilities justify their leave by canonical law and, therefore, must be considered and conceded.

8

Sacred Performances

Practices in Faith

1. The best portion of the earth in the sight of Allah is that upon which a mosque is raised. The distinctive feature of the devotee of Allah is that he loves the mosque also. On the terrific day of doom when there will be no shade anywhere, Allah will keep that person under the shade of His Heaven whose heart is devoted to the mosque. The Holy Prophet [S.A.W.] has observed:

"The man whose heart is devoted to the mosque will rest under the shade of Heaven." (Bukhari)

2. Render service to the mosque; keep the house of Allah populated. To render service to the mosque and keep it populated is a sign of faith. Allah affirms:

"He shall tend Allah's sanctuaries who believeth in Allah and the Day of reckoning." *(Al-Tauba: 18)*

3. Always say your obligatory prayers in congregation in the mosque. Maintain a regular system of congregation and announcement of the Prayer-call in the mosque and correlate your whole life with the mosque. Mosque is the pivot around which the life of a true believer revolves. The Holy Prophet [S.A.W.] observed:

"There are certain people among the Muslims who stay in the mosque permanently and do not leave the place. They have angels as their companions. If such people disappear from the mosque, the angels go about looking for them. If these people fall ill, the angels enquire after their health and when they are engaged in some task, the angels aid them - A person who sits in the mosque anticipates blessings of the Lord." (Musnad Ahmad)

4. Go to the mosque with eagerness and enthusiasm to say your prayers. The Holy Prophet [S.A.W.] affirmed: "The act of going to the mosque morning and evening is like going to fight in the cause of Allah." And further observed: "The people who go towards the mosque in the dim light of the dawn will be accompanied by full radiance of light on the Day of Doom." In addition, the Holy Prophet [S.A.W.] affirmed: "Each step that a man takes towards the mosque to say his prayers with the congregation, debits one sin and credits one virtue to his account." (Ibn Habban)
5. Keep the mosque clean and tidy. Sweep the place and clean out all dust or filth. Burn incense, especially on Fridays so that the whole mosque becomes fragrant with the aroma of the incense. The Prophet [S.A.W.] observed: "To sweep the mosque; to keep it tidy and clean; to cast out all dust and filth from the mosque; to burn incense in the mosque, especially to make the place fragrant with the aroma of the incense on Fridays- all these are acts which lead to Paradise."

(Ibn Majah)

Moreover, the Holy Prophet [S.A.W.] said: "To clean out the dirt and dust of the mosque is the mehr (dower) of a pretty-eyed Houri." (Tibrani)

6. Go to the mosque in a state of awe and trepidation. Say 'Assalamo 'Alaikum' [peace be on you] on entering the

mosque. Sit down quietly and pray in such a manner that your heart should be filled with the awe of the Greatness and Glory of Allah. Those who enter the mosque laughing and talking are careless and impudent. The hearts of such people are devoid of the fear of Allah. Some people in their bid to join the congregation lest they miss any Rakat rush forward into the mosque. This act is contrary to the sanctity of the mosque. Whether you are able to join the 'Rakat' or not, walk in the mosque with poise, dignity and in humility; avoid hurried movement.

7. Sit down in the mosque in peace and avoid worldly talk. To shout or make a noise, to cut jokes and laughter, to discuss bazar rates, to comment on the world affairs or to strike business deals in the mosque is an act of sacrilege. Mosque is a place for Worship; use it for the purpose of offering devotions to Allah only.
8. Do not take such small children with you in the mosque who have not yet attained awareness of the sanctity of the mosque lest they should discharge urine, defecate or spit in the mosque.
9. Do not use the mosque as a thoroughfare. On entering the gate of the mosque it becomes obligatory upon you to say prayers, or sit down and engage in the remembrance of Allah or recite the Holy Quran.
10. If you lose something somewhere else, do not make an announcement of your loss in the mosque. Whenever someone made such an announcement in the mosque of the Prophet [S.A.W.] the Holy Prophet [S.A.W.] was offended and used to remark:

"May Allah restore not the lost thing to thee!"

11. On entering the mosque put your right foot first in and say 'peace and blessings of Allah be on the Holy Prophet' [S.A.W.] and then say the following prayer. The Holy

Prophet [S.A.W.] observed: "Whenever any of you enters the mosque, he should say 'peace and blessings of Allah be on the Holy Prophet' [S.A.W.] and then say this prayer:

"O Allah! Open the gates of Thy Mercy for me."

(Muslim)

After entering the mosque, say two Rakat' of supererogatory prayers. These two Rakat are described by the term "Tahiyyat ul-Masjid'. Similarly, whenever you return from a journey, go first to the mosque and say two Rakat of supererogatory prayers and then proceed to your house. On return from a journey, the Holy Prophet [S.A.W.] used to go first to the mosque and offered supererogatory prayers and afterwards proceeded home.

12. On coming out of the mosque, put your left foot out first and say this prayer:

"O Allah! I seek your Favour and Blessings."

(Muslim)

13. Maintain a regular system of announcing the prayer-call and holding of congregational prayers. Appoint only such persons as Muaddhin (one who gives adaan i.e. call for prayers) and Imam (one who leads the prayers) as are on the whole better than others in their devotion to religion and possess superior character. If possible try to appoint such people as Muaddhins and Imams who demand no remuneration for their services and are willing to discharge these duties voluntarily in anticipation of the reward in the Hereafter.

14. Say this prayer after hearing the prayer-call. The Holy Prophet [S.A.W.] observed: "The man who after hearing the prayer-call recites the following prayer will thereby acquire a right over me to pray for him on the Day of Doom."

(Mishkat)

"Allah! The Master of this Perfect Call and this Congregation standing for Prayer! Grant Muhammad [S.A.W.] Thy closeness and Excellence and appoint him to that exalted state the promise of which Thou gave him and grant us the favour of Muhammad's [S.A.W.] intercession with Thee on our behalf. Undoubtedly Thou never goes back on Thy promises."

15. When the Muaddhin is announcing the prayer-call, repeat his utterances after him. However, when he says ... Hayya 'alassalah and Hayya'alal falah say in reply *La haula wala quwwata illa billahil 'aliyyil 'azim.*1 In the course of announcing the call for dawn prayers when the Muaddhin says. *Assalatu Khairum min-annaum.* (Prayer is better than sleep) say these words in reply *Sadaqta wa bararta.* (You spoke the truth and good).
16. When the announcer of *Takbir* says (*Qadqamatissalah*) says these words in reply *Aqamahallahu wa adamaha.* (May Allah maintain it for ever).
17. The women should say their prayers in the home instead of going to the mosque. On one occasion the wife of Hadrat Abu Humaid Saadi [R.A.A.] submitted: "O Prophet [S.A.W.]! I cherish a great desire to say prayers in your company." The Holy Prophet [S.A.W.] observed: "I am aware of your eagerness. But it is better for you to say prayers in your room than in the verandah outside your room and saying prayers in the verandah of your house is better for you than saying prayers in the courtyard of your home."

However, the women should try their best to cater to the requirements of the mosque. They should arrange for the supply of water, mats, incense and perfumes and other articles of use in the mosques and should cherish feelings of deep attachment to the mosque in their hearts.

18. Take grown up children with you to the mosque. Mothers ought to persuade their children to go to the

mosque so that they may develop eagerness and enthusiasm for prayers. Show tenderness, love and affection to children in the mosque. If they commit any wrong or an act of mischief, do not rebuke or bully them. Make them understand the proper etiquettes with love and affection and instruct them in virtue.

Performance of Prayers

1. Observe perfect cleanliness and purity for the purpose of saying the prayers. Brush your teeth (use miswak) also when performing ablutions. The Prophet [S.A.W.] said: "The distinctive mark of the members of my Ummah on the Doomsday will be that their brows and organs of ablution will be glowing with the radiance of Divine Light. Hence it is open to everyone to enhance his share of the Divine Light as much as he wants."
2. Put on clean, neat, respectable civilised and proper dress for observing prayers. The Holy Quran affirms:

"O sons of Adam! Adorn yourself properly at each hour of prayer."

3. Say prayers at the prescribed hours.

The prayer has been made obligatory for the believers to be observed at prescribed hours. Hadrat 'Abdullah b. Masud [R.A.A.] once asked Holy Prophet [S.A.W.]:

"O Prophet of Allah [S.A.W.]! Which deed is the most favourite one to Allah?" The Holy Prophet [S.A.W.] replied: "To say prayer at the proper time." Furthermore, the Holy Prophet [S.A.W.] observed: "Allah has made five prayers obligatory. A person who after performing ablutions carefully observes these prayers in perfect humility at their proper hours acquires a right of salvation by Allah; but he who shows carelessness in prayers has no right to anticipate forgiveness and salvation by Allah. In this case, it is entirely up to the Will of Allah to forgive him or to punish him." (Malik)

4. Always say your prayers in congregation. At times when you miss the congregation for any reason, try to say the obligatory (Fard) prayers in a mosque. However, offering of Sunnah prayers is permissible at home also. The Holy Prophet [S.A.W.] said: "The person who joins the congregation for prayer at the start i.e. first Takbir for forty days at a stretch is secured from the torments of Hell as well as from the evil of discord." (Tirmidhi)

In addition to this, the Holy Prophet [S.A.W.] also said: "If the people become aware of the rewards and blessings of offering prayers in a congregation, they would hasten to join the congregation for prayer despite a thousand hindrances. The first row of a congregation for prayer is like the row of angels.. It is better for two men to offer prayers together than separately. The larger the congregation the dearer it is to Allah." (Abu Daud)

5. Say prayers with peace of mind. Perform bows (Ruku') and prostrations (Sajda) calmly. Rising from a bow, stand straight with ease and then go into prostration. Keep a suitable interval between two prostrations and in this interval, say the following prayer:

"O Allah, forgive me, be Merciful to me, set me on the right path, remove my misery, grant me peace and provide for my sustenance." (Abu-Daud)

The Holy Prophet [S.A.W.] has observed: "The person who observes prayer properly, the prayer itself blesses him with good wishes in these words `May Allah protect thee in the same manner in which they took care of me."

And the Holy Prophet [S.A.W.] also said: "The worst form of theft is the theft of prayer." The people asked: "O Holy

Prophet [S.A.W.]! How can one commit a theft in prayer." The Holy Prophet [S.A.W.] answered: "By skipping over the complete performance of bows and prostrations."

6. Start making preparations for the prayer at once on hearing the prayer-call (adaan). Perform ablutions and reach the mosque well before time. Sit down quietly in the line and wait for the congregation to form. It is symbolic of hypocrites to be sluggish, to try and go for the prayers in a languid manner after hearing the prayer-call.
7. Announce the prayer-call with eagerness and zest. A person asked the Holy Prophet: "O Prophet of Allah [S.A.W.]! Tell me a deed that can lead me to Paradise." The Holy Prophet [S.A.W.] said: "Announce the call for prayer." The Prophet [S.A.W.] further said: "Within the extent to which the call of the Muaddhin reaches each man who hears the call will be witness in favour of the Muaddhin on the Day of Judgement . A shepherd who grazes his flock in the pasture and pronounces the adaan in a loud voice at the fixed hour, all things within the radius of the area in which his voice vibrates will stand testimony in his favour on the Day of Judgement." (Bukhari)
8. If you are acting as an Imam, discharge your responsibility in relation to the saying of prayer with all the manners and rules prescribed by religion. Keep in view the interests of the congregation and perform your duty as a leader well. The Holy Prophet [S.A.W.] said: "The Imams who lead the prayer in a proper manner and entertain a high sense of personal responsibility for the good will obtain reward for the prayers of their congregation also. The Imam's reward in this case will be equal to the combined reward of the congregation. However, the reward and virtue

of the members of the congregation is not curtailed thereby." (Tibrani)

9. Say your prayers with humility in such a state that the heart should be filled with a sense of awe of the Greatness and Glory of Allah and your entire being should be overwhelmed with trepidation and solemnity. It is a great sacrilege to make unnecessary movements of hand and foot, scratching any part of the body, to pass fingers through the beard, to plug the nose with a finger or to fold up your dress. Take the utmost care to avoid such actions.

10. Seek to gain nearness to Allah through prayers. Say prayers in such a state of mind as if you are standing before Allah or at least be mindful that Allah is watching you. The Holy Prophet [S.A.W.] said:

"The bondman is nearest to Allah at the moment when he is lying in prostration (Sajdah) before Him. Hence while you are performing Sajdah pray fervently." (Muslim)

11. Say prayers with eagerness and zest. The formal observance of prayers as if prayer were a burden or a compulsion is no genuine form of worship. Having said prayers of one time, look forward to the next hour of prayers with eagerness and fervour. One day after having offered the Maghrib prayers, some people stayed waiting for the hour of 'Isha prayers. The Holy Prophet [S.A.W.] arrived with such hurried steps that he was panting for breath. The Holy Prophet [S.A.W.] observed: "O people! Be happy, your Lord opened a gate of the heavens and showed your view to His angels and said with pride: "Look my devotees have finished one prayer and are awaiting the next hour of worship'."

(Ibn Majah)

12. Do not say prayers in a hurried manner with a sense of 'Let us get over with it', like the careless and carefree persons. Remember Allah with a sincere beau and say prayers with complete devotion and a solemn awareness of duty and direct your heart, mind, feelings, passions, thoughts and ideas towards Allah. Prayer, in order to become a genuine form of worship, must contain remembrance of Allah. The prayer of the hypocrites is always devoid of the remembrance of the Lord.

13. Discharge the duty enjoined upon you by prayer even after the prayer and manage your whole life in such a manner that it should fully reflect the injunctions contained in the prayers. The Holy Quran says: "Prayer serves as a deterrent to immorality and contumacy." The Holy Prophet [S.A.W.] elucidated the same point through a deeply impressive simile: The Holy Prophet [S.A.W.] shook a dry branch of a tree briskly so that all the leaves of the branch fell off. Thereupon the Holy Prophet [S.A.W.] observed: "The sins of those who say prayers drop off as the leaves of this dry branch fell off." Afterwards the Holy Prophet [S.A.W.] recited this verse of the Holy Quran:

> "Establish worship at the two ends of the day and in some hours of the night. Lo! good deeds annul ill deeds. This is a reminder for the mindful."
>
> (11: 114)

14. Recite the Quran slowly in the course of prayers and observe other narrations of the prayer at a slow pace with careful attention and devotion of heart and mind. The practice of reciting the Quran and saying other words of the prayer with understanding augments your fervour and the prayer then attains the form of genuine worship.

15. Observe prayers regularly and don't ever miss any

prayer. It is the basic attribute of the believers to be regular and punctual in observing prayers:

"Save worshippers who are constant at their worship."
(70: 22-23)

16. Along with regular observance of obligatory prayers, you should offer supererogatory worship and offer praises to Allah frequently. The Holy Prophet [S.A.W.] said: "Any man who offers twelve Rakats (supererogatory prayers) during a period of day and night in addition to the five obligatory prayers, Allah ordains a dwelling to be built for this man in Paradise."
(Muslim)

17. Say your supererogatory prayers (Sunnah and Nawafil) off and on in your homes also. The Holy Prophet [S.A.W.] has said: "Offer some supererogatory prayers at home after saying obligatory prayers in the mosque. Allah shall bestow goodness in your homes as a reward for these prayers." (Muslim). The Prophet of Allah [S.A.W.] himself frequently offered Sunnah and Nawafil at home.

18. When you set out from the house for dawn prayers, say this prayer:

"O Allah! Make Light in mine heart, Light in mine eye, Light in mine ear, Light on my right, Light on my left, Light above me, Light beneath me, Light before me, Light behind me, and make thou for me Light. Light in my tongue, Light in my sinews, Light in my flesh, Light in my blood, Light in mine hair, Light in my body, Light in my soul and magnify for me Light! O Allah bestow upon me Light!
(Hisn, Hasien)

19. When you have finished the performance of dawn and evening prayers, repeat the following prayer seven times before engaging in conversation.

"O Allah! Protect me from the Fire."

The Holy Prophet [S.A.W.] said:

"After the dawn and evening prayers, repeat the following prayer seven times before engaging in conversation. If perchance you die in the course of that day or night, you shall certainly be saved from Hell." (Mishkat)

20. After each prayer, repeat Astaghfirullah three times and then say this prayer:

"O Allah! Thou art the peace and from Thee is the peace. Blessed art Thou, O Lord of Majesty and Glory." (Muslim)

Hadrat Thauban [R.A.A.] reports:. "The Holy Prophet [S.A.W.] used to repeat (I seek forgiveness from Allah) three times after finishing each prayer and afterwards said this prayer." (Muslim)

21. Observe proper care in keeping the lines straight for offering the prayer in congregation. Keep the lines perfectly straight and stand shoulder to shoulder close to each other, leaving no space in between. Do not form lines in the rear unless the front lines are filled. On one occasion in a congregation for prayer, a man was standing in line in such a manner that the position of his chest was inclined forward. On seeing the man standing in this fashion, the Holy Prophet [S.A.W.] warned: "O people of Allah! you must stand in straight lines in a proper manner else Allah shall cause you to stand in opposite directions to each other." (Muslim, Vol. I)

On one occasion, the Holy Prophet [S.A.W.] said: "Any man who arranges the line in a formation, Allah shall bestow Grace on him; and any man who causes disarray in the line, Allah shall cause him to suffer chaos." (Abu Daud, Vol. I)

22. The line of the children must be formed behind the lines of men. Do not let the children stand with their elders. However, in the 'Idgah, where certain difficulties might be faced or where the possibility of the loss of children exists, there is no need to send the children to form lines in the rear. Make them stand with you. The lines of women should be formed either at the farthest rear or separately if a separate enclosure has been built in the mosque for women. Similarly, in the 'Idgah make separate arrangements for the congregation of women.

Quran's Recitation

1. Recite the Holy Quran with eagerness and fervour and put all your heart and soul in the recitation. Be sure that love of the Quran means love of Allah. The Holy Prophet [S.A.W.] said: "The best form of worship for my Ummah is recitation of the Quran."
2. Engage yourself in the recitation of the Quran off and on and never feel weary of reciting the Holy Book. The Holy Prophet [S.A.W.] said: "Allah has ordained that any man who engages himself in the recitation of Quran so oftenly that he finds no time for supplication I shall provide him more without asking than those who ask." (Tirmidhi)

Further than this, the Prophet of Allah [S.A.W.] observed: "The servant gets nearest unto Allah by reciting the Quran." (Tirmidhi)

Advising the people to recite the Holy Quran, the Holy Prophet [S.A.W.] also said: "The man who has studied the Quran and recites it daily is like a basket full of musk whose sweet smell is making the whole atmosphere fragrant. And the man who has studied the Quran but does not recite it is like a bottle full of musk whose mouth has been sealed with a stopper." (Tirmidhi)

3. Recite the Quran with the sole motive of seeking guidance and not for the sake of gaining popularity, or establishing a reputation for good, harmonious recitation or making a name for piety. These are base motives and he who recites the Quran with these motives in mind can obtain no guidance from the Quran.
4. Take care to be completely neat and clean before you sit down for recitation. Do not touch the Holy Book without performing ablution and recite it sitting in a clean and tidy place.
5. Sit cross-legged with your face towards the Qiblah and recite the Quran with your head bowed, with utmost care, complete attention, eagerness of heart and in a proper manner. Allah says:

"(This is) a scripture that We have revealed unto thee, full of blessing, that thee may ponder over its revelations, and that men of understanding may get guidance from it." (38: 29)

6. As far as possible recite the Quran in a clear and distinct manner and read the letters correctly and utter the syllables in proper style and recite slowly. The Holy Prophet [S.A.W.] said: "Use your voice and style to recite the Quran in the best manner."

(Abu Daud)

The Holy Prophet [S.A.W.] used to recite each word in a clear and distinct manner and read each verse separately.

The Holy Prophet [S.A.W.] said:

"He who recites the Quran will be told on the Day of Judgement. Recite the Quran now in the same clear and distinct manner and in the same harmonious style in which you used to recite it with care and propriety in the world and as a reward for the recitation of each verse you shall be elevated one degree higher and your ultimate place is near the end of the final verse." (Tirmidhi)

7. Do not recite the Quran in an extremely loud or very low voice. Keep your voice at a medium pitch. Allah ordains:

"Be not loud voiced in thy prayer nor too low voiced but follow a way between." (17.110)

8. Recite the Quran whenever you find time, but do try to recite Quran in the course of Tahajjud prayer at dawn. This recitation of the Quran entails the reward of highest degree and it should be the aspiration of a true believer to attain the apex of excellence in reward for recitation.

9. Do not complete the reading of the whole of the Holy Quran in less then three days. The Holy Prophet [S.A.W.] observed: "He who completes the recitation of the full text of the Quran in less than three days does not understand the meanings of the Quran at all."

10. Keep in mind the glory and value of the Quran and as you observe the etiquette of keeping your person neat and clean while reciting the Quran, so also you must purge your heart of evil thoughts, wicked passions and impure purposes. The heart that is tainted with evil and wicked thoughts and passions cannot appreciate and admire the glory and value of the Holy Quran, nor can the bearer of such an evil heart grasp the meanings and realities of the Quran. Hadrat 'Ikrama [R.A.A.], whenever opened the Quran, he often fainted. He used to say: "These are the words of my Great and Glorious Lord."

11. Recite the Quran with the conviction that on this earth this Book is the only source of guidance for mankind. Meditate and reflect deeply over the meanings of the Quran from this viewpoint and try to grasp the realities

and learn the wisdom contained in this Book. Do not recite it hurriedly but form the habit of reading slowly, distinctly and with careful understanding of the meanings and try to ponder over the message conveyed to us. Hadrat 'Abdullah b. 'Abbas [R.A.A.] often remarked: "I consider it far better to recite small Surahs like Al-Qariah with understanding and care than to read through the longer Surahs of Al-Baqarah and Ali-'Imran speedily without careful understanding of the meanings of the words. The Holy Prophet [S.A.W.] once recited this one verse over and over again all through the night.

"If Thou punisheth them, Lo! they are Thy slaves, and if Thou forgiveth them, Lo! Thou only Thou art the Mighty, the Wise." (5.118)

12. Recite the Quran with full determination to adapt your life to the injunctions of this Holy Book and to reform the pattern of your living in the light of the guidance provided by it. Make constant endeavours to order your life in conformity with the Quranic injunctions and purge your life of all impurities. The Holy Quran like a mirror will clearly reflect each blot and spot on your character. It is entirely your own responsibility to wash off these blots and stains from your life.

13. Feel the full impact of the verses of the Holy Book during recitation. Rejoice and feel happy on reading about the narrations of Divine Mercy, Forgiveness and the Everlasting bounties of Paradise. And on reading about the narrations of the wrath, anger and the terrific punishments of Hell your body should tremble, eyes should flow and the heart should melt with the sentiments of repentance and shame. Your face should glow with the light of happiness on reading about the successes of the pious and faithful people and you

should be seized with deep sorrow on reading about the destruction of nations. The study of verses containing warnings and forebodings of torments should make you tremble and your soul should be filled to the brim with the sentiments of gratitude on reading the verses which bear glad tidings.

14. After reciting the Holy Quran offer a prayer. The words of one of the prayers offered by Hadrat 'Umar [R.A.A.] are as follows:

"Allah! Whatever my tongue recites from Thy Book, grant me the favour to reflect upon it. Allah! bestow upon me the understanding of it. Vouchsafe to me the knowledge of its meaning, and spirit, and the vision to see its niceties. Grant me the favour to act according to its injunctions as long as I live. Your Being is without doubt Omnipotent."

Friday Manners

1. Take full measures to clean and purify yourself on Fridays. Bathe and adorn yourself in the best possible manner.

Hadrat 'Umar [R.A.A.] reports that the Holy Prophet [S.A.W.] observed: "The person who comes to offer prayers in the Friday congregation should bathe himself first." (Bukhari, Muslim)

According to the statement of Hadrat Abu Hurrayrah [R.A.A.] the Holy Prophet [S.A.W.] observed: "Every Muslim owes duty to Allah that he should take bath every week and wash his head and body."

Hadrat Abu Said Khudri [R.A.A.] relates that the Prophet of Allah [S.A.W.] observed: "It is obligatory upon every adult youth to take bath on Friday and to brush the teeth and use perfume if available."
(Bukhari, Muslim)

Hadrat Salman [R.A.A.] states that the Holy Prophet [S.A.W.] said: "Any man who bathes on Friday and takes full care to keep himself neat and clean and uses hair oil and perfume and then reaches the mosque just after mid-day and does not part two men sitting in a line in the mosque and then offers the prayer which Allah had decreed to him and afterwards listens to the sermon seated calmly when the Imam ascends the pulpit, Allah shall pardon all the sins committed by him during the internal between this Friday and the preceding one." (Bukhari)

2. Take care to perform good deeds on Friday such as most frequent remembrance of Allah, recitation of the Holy Quran, prayer, Sadaqa, charity, enquiring after the welfare of the sick, joining the funerals, visit to the graveyard and other pious acts.

Hadrat Abu Hurrayrah [R.A.A.] reports that the Holy Prophet [S.A.W.] said:

"The most important day that ever dawned is the Friday. It was on this day that Adam [A.S.] was created and on this day he was admitted to Paradise and it was on Friday when he was expelled from there (and was appointed the vicegerent of Allah and it is on this day that the Doom will descend." (Muslim)

Hadrat Abu Said Khudri [R.A.A.] reports that the Holy Prophet [S.A.W.] said: "There are five such acts that if a man shall perform them in the course of a single day, Allah shall write his name among those destined to enter Paradise. These acts are:

(i) To enquire after the welfare of the sick. (ii) To join a funeral. (iii) To keep a fast. (iv) To offer Friday Prayer. (v) To emancipate a slave." (Ibn Habban)

It is evident that the performance of all these five acts together is possible only on a Friday.

In another tradition Hadrat Abu Said Khudri [R.A.A.] reports that the Holy Prophet [S.A.W.] observed: "Any man who recites Surah Kahf on Friday, a radiant light will glow for him in the space between two Fridays." (Nasai)

And Hadrat Abu Hurrayrah [R.A.A.] states that the Holy Prophet [S.A.W.] said: "Seventy thousand angels beg mercy for the man who recites Surah Ad-Dukhan on Friday night and all of his sins are pardoned." (Tirmidhi)

The Holy Prophet [S.A.W.] has affirmed: "There is a certain blessed moment in the course of Friday that any prayer said in by a believer is accepted by the Almighty." (Bukhari)

Which blessed moment is this? The opinion of the *'Ulama* is at variance on this point, because of the reason that traditions mention different times in this respect. However, the *'Ulama* agree that two statements are more correct than the others. According to one statements, the intervening time from the moment the preacher ascends the pulpit to deliver the sermon to the end of the prayers is the most propitious one. Another version holds that blessed moment is the end of Friday when the sun is about to set in the horizon. It is advisable, therefore, that you should pass both the times in offering prayers and supplications in utter humility and reverence to the Lord. It is better to add the following prayer with your other prayers:

"Allah! You are my Lord. There is no deity except You. You created me. I am Your servant and I hold firm to my promise and allegiance to You as far as it lies in my power. I acknowledge all the bounties and favours that You have conferred on me. I confess my sins; forgive me, for there is no one else except You Who has the power to grant pardon for sins and I beseech protection against the evil effects of my own sins." (Bukhari, Nasai)

3. Observe Friday prayers according to all the prescribed etiquettes. Friday prayer is obligatory upon every adult, healthy, resident and sane Muslim male. If there be two men beside the Imam present at a place, the Friday prayer must be offered. The Holy Prophet said:

> "The people ought not to miss Friday prayer under any circumstances or else Allah shall seal their hearts (and having been denied Divine Guidance) they will become one with those who are forgetful (of Religion)."
>
> (Muslim)

According to the testimony of Hadrat Abu Hurrayrah [R.A.A.] the Prophet of Allah [S.A.W.] said: "Any man who comes to the mosque for saying the Friday prayer after bathing and washing himself clean and then offers 'Sunnah' prayers which Allah had decreed and then sits quietly till the end listening to the sermon of the Imam and afterwards offers obligatory prayers with the Imam, Allah shall grant him pardon for the sins which he committed between the preceding Friday and this one and the sins committed till three days before."

"Hadrat Yazid b. Mariym [R.A.A.] relates: "I was going to offer Friday prayers when I chanced to meet Hadrat 'Abay b. Rifaah [R.A.A.] on the way. He asked me: "Where are you going?" I said: "I am going to offer Friday prayers". Hadrat 'Abaya [R.A.A.] remarked: "I congratulate you. Every step you move, you move on the path leading towards Allah." The Holy Prophet [S.A.W.] said: "Fire is made unlawful for the man whose feet are soiled with dust while walking along the path of Allah."

4. Hasten towards the mosque the moment you hear the call for Friday prayer. Close your business and stop your other activities at once. Listen to the sermon and say prayers with perfect devotion. Resume your business as soon as the Friday prayer is over. The Holy Quran says:

> "O ye who believe! When the call is heard for the prayer of the day of congregation hasten unto remembrance of Allah and leave your trading. That is better for you if ye did but know. And when the prayer is over, then disperse in the land and seek Allah's bounty, and remember Allah much, that ye may be successful." (Al-Jumah 9-10)

These verses contain the following injunctions for the true believers:

(i) A true believer should offer Friday prayers with complete devotion and utmost awareness of the etiquettes of this prayer. He should stop all other engagements on hearing the prayer-call and hasten towards the mosque.

(ii) It is unlawful for the true believer to carry on business or to engage in other worldly interests after hearing the announcement of the prayer-call and thus having forsaken the memory of Allah to turn into a world-loving creature.

(iii) The secret of a pious man's salvation lies in his living as a servant and slave of Allah in this world. Whenever the call of Allah reaches him, he should, as a devoted and obedient servant forsake all interests and set aside all worldly advantage and rush to respond to the call of his Master. He should proclaim by deed that the sacrifice of worldly advantage for the sake of fulfilling the demands of religion does not signify ruin and failure. On the other hand, destruction and failure lies in transgressing the bounds of religion in his lust for gaining worldly interests.

(iv) The theory of renouncing the world altogether is fallacious. Man should not be so much immersed in spiritual pursuits that he should become incapable of dealing with worldly affairs. The Holy Quran, in fact, enjoins upon the faithful to disperse on the earth as soon as the prayer is over and to take full advantage of all the resources and means of livelihood that Allah has provided on the earth. The Quran affirms that the pious should exert all their energies and employ all faculties in the business of earning their share of the subsistence provided by Allah. It is not proper for a true believer to be dependent on others for his needs, nor is it advisable for him to neglect his duty of providing for the needs of his dependents and to cause them suffering and dismay.

(v) The final and important injunction is that the true believer should not be engrossed in worldly affairs so deeply that he should forget Allah. He should remember under all circumstances that the real gain and essence of his life is the remembrance of Allah. Hadrat Said b. Jubayr [R.A.A.] remarks: "The remembrance of Allah is not only announcing the greatness of Allah or uttering praises of Allah but all those are engaged in the remembrance of Allah who are busy ordering their lives in conformity with the Commands of Allah."

5. Try to reach the mosque for the Friday prayer as early as possible to get a seat for yourself in front line.

According to the statement of Abu Hurrayrah [R.A.A.], the Holy Prophet [S.A.W.] said: "Any man who bathes himself and washes his whole body to cleanse it of all impurities and then reaches the mosque first is like the person who offers the sacrifice of one camel, and he who arrives next to him is like the person who sacrifices one cow (or buffalo) and the one who reaches in the third place is like a person who offers the sacrifice of a horned ram. Coming next to him is like a person who gives away as it were one egg in the way of Allah. Later when the Imam comes forward to deliver the sermon, the angels leave the gate of the mosque and come over to sit in the mosque to hear the sermon and say the prayers."

(Bukhari, Muslim)

Hadrat 'Irbad b. Saria [R.A.A.] states: "The Holy Prophet [S.A.W.] used to invoke mercy of Allah three times upon those who formed the first line and only once upon those who were in the second line."

(Ibn Majah, Nasai)

Hadrat Abu Hurrayrah [R.A.A.] observes: "The people do not know the high degree of reward and blessings reserved for the people who form the first line of prayer. If they knew it, they would start drawing lots for the privilege of joining the first line."

(Bukhari, Muslim)

6. Offer your Friday prayers in a Big mosque (Jama Masjid). Take your seat wherever it is available. Do not jump over people's heads and shoulders in an effort to get a seat in front. This causes considerable mental and physical discomfort to the people, disturbs their peace of mind and diverts their attention.

Hadrat 'Abdullah b. 'Abbas [R.A.A.] relates that the Holy Prophet [S.A.W.] said: "The person who retreats from the first line of prayer and stands in the second line with the intention that his Muslim brother may suffer no inconvenience, Allah will grant such a man reward and blessing twice as much as to people in the first line." (Tibrani)

Hadrat Salman [R.A.A.] reports that the Holy Prophet [S.A.W.] said: "The person who bathes himself on Friday and cleanses and purifies himself as much as he can, and then use oil and applies perfume and reaches the mosque just after mid-day and does not part two men sitting together (in other words he does not commit the error of jumping over the heads and shoulders of people, or making his way through the lines or sitting between two men by pushing them apart, but sits down quietly wherever he finds room) and offers prayer and Sunnah which Allah had decreed upon him and afterwards listens quietly to the sermon when the Imam takes the pulpit, Allah will pardon all his sins which he committed during the period between that Friday and the preceding one."

(Bukhari)

7. The sermon should be brief as compared to the prayer. The sermon in fact is meant to induce people to offer devotions and worships and worship to Allah, while prayer is not only worship in itself, but the best worship. Hence it is in no way proper to prolong the sermon and go through the prayer quickly in a shorter period of time. The Holy Prophet [S.A.W.] said:

"To prolong the prayer and deliver a brief sermon is an attribute of the wise preacher. Hence say prayers for a longer period of time and make the sermon brief." (Muslim)

8. Listen to the sermon in silence with rapt attention and eagerness in a receptive mood. Make up your mind with all sincerity to act upon the injunctions of Allah and His messenger [S.A.W.] that you have come to know through the sermon. The Holy Prophet [S.A.W.] said:

"The man who bathes and comes to offer Friday prayer and says the prayer which Allah has destined for him and then sits quietly and listens to the sermon in rapt attention and with perfect devotion till the preacher has finished the sermon and afterwards says obligatory prayer with the Imam, Allah shall pardon all his sins which he committed during the period between that Friday and the preceding one and his sins even committed during three days before it."

(Muslim)

According to another tradition: "When the preacher comes forward to deliver the sermon, then it is improper to say any prayer or engage in conversation."

9. The second sermon must be delivered in Arabic. However, in the first sermon describe some injunctions of Allah and His Messenger [S.A.W.], give some advice, provide guidance and remember Allah in the local language of the participants of the congregation. The sermons which the Holy Prophet [S.A.W.] delivered on Fridays reveal that the preacher should provide advice and guidance to the Muslims in regard to the prevailing circumstances. This purpose can only be achieved if the preacher delivers his sermon to the congregation in the people's own language.
10. It is highly propitious to recite Surah al-Ala and al-Ghashiya or surah Munafiqun and Surah al-Jumah in the obligatory prayers on Friday as was the practice of the Holy Prophet.
11. Make it essential to offer Darood as much as possible and pray for Allah's peace and blessings upon the Holy Prophet on Fridays.

The Holy Prophet [S.A.W.] has observed:

"Recite as much Darood for me as possible on Fridays. The angels join this 'Darood' Prayer and Darood is presented to me. (Ibn Majah)

Prayer for the Demised

1. Do join the funeral prayers. The funeral prayer is a petition of mercy for the deceased and this is a duty

which every one owes to the dead. If you fear the funeral prayer will be over by the time you have performed ablution, then perform Tayammum and join the prayers at once. The Holy Prophet [S.A.W.] said: "Do say the funeral prayers. May be this prayer induces feelings of sorrow in you. A sorrowful man remains under the shadow of Allah and welcomes every pious deed." (Hakim)

The Holy Prophet [S.A.W.] also said: "The deceased whose funeral prayers are offered by three lines of Muslims will certainly be admitted to Paradise." (Abu Daud)

2. At the time of saying funeral prayers, put the bier on the ground so that the head is towards the north, the feet towards the south and the face of the dead is turned in the direction of the Qiblah.
3. If you are leading the funeral prayer, stand facing the bosom of the dead.
4. The number of lines in a funeral prayer must be odd. A single line would suffice if those present at the funeral prayer are few, but if there are enough present, fall in three. As the number of people increased, form more lines, yet the number of lines should be kept odd.
5. Make a resolve in your mind before starting the funeral prayer that you are saying the funeral prayers to beg Mercy from the Kind and Beneficent Lord for the deceased. The Imam as well as the followers should make this resolve.
6. Whatever the Imam says in the funeral prayer, the followers must repeat the same. The followers should not keep silent. However, the Imam should say Takbirs in a loud voice and the followers should repeat them in a low sound.

7. Say four Takbirs in the funeral prayer. Raise your hands up to the ears while saying the first Takbir and then fold them on you abdomen and offer praise to Allah:

"Allah! Thou art Pure and Supreme. High Praise and Thanksgiving is due to Thee. Thy Name is the Most Blessed one and the Bestower of Good. Thy Exaltedness and Glory art Most High. Thy Praise is Great and there is no deity except Thee."

Now say the second Takbir, but do not raise your hands, nor make a motion of the head. At the end of the second Takbir, recite the Darood:,

"Allah! May Thy peace and blessings be upon Muhammad and his family, as Thou sent Thy peace and blessings upon Ibrahim and his family. Without doubt Thou possesseth the greatest attributes and art Most High. Allah! May Thy peace and blessings be upon Muhammad and his family, as Thou sent peace and blessings upon Ibrahim and his family. Without doubt Thou possesseth the greatest attributes and art Most High."

Now say the third Takbir without raising your hands and offer a prayer with prescribed supplication to beg mercy from the Lord for the dead. Finally, say the fourth Takbir and say Salam turning the head to right and left.

8. If the deceased is an adult male or female, say this prayer after the third Takbir.

"Allah! Show mercy to our living, to our dead, to those who are present with us here and to those who are not present, to our youngster, to our elders, to our men and to our women. Allah! Whomsoever it pleases Thee to keep alive among us, keep him alive as faithful of Islam and upon whomsoever it pleases Thee to send death, let him die in faith."

If the deceased is a minor boy, say this prayer:

> "Allah! Let this boy serve as a means of Thy grant of salvation to us and let him be a repository of our reward and welfare in the eternal world and let him be our successful intercessor."

If the deceased is a minor girl, say this prayer. The meaning of this prayer is identical with the prayer offered for the boy.

9. While going along with a funeral procession think over your own end and visualise that as you are proceeding to commit the deceased to earth, in the same way others will be proceeding one day to bury you in the earth. In this pensive and thoughtful frame of mind, you will gain the favour of remembering your ultimate end for some time at least and the worries and cares of the world will vanish from your mind.

Attending the Death-bed

1. When you visit a person whose end is near, keep on reciting the Kalima (There is no god but Allah and Muhammad is His Apostle) in a loud voice. Do not press the patient to utter the Kalima. The Holy Prophet [S.A.W.] said: "When you sit by the death-bed of any Muslim, keep reciting the Kalima." (Muslim)
2. Recite Surah Yasin when the patient is heaving last breaths. The Holy Prophet [S.A.W.] observed: "Recite 'Surah Yasin' by the death-bed." (*Fatawa-e-Alamgiri*, p. 100, Vol. I). When the person has breathed his last, do not recite the Quran near the deceased till his body has been given bath. The man who needs a bath and the woman who is passing through the period of her menses or the after-birth course should not go near the dead.
3. Say ("We are for Allah and we shall return to Him.) "The Holy Prophet [S.A.W.] said: "The following three rewards are conferred on a man who recites (We are

all creatures of Allah and we shall return to Him) in the moment of distress:

(i) Firstly, blessings and salvation descend on him from Allah. (ii) Secondly, he receives the reward for seeking the Truth. (iii) Thirdly, his loss is compensated and a better reward in lieu of the dead and lost one is conferred on the bereaved person who says:

(Tibrani)

4. Abstain from loud lamentations and wailing for the deceased person. However, if the eyes are filled with tears out of grief it is but natural. When the Holy Prophet's [S.A.W.] son Hadrat Ibrahim [R.A.A.] expired, the eyes of the Holy Prophet [S.A.W.] were filled with tears: Similarly, when his grandson, the child of his daughter Zainab [R.A.A.] passed away, the Holy Prophet [S.A.W.] shed tears. The people asked: "O Prophet of Allah [S.A.W.]! How is it?" The Holy Prophet [S.A.W.] said: "This is a blessing which Allah has bestowed upon the hearts of His creatures. Allah shows mercy to those among His creatures who are tender hearted and kind." The Holy Prophet [S.A.W.] further said: "He who slaps his face, tears his clothes and indulges in lamentation like the pagans, has nothing to do with us."

5. As soon as one expires, straighten out his arms and legs; close the eyes and pass a wide bandage below the chin and tie its ends over the head. Both toes of the feet should be tied together with a strip of cloth. Wrap the body in a shroud and keep on reciting 'In the name of Allah' and according to the custom of the followers of the Prophet of Allah [S.A.W.]. Pass around an obituary notice among the people. At the moment of lowering the corpse in the grave, continue to say the same prayer.

6. Mention the virtues of the dead and avoid narration of his ills. The Holy Prophet [S.A.W.] said: "Do mention the virtues of your dead and keep silent about their vices." (Abu Daud). In addition, the Holy Prophet [S.A.W.] said: "When a man dies and a few of his neighbours testify that he was a good man, Allah observes - "I accept your testimony and I grant him pardon even for those of his acts which remained a secret to you." (Ibn Habban)

On one occasion the companions [R.A.A.] praised the virtues of a dead man in the presence of the Holy Prophet [S.A.W.] whereupon the Prophet of Allah [S.A.W.] said: "This dead person's abode has been made in Paradise. O people, you are the witnesses of Allah on earth. If you testify that a certain man is good, Allah admits him to Paradise and if you bear witness that a certain man is wicked, Allah consigns him to Hell." (Bukhari, Muslim)

And the Holy Prophet [S.A.W.] also said: "When you visit a patient to enquire after his welfare or join a funeral procession, "do utter good remarks, for the angels say 'So be it' (Amin) after each good remark you make." (Muslim)

7. Always show patience and fortitude on the death of your near and dear ones. Do not utter any ungrateful remark. The Holy Prophet [S.A.W.] has said:

"When a man observes patience on the death of his child, Allah enquires from His angels, "Did you extract the soul of the child of my servant?" The angels submit: "Yes." Allah then asks: "And what did my servant say?" They submit: "Lord! He offered praise to Thee and recited (We all belong to Allah and to Him shall we return, thereupon Allah ordains the angels: "Build a dwelling in Paradise for this servant of mine and name this dwelling 'Bait-al-Hamd' (House of Thanksgiving)." (Tirmidhi)

8. Do not delay washing the body of the deceased. It is better to put some leaves of the 'plum tree' in the bath water and heat it a little. Stretch the body on a clean wooden board; take off its garments and wrap a sheet round the lower part of the body. Cover your hand with a cloth and clean the front and back private parts of the body. Take care that the wrapping sheet does not slip off. Then perform ablution on the body. There is no need, however, to rinse the mouth or pass water into the nose of the body during the performance of ablution. When washing the corpse block the ears and nostrils with cotton wool so that water does not enter into them. Then wash the head clean with soap or something else. Turn over the corpse towards the left side and pouring water from the right side bathe the body from head to foot. Similarly, pouring the water from the left side wash the body from head to foot. Take off the water soaked sheet and wrap a dry sheet round the lower part of the body. Now lift the body from the board, and place it in the coffin on the cot. The Holy Prophet [S.A.W.] said: "Allah shall pardon forty capital sins of man who bathes a corpse and conceals the sins of the dead person; and the man who lowers the corpse in the grave, provides, as it were, a home to the deceased to live in until the Day of Doom." (Tibrani)

9. Use a white cloth of average quality as a shroud for the body; don't use a very costly cloth nor a cloth of very low quality. For men the shroud should consist of three garments; one sheet, one 'Tehband' (a sheet for wrapping round the lower part of the body) and a 'Kafni' or 'shirt' (a covering for the upper portion of the body). The length of the sheet should exceed the stature of the dead in measurement so that its ends may be tied

on the side of the head as well as on the side of the feet. The measure of the width of the sheet should be adequate to cover the body well. For women, include an additional apparel 'sarband', a piece of cloth to cover the head and conceal the hair in the coffin. It should be one yard long and measure a little less than a yard in width. A 'Chest Band', a cloth to provide an additional covering from armpits to the knees, should also form part of a woman's coffin. The Holy Prophet [S.A.W.] said: "Allah will provide dresses made of Sundus and Astabraq in Paradise for him who puts the body of a deceased in coffin." (Hakim)

10. Keep your pace quick while taking the bier to the graveyard. The Holy Prophet [S.A.W.] has observed; "Make haste in the matter of funerals." Hadrat Ibn Masud [R.A.A.] submitted to the Holy Prophet [S.A.W.]: "O Prophet of Allah [S.A.W.]! What should be the pace of our steps while taking the bier to the graveyard?" The Holy Prophet [S.A.W.] said: "Keep the pace of your steps short of running. If the deceased was a good man, carry him to his good end quickly. If he was wicked one, make haste to remove his evil from your midst." (Abu Daud)

11. Accompany the funeral on foot. On one occasion, when the Holy Prophet [S.A.W.] was walking with a funeral procession, he [S.A.W.] saw a few participants riding along. The Holy Prophet [S.A.W.] reprimanded them thus: "Don't you feel ashamed of yourselves! The angels are walking on foot, while you are riding on the backs of the beasts." However, on your way back from the burial, you can use a transport. The Holy Prophet [S.A.W.] went with the funeral procession of Abu Wahidi [R.A.A.] on foot and returned on horseback.

12. Stand on your feet on seeing a funeral approaching and if you do not wish to accompany it, wait till the

procession has moved on to some distance before resuming your journey or other activities. The Holy Prophet [S.A.W.] said:

"Stand on your feet on seeing a funeral procession approaching. Those who accompany the funeral procession should not sit down until the bier has been placed on the ground."

13. Do offer funeral prayers. You should also participate in funeral processions and put your shoulder under the bier for sometime. The Holy Prophet [S.A.W.] said:

"Every Muslim owes a duty to accompany the funeral procession of a deceased Muslim." The Prophet of Allah [S.A.W.] further said: "A man who participates in the funeral procession and offers funeral prayers will get a reward equal to one Carat. He who attends the burial also after saying the funeral prayers will receive a reward equal to two Carats." Some one submitted: "What will be the size of these two Carats?" The Holy Prophet [S.A.W.] said: "It will be equal to the mass of two mountains."

(Bukhari, Muslim)

14. Let the grave be excavated from north to south lengthwise. Keep the body of the deceased turned towards the Qiblah when lowering it in the grave. If the body is light, two men are enough, otherwise three or four men may join in entering a body into the grave. At the moment of internment, untie the knots of the shroud and turn over the body towards the Qiblah.

15. Do observe purdah when interning a female body into the grave.

16. Start filling the grave with earth from the side of the head. Pick up the earth in both hands and throw it into the grave. Repeat the act three times. When throwing in the earth the first time say 'Minha Khalaqnakum,

"We created you out of this earth." When throwing in the earth the second time, say. 'Wa fiha nuidukum'. "And We return you to the same earth." And when you throw in the earth the third time, say *'Waminha nukhrijukum taratan ukhra,* "And We shall resurrect you from the same earth."

17. Do not raise the grave very high, nor make it in the form of a square. Fill the grave with the same amount of earth which was excavated from it. Sprinkle some water over the grave after filing it with earth.

18. Stay a while near the grave after burial. Offer prayers begging mercy for the deceased. Recite some verses of the Quran and send its blessings for the departed soul. Ask other people to offer prayers to Allah to show mercy to the dead person. The Holy Prophet [S.A.W.] himself used to offer prayers to Allah for the grant of mercy to the deceased and said to other people: "Pray to Allah that your brother may remain steadfast and beg mercy for him from the Lord as now is he to account for every moment of his worldly life."

    (Abu Daud)

19. If a bereavement occurs among the kin, relatives, or in the neighbourhood, send cooked food for one or two times to their house, because they will be too overcome with grief to think of cooking meals. 'Jami' Tirmidhi' records that when the martyrdom of Hadrat Jafar [R.A.A.] was reported the Holy Prophet [S.A.W.] commanded: "Prepare some food for the family of Jafar. They are preoccupied with grief today."

20. Do not mourn for the dead for a period of more than three days. However, for a woman whose husband is dead, the prescribed period of mourning is four months and ten days. When Abu Sufyan [R.A.A.], the father of Umm-ul-Mominin Hadrat Ummi Habiba [R.A.A.]

expired, the illustrious lady Zainab [R.A.A.] came to offer condolences to her. Hadrat Ummi Habiba [R.A.A.] asked for perfume in which some quantity of yellow saffron had been mixed. Umm-ul-Mominin rubbed that perfume on her slave-woman and then applied some to her own face. She then said: "Allah knows I did not need perfume, but I have heard the Prophet of Allah [S.A.W.] say: "No woman who believe in Allah and the Day of Judgement should observe mourning for more than three days for any man. However, the period of mourning in the case of her husband's death is four months and ten days." (Abu Daud)

21. Offer some charity on behalf of the deceased according to your means. However, strictly avoid performance of unpropitious and improper rites in this case.

Visiting Graveyards

1. Accompany the funeral procession to the graveyard and attend the burial. Do pay visits to the graveyard off and on. These visits remind one of the life Hereafter and induce one to start making preparations for the life after death. On one occasion the Holy Prophet [S.A.W.] accompanied a funeral procession to the graveyard and sitting down beside a grave shaddad so much tears that the earth became wet. Then addressing the companions [R.A.A.], the Holy Prophet [S.A.W.] said: "Brothers! Prepare yourself for this day." (Ibn Majah)

Once when he was seated near a grave, the Holy Prophet [S.A.W.] said: "Every grave proclaims in the most terrific voice; 'O Progeny of Adam! Have you forgotten me? I am the house of loneliness. I am a strange land of wilderness! I am a hole of mites and worms. I am a place of hardship and trial. Save those fortunate one for whom Allah makes me commodious and wide, I am for all other human beings a tortuous place." In addition, the Holy Prophet [S.A.W.] observed: "The grave is either one of the pits of Hell or a small flower-garden out of the gardens of Paradise." (Tibrani)

2. Take a lesson on seeing the graveyard and form the habit of concentrating your thoughts and imaginative powers on the meditation on life after death. Once upon a time, Hadrat 'Ali [R.A.A.] visited a graveyard. Hadrat Kameel [R.A.A.] accompanied him. On reaching the graveyard, Hadrat 'Ali [R.A.A.] looked at the graves and then addressing the inmates of the graves, said:

'O inmates of graves! O inhabitants of ruins! O those who live in isolation in a land of wilderness! Say, how you are? As regards conditions over here, the assets left over have been divided, the offspring are rendered orphans, the widows have entered into new marriage contracts. This is the state of affairs in our world. Now tell us what is happening to you." Hadrat 'Ali [R.A.A.] then remained silent for some time and then turning towards Hadrat Kameel [R.A.A.] observed: "Kameel, if the inmates of these graves were allowed to speak, they would say: "Piety is the most valuable treasure." Having said this, Hadrat 'Ali [R.A.A.] wept and continued to weep for a long time. Later Hadrat 'Ali [R.A.A.] remarked: "Kameel, the grave is an enclosure where only deeds matter and as soon as one meets death he realises this fact."

3. Say this prayer on entering the graveyard:

"Peace be on you, O pious and faithful inmates of this set habitation. Allah willing, we shall soon join company with you. We pray to Allah for our sake and for your sake, that He may protect us from His torture and Wrath."

4. Don't laugh, crack jokes or engage in wordly talk in the graveyard like careless and carefree person. Grave is the gateway to Eternity. Let the sight of this gateway turn your thoughts to the next world and overcome by feelings of care and remorse. Let your eyes shed tears of repentance. The Holy Prophet [S.A.W.] said: "I had forbidden you to visit graveyards (so that faith in one Allah may take firm roots in your heart). But now if you wish you may go to the cemeteries, for the sight of graves makes one remember the life Hereafter." (Muslim)
5. Avoid building graves of bricks and mortar and do not embellish them. When the Holy Prophet [S.A.W.] was close to the end of his [S.A.W.] earthly life, he was restless with physical pain. In this state, he would sometimes draw the sheet over his holy face and then remove it. While the Holy Prophet [S.A.W.] was in this turbulent condition of restlessness, Hadrat 'Aishah [R.A.A.] heard him uttering the following words: "Allah's curse be on the Jews and Christians. They turned the sepulchres of their Prophet's into places of worship."
6. Do pray that Allah may bestow rewards on the dead and grant them mercy, whenever you visit the graveyard. Hadrat Sufyan [R.A.A.] states: "Just as the living stand in need of eating and drinking, so do the dead stand in dire need of prayers for their salvation."

Tibrani records the following tradition: When Allah elevates a pious man one degree higher in Paradise, the man submits: "O Creator! How did I come to deserve this reward?" Allah thereupon affirms: "This reward has been conferred upon you by virtue of your son's petitions of mercy on your behalf."

Eclipse of Sun or Moon

1. When the sun or the moon is eclipsed, do engage

yourself in the remembrance of Allah. Offer prayers to Him. Praise Him, and give charity. As a blessing for these pious deeds, Allah puts off all trials and calamities. Hadrat Mughira b. Shobah [R.A.A.] relates that the Holy Prophet [S.A.W.] said: "The sun and the moon are the two signs of Allah. They do not go under eclipse on the birth or death of anyone. Do call for the grace of Allah, offer prayers to Him, worship Him when you see the sun or the moon in eclipse and continue to offer devotions to the Almighty until the eclipse clears off."

(Bukhari, Muslim)

2. When the sun is under eclipse, offer prayers in a congregation in the mosque. However, do not announce the prayer-call, nor say Iqamat : Call the people together by some other means. When the moon is in eclipse, offer supererogatory prayers (Nawafil). Do not assemble a congregation.

3. When the sun is eclipsed, say two 'Rakats' of supplementary prayers well in a congregation and recite long from the Holy Quran and continue your prayers until the sun is clear. Recite the Holy Quran loudly during the prayers. In the days of the Holy Prophet [S.A.W.] once the sun came under eclipse. The same day Hadrat Ibrahim [R.A.A.], the infant son of the Holy Prophet [S.A.W.] expired. The people began to say to each other that since Hadrat Ibrahim, the son of Muhammad [S.A.W.] has passed away, the sun has gone under eclipse. The Holy Prophet [S.A.W.] assembled the people in a congregation and led them in prayer consisting of two Rakats. The Holy Prophet [S.A.W.] engaged in long recitation of the Holy Quran in the course of his prayer and read through the whole of 'Surah al-Baqarah'. The Holy Prophet [S.A.W.] then told the people: "The sun and the moon are the two Signs of Allah. They do not go into eclipse on the birth or death

of anyone. O People! Whenever such an event occurs, do engage in devotion to Allah. Offer prayers to Him, praise Him, hymn His greatness and oneness. Say prayers and give charity." (Bukhari, Muslim)

Hadrat 'Abdul Rahman b. Samurah [R.A.A.] says: "During the propitious days of the Holy Prophet [S.A.W.] the sun went into an eclipse once. I was at that time practising archery outside Medina. I at once flung away the arrows to see what would the Holy Prophet [S.A.W.] do at the occurrence of this event. So I went to the presence of the Holy Prophet [S.A.W.]. He was occupied in offering praises to Allah and repeating His Attributes and uttering Takbir[5] and Tahlil and observing prayers and making supplications with his hands raised to the Heavens. Then the Holy Prophet [S.A.W.] offered prayer consisting of two Rakats and recited two long Surahs of the Quran in the course of the prayers and continued to offer devotions till the sun cleared off the eclipse."

The illustrious companions [R.A.A.] also used to offer prayers during 'Kusuf' and 'Khusuf. Hadrat 'Abdullah b. Zubayr [R.A.A.] offered prayers on the appearance of an eclipse in Medina. Similarly, on another occasion when an eclipse appeared Hadrat 'Abdullah b. 'Abbas [R.A.A.] assembled the people and offered a prayer in congregation.

4. In the course of the prayer on the occasion of an eclipse of the sun, recite Surah 'Ankabut and Surah Fatiha in the first Rakat and recite Surah al-Room in the second Rakat. It is propitious to recite these Surahs, but not obligatory. Surahs other than those mentioned above may also be recited.

5. If the women wish to join the congregation for prayer on the occasion of an eclipse of the sun and the facility for including them in the congregation exists, do let them join. Persuade the children also to join prayers so that faith in one Allah takes firm roots in their hearts

in their early years and no other notions derogatory to the belief in one Allah may infiltrate their minds.

6. If the eclipse of the sun occurs during those hours in which the saying of prayers is forbidden i.e., the hours of sunrise, sunset and the declining hours of the day, avoid offering 'Namaz', Do offer praises to Allah however and give charity to the poor and the destitute. If the eclipse continues even after the hour of sunrise or the declining hour of the day have passed, then say prayers also in addition to performing the above-mentioned deeds.

The Fasting

1. Start preparing your mind from the month of Shaban for according a befitting reception to Ramadan. Keep fasts frequently before the fifteenth of Shaban. Hadrat 'Aishah [R.A.A.] relates: "The Holy Prophet [S.A.W.] used to keep fasts more often in Shaban than in any other month."
2. Make an effort to sight the Ramadan moon with full attention and eagerness and say this prayer on sighting the moon:

   "Allah is the greatest! O Allah! Do make the appearance of this moon a token of peace, faith, salvation and Islam (obedience) for us. Do make this moon arise as a favour to us so that we may perform deeds which conform to Thy Will and are dear to Thee. Our Lord and thy Lord is Allah!"

   And say the same prayer on sighting the moon of each month. (Tirmidhi, Ibn Habban, etc.)
3. Do take special interest in offering devotions during the month of Ramadan. In addition to obligatory prayers, make it a point to observe supererogatory prayers (Nawafil) also. Make a firm resolve to win the maximum

favour of Allah. Allah has reserved His special favours and blessings for this great and propitious month. On the final day of Shaban, the Holy Prophet [S.A.W.] in a discourse on the blessings of the month of Ramadan said:

"O people! A great and blessed month is going to set in on you. Each night of this month is better than a thousand months. Allah has made fasting obligatory during this month and has ordained Taravih as a supplementary prayer. Any one who performs a good deed during this month of his own free volition will receive a reward equal to the reward for obligatory deeds performed during other months. And any one who performs a single obligatory act during this month, shall receive a reward equal to the reward of seventy obligatory acts during other months."

4. Keep fasts whole of the month with deep eagerness and zeal. Even if you can't observe fast due to some serious illness or for any other reason permissible in Shariah, strictly avoid eating before others out of respect for the sanctity of Ramadan. To all intents and purposes, you must appear as if you are fasting.
5. Make it a point to recite the Holy Quran. The month of Ramadan has a special connection with the Holy Quran. The Holy Quran was revealed in this month and the other Divine Books also descended in the same month. Hadrat Ibrahim [A.S.] received scriptures on the first or the third day of this month. 'Zabur' descended on Hadrat Daud [A.S.] on the twelfth or eighteenth day of this month. Torah was revealed to Hadrat Musa [A.S.] on the sixth day of this propitious month. On the twelfth or thirteenth day of the same blessed month, the Bible was transmitted to Hadrat 'Isa [A.S.]. Hence recite Quran as many times as possible

in the course of this month. Hadrat Jibbrail [A.S.] used to recite the Holy Quran to the Holy Prophet [S.A.W.] and also heard recitation of the Quran from the Holy Prophet [S.A.W.] every year during the month of Ramadan. In the final year of the Holy Prophet's [S.A.W.] earthly life Hadrat Jibbrail [A.S.] completed the whole text of the' Quran twice during the month of Ramadan.

6. Try to recite the Quran distinctly and with understanding. Along with frequent recitation, be careful to grasp the meaning of the Holy Quran with a clear impact of its message on your mind and heart.
7. During 'Taravih' do listen to the recitation of the whole text of the Quran. The Holy Prophet [S.A.W.] used to listen to the whole text of the Holy Quran at least once during Ramadan.
8. Say 'Taravih' prayers with humility, eagerness and devotion. Do not just complete the number of Rakats in a mechanical fashion. Offer prayer with understanding and devotion so that your life may be influenced by the propitious influence of Namaz and your devotion to Allah may become firm and deep. Do offer Tahajjud prayers also by the favour of Allah.
9. Give charity and spend whatever you can in the way of Allah. Look after the needs of the poor, the widows and the orphans and arrange provisions for them for 'Sahri' and 'Iftar'. The Holy Prophet [S.A.W.] has affirmed: "This is a month of Maswat." Hadrat Ibn 'Abbas [R.A.A.] reports: "The Holy Prophet [S.A.W.] was by nature generous and munificent, but his [S.A.W.] munificence knew no bounds during the month of Ramadan. When Hadrat Jibbrail [A.S.] visited the Holy Prophet [S.A.W.] each night and recited the Holy Quran to the Prophet [S.A.W.] and heard the recitation of the

Holy Book from the Prophet [S.A.W.], during that period the Holy Prophet [S.A.W.] became even more generous than the blowing wind."

10. Do offer maximum rakats of supplementary prayers during 'Shab-e-Qadr, and recite the Holy Quran. The importance of this night is affirmed by the fact that the Holy Quran was revealed during this night. The Holy Quran says:

"Lo! We revealed it in the Night of Power. And do you understand what the Night of Power is! The Night of Power is better than a thousand months. The angels and the spirits descend therein, by the permission of their Lord with all decrees. (That night is) Peace until the rising of dawn."

The traditions record that 'Shab-e-Qadr' is one among the odd nights in the last week of Ramadan. Say this prayer during this night:

"Allah! Forgiveness is Thy Greatest Attribute, for Thou likest to forgive. So forgive me."

Hadrat Anas [R.A.A.] relates that once in the month of Ramadan, the Holy Prophet [S.A.W.] observed: "A month has come upon you people in which there is one night which is better than a thousand months. The person who misses offering devotions in the course of this night deprives himself of all the bliss. And only that person remains deprived of the Grace and Blessings of this month who really deserves deprivation." (Ibn Majah)

11. Observe Itikaf in the last week of the month of Ramadan. The Prophet of Allah [S.A.W.] used to perform Itikaf during the last ten days of Ramadan.

Hadrat 'Aishah [R.A.A.] reports: "When the last week of Ramadan approached, the Holy Prophet [S.A.W.] used to keep awake during most part of the nights and devoted himself to worship. He [S.A.W.] also decreed the female of the household to remain awake and engaged himself in the worship of Allah with full zeal and perfect devotion."

12. Show utmost tenderness and erection to people in the month of Ramadan. Provide maximum facilities to your employees and supply their needs with extreme liberality. Deal with members of your household with kindness and generosity.
13. Say the maximum Rakats of prayers with humility, zeal and devotion. It is related in 'Durr-e-Munthur' that when the Holy Month of Ramadan came, the pattern of the Holy Prophet's [S.A.W.] life underwent a change. The number of the Rakats of supererogatory prayers offered by him [S.A.W.] increased. He [S.A.W.] observed deeper humility in prayers and appeared totally overcome with fear of Allah.

The traditions record: "In the month of Ramadan, Allah ordains the heaven supporting angels to give up their supplications and say Amin (So be it!) after the prayers of the fasting persons."

14. Pay 'Sadaqa-tul-Fitr' (charity ordained before Eid prayers and at the end of Ramadan) with a willing heart and give it away before saying 'Eid prayer. If possible pay it well before the 'Eid so that the needy and destitute may also buy necessary provisions for the 'Eid and go to the 'Idgah with everybody else and join in the festivities of the 'Eid. It is reported in the traditions that the Holy Prophet [S.A.W.] made the payment of 'Sadaqa-tul-Fitr' obligatory for his followers for two reasons: first, as an atonement for any improper or licentious deed that the fasting people may have committed unconsciously in the period of their fast; and secondly, 'Sadaqa-tul-Fitr' is to be paid to make

provisions of food for the poor and the indigent to afford them to enjoy the auspicious Eid day.

(Abu Daud)

15. Besides practising maximum possible piety yourself in the holy days of Ramadan, persuade others also with fervour, zeal, tenderness and tact to do acts of piety, so that the fear of Allah, love of piety and goodness may reign supreme all over the society, and as a whole, may derive the greatest benefit from the limitless blessings of the holy month of Ramadan.

Observing Fasts

1. Keeping in view the great reward and great blessings of Fasting, make arrangement for observing fasts with full zeal and complete earnestness. No other form of worship can serve as an alternative to Fasting. For this reason, Allah made Fasting obligatory for every Ummah (Followers of a Prophet). Allah affirms:

"O ye who believe! Prescribed for you is fasting, as it was prescribed for those before you so that you may become God-fearing."

The Holy Prophet [S.A.W.] elucidated this sublime objective of Fasting as follows:

"A person who does not renounce false speech and practising falsehood while he fasts, Allah cares not for his abstinence from food or drink." (Bukhari)

The Holy Prophet [S.A.W.] further observed:

"The person who fasts with a perfect sense of devotion to faith and 'Ihtisab' (sense of accountability), Allah will pardon all the sins which he may have committed in his previous life." (Bukhari)

2. Observe all fasts of Ramadan with full care and miss not any fast save in case of severe illness or on the

ground of some religious excuse. The Holy Prophet [S.A.W.] said:

"Anyone who misses a single fast during Ramadan except in case of severe illness or on ground of religious excuse cannot make amends for this offence by keeping fasts on all the remaining days of his life." (Tirmidhi)

3. Keep yourself busy in your daily occupation and be active and cheerful in work so as to avoid hypocrisy and false appearances during fasting. Do not show weakness or lethargy in your behaviour during the fast. Hadrat Abu Hurrayrah [R.A.A.] remarked: "When a man observes fasts he ought to anoint himself with oil as usual so that the effects of fasting do not show off."

4. Make your best efforts to avoid all forms of evil during the fast, because the very objective of the fast is to purge the life of man of all evil and make it righteous. The Holy Prophet [S.A.W.] has affirmed:

"Fast is seen as a shield. When any of you is in a state of fasting, he should take care not to utter any evil speech by his tongue or to start an affray. In case someone starts railing at him or is inclined to start a fight with him, the man who is fasting should reflect that he is in a state of fasting (how can he reciprocate offensive language?) (Bukhari, Muslim)

5. Covet the great reward for fasting as reported in the Traditions. Offer a prayer to Allah especially near the hour of Iftar (breaking the fast). "O Allah! Be gracious to accept my fast and grant me that favour and reward which You have promised." The Holy Prophet [S.A.W.] affirmed: "Those who observe fasts will enter Paradise through a special gateway. The name of this gate is 'Rayyan'. When the entire number of all those who

observe fasts have gone in, the gate will be closed and no one will be allowed to enter it afterwards."

(Bukhari)

The Holy Prophet [S.A.W.] also observed: "On the Day of Judgement, Fast will intercede with Allah and say: "O Creator! I restrained this man from eating, drinking and taking other pleasures during the day. O Allah! Be gracious to accept my intercession on behalf of this man." And Allah shall grant this petition." (Mishkat)

In addition, the Prophet of Allah [S.A.W.] observed: "Any prayer which a fasting person offers at the hour of Iftar (time of breaking the fast) is granted and is never refused." (Tirmidhi)

6. Bear the hardships of the fast in good cheer. Do not degrade the sanctity of the fast by complaining of the pangs of hunger or thirst or weakness.

7. If you are unable to observe fast during a journey or because of severe illness, you can forego it, but atone for it on other days. The Holy Quran affirms:

"But whosoever among you is sick or on a journey (he is required to observe fast instead of these days) the same number on other days." (2: 185)

Hadrat Anas [R.A.A.] reports: "On occasions when we went on journeys with the Holy Prophet [S.A.W.], some of the companions observed fast and others did not. However, neither those who had kept fast criticised those who had missed the fast nor the latter objected to the fasting of the former." (Bukhari)

8. Avoid back-biting and casting an evil eye strictly during the fast. The Holy Prophet [S.A.W.] has observed:

"The person who keeps fast is in fact offering devotion to Allah from morning till evening unless, of course, he backbites Etiquette of Life in Islam against someone. When he indulges in backbiting, his fast is broken." (Ad-Dailmi)

9. Earn a lawful living. No devotion of the body fed on illicit earnings is admissible. The Holy Prophet [S.A.W.] has affirmed: "The body fed on illicit earnings is a proper fuel for Hell-Fire." (Bukhari)

10. Do eat 'Sahri' meal. This alleviates the hardship of fasting as well as safeguards against weakness and lethargy. The Holy Prophet [S.A.W.] has observed: "Do eat the 'Sahri' meal, for the eating of 'Sahri' meal entails blessing." (Bukhari)

Moreover, the Holy Prophet [S.A.W.] observed: "Eating of 'Sahri' meal entails blessing; Take a few draughts of water, if nothing else. The angels of Allah send peace and blessings upon those who eat the 'Sahri' meal." (Ahmad)

Furthermore, the Holy Prophet [S.A.W.] observed:

"Take some rest at noon and get some ease in the night prayers. Eat Sahri meal to obtain nourishment during fast in the day time." (Ibn Majah). 'Sahih Muslim' records: The Holy Prophet [S.A.W.] observed: "The only difference between our fasting and the fasting observed by other people of the Book is that we begin the fast by eating the Sahri meal."

11. Do not delay in ending the fast after sunset, for the main objective of fasting is to inculcate the spirit of submission rather than abstinence from food and drink. The Holy Prophet [S.A.W.] affirmed:

"The Muslims will remain in good condition if they hasten to do Iftar (meal taken at sunset to end the fast)." (Bukhari)

12. Say this prayer at the time of Iftar:

"O Allah! it is for thee that I observe fast and it is with Thine blessing that I break it." (Muslim)

After ending the fast, say this prayer:

"No more was the thirst, moistened were the veins and reward became due if the Lord so Willed." (Abu-Daud)

13. When you perform Iftar (ending the fast) at the house of some body else, say this prayer:

"May it please Allah that the fasting people may perform Iftar at your house and pious people may enjoy the hospitality of food provided by you! May the angels invoke blessings upon you by their prayers!" (Abu-Daud)

14. Do arrange Iftar parties. This act entails a high reward. The Prophet of Allah [S.A.W.] has observed:

"Any man who supplied meal to a fasting person to perform Iftar, Allah shall pardon his sins in reward for this act and grant him salvation from Hell-Fire. The man who supplies meal for Iftar to a fasting person will receive an equal reward with him. The reward of the fasting person will not, however, be curtailed.". The people submitted: "O Prophet of Allah [S.A.W.]! Where shall all of us end the wherewithal to make provision for the Iftar of a fasting person and to feed him." The Holy Prophet [S.A.W.] observed: "It is enough to feed a fasting person at Iftar with a date or some quantity of milk or even supply him a single draught of water for Iftar." (Ibn Khuzaima)

Alms Giving and Charity

1. Give away in the way of Allah with the sole motive of winning the favour of Allah. Do not waste your virtuous deed by keeping in view some ulterior purpose or motive. Do not expect the beneficiaries of your deed to

offer thanks to you or acknowledge your favour or testify to your magnanimity. The true believers anticipate reward for their deeds from Allah only. The Holy Quran expressed the sentiments of the true believers in these words:

"We feed you for the sake of Allah only. We wish for no reward nor thanks from you." (76: 9)

2. Avoid display, ostentation and showing off. Hypocrisy destroys the virtue of the best of deeds.
3. Pay Zakat openly, so that others may also be induced to perform their duty. However, offer other Sadaqat (charitable acts) secretly so as to promote feelings of deep sincerity in your heart. Deeds performed with true sincerity are of great value in the eyes of Allah. On the Day of Judgement in that terrible field where there will be no shade, Allah shall keep under the shadow of heaven that man who spends in the way of Allah in such extreme secrecy that the left hand does not know what the right hand has spent." (Bukhari)
4. After spending in the way of Allah avoid reminding the beneficiaries of the favours you have done to them nor cause them any distress. To administer shocks to the self-respect of the indigent and poor, to injure their feelings by reminding them of favours done to them and to expect that they should acknowledge their obligation to you, that they should always humbly bow to you and regard you as their superiors - such sentiments when you have given away charity in the way of Allah, are wicked and despicable. The heart of the true believers should be free of such notions. Allah ordains: "Ye who believe! Render not vain your alms giving by reproach and injury like him who spendeth his wealth only to be seen of men."
5. Do not take pride or assume an air of arrogance after

spending in the way of Allah. Do not advertise your magnanimity among the people. You should rather tremble at the thought whether your sacrifice has been accepted by Allah or not. Allah ordains:

"And those who give what they give while their hearts are full of fear that to their Lord they shall return."

6. Show tenderness to the poor and destitute. Do not rebuke them, nor rule over them nor show off your superiority over them. In case you have nothing to give to a supplicant, excuse yourself with extreme humility and politeness, so that he may depart silently invoking blessings upon you even without receiving anything from you. The Holy Quran says:

"But if you turn away from them seeking means from thy Lord, for which thou hopest, then speak unto them a reasonable word." (17.28)

And Allah also ordains:

"Therefore the beggar drive not away."

7. Spend in the way of Allah liberally with eagerness. Do not spend with a stingy or grudging heart, nor consider it an oppressive fine. Only those people deserve grace and success who forswear miserliness, narrowmindedness and stinginess.

8. Spend only 'Halal' (earned by righteous means) goods in the way of Allah. Allah accepts only those goods which are pure and have been earned through righteous means. How can a believer who is eager to spend in the way of Allah bear that his lawfully earned goods should be mixed with illicit gains? Allah ordains:

"Ye who believe! Spend of the good things that you have earned."

9. Give away the best goods in the way of Allah. Allah ordains:

> "You shall never attain righteousness until you spend of that which you love." (3: 92)

Goods given away as Sadaqa (charity) are being accumulated for the benefit of eternal life in the Hereafter. How can a believer bear the thought of defective goods for his everlasting life.

10. If you are liable to pay the Zakat (poor-due), do not delay the payment. Pay it at once after careful accounting so that, Allah forbid, nothing remains due in your account.
11. Pay the Zakat (poor-due) under a collective system and spend it under the collective system. Where Muslim governments do not exist, the Muslim citizens can form parties and create a Baitul Mal for the receipt and expenditure of Zakat (poor-due).

Holy Pilgrimage

1. Do not delay or keep putting off the performance of Hajj. Whenever Allah bestows enough means on you for the fulfilment of this interesting obligation set out for Hajj at the earliest opportunity. You do not know how much longer life will last, so why should you keep putting off the performance of this duty from one year to the next. The Holy Quran affirms:

> "And the people owe this duty to Allah that whoever has the means to journey to his House should make a pilgrimage to it. And whoever refuses to obey this command should know that Allah needs no favour from any one in the world."

A greater ruination and deprival of man cannot be imagined than that Allah should thus openly proclaim His indifference and disconcern to man.

The Traditions relate: "The person who makes up his mind to go on the pilgrimage should make haste to perform this obligation. It is possible that he may be taken ill; or his she-camel may get lost, or perhaps an event occurs which makes it impossible for him to go to the Hajj." (Ibn Majah)

The implication is that when means are available a person should not evade the performance of this duty without sufficient reason, for one never knows if these means, freedom and facility will still be available to him in the near future, Allah forbid, the man may remain deprived of the blessing of performing the Hajj forever. May Allah save every believer from this deprival! The Holy Prophet [S.A.W.] has reprimanded such persons in very strict terms. The Tradition records that the Holy Prophet [S.A.W.] observed:

"A man who is not prevented by illness or genuine need or is free from the restraints of a tyrannical and despotic ruler and yet does not perform the Hajj may die a Jew or a Christian for aught we care."
(Sunan Kubra, Vol. 4)

Hadrat 'Umar [R.A.A.] was heard as saying. "I wish to summon those who, despite having means, do not perform the Hajj, for they are not Muslims, they are not Muslims at all."

2. Go on a pilgrimage to the House of Allah and perform Hajj to please Allah alone. Do not stain this pure objective with any worldly motives or interests. The Holy Quran affirms:

"And hinder not those who are proceeding to the Sacred House seeking the graces and pleasure of Allah." (5: 2)

"And complete the Hajj and 'Umrah for Allah's (sake)." (2: 196)

And the Holy Prophet [S.A.W.] has affirmed: "The reward for the performance of 'Hajj Mabrur, is certainly no less than admission to Paradise."

3. Do not circulate the news of your going to the pilgrimage. Keep your departure for Hajj and your return a private matter. Avoid strictly all those customs and ceremonies which smack of ostentation or display. Even though the real test of righteousness and acceptability of a deed is that it should be performed with the sole intention of pleasing Allah, and that the motive of the act should be free from all taint of any extraneous desire; but this point should be especially borne in mind in the case of Hajj, for Hajj is the last resort for effecting a spiritual revolution and the purification of soul and the moral conduct of man. The 'spiritual patient' who is not successfully cured by this efficacious treatment has no hope of healing by any other means.
4. Even if you have no wherewithal to proceed to the pilgrimage, you should cherish the desire to view the House of Allah, to offer 'salam' (peace and blessing) on the Mausoleum of the Holy Prophet [S.A.W.] and keep the Ibrahimi sentiments of sacrifice which are produced in the souls of the believer by Hajj ever afresh in your heart. The heart which is devoid of these sentiments is not that of a true believer but resembles to a desolate ruin. The Holy Prophet [S.A.W.] has affirmed:

"Those who go to perform Hajj or 'Umrah' are the special guests of Allah. Their prayers are granted by Allah and if they supplicate for mercy, He forgives them." (Tibrani)

5. Take the best provisions with you when you go for Hajj. The best provision in this case is fear of Allah. In this journey of righteousness, the man who avoids transgressing the Commands of Allah and who reaps the maximum benefit of the blessings of pilgrimage is the one who fears Allah under all circumstances, and

has a burning zeal to win the favour of Allah. The Holy Quran says:

"And take provisions for the journey (to perform Hajj) for verily the best provision is the fear of Allah."
(2: 197)

6. Having resolved to go to Hajj, start making preparations with singleminded devotion. Keep the date of the Hajj constantly in view. Reflect upon each article of the obligation of pilgrimage. Try to realise the feelings which Allah intends to promote in the heart of the believer through the observance of these articles of the obligation of Hajj. Like a conscious and knowledgeable believer, observe all the articles of Hajj with full awareness and imbibe the realities contained in the articles of Hajj and endeavour to bring about a righteous revolution in your life in conformity with these realities. It is for this reason that Allah has ordained the performance of Hajj obligatory for the believers. Allah ordains:

"And remember Him as He has guided you and verily prior to it you were of those gone astray."
(2: 198)

For this purpose, deeply reflect upon those portions of the Holy Quran which describe the reality, importance and the sentiments created by the performance of Hajj. A careful study of the Traditions of the Holy Prophet [S.A.W.] and those books which deal with the date of the Hajj and discuss the articles of Hajj will also prove useful in this respect.

7. Memorise the propitious prayer which should be offered during the Hajj. These may be found in the Books of Traditions. And in the words of the Holy Prophet [S.A.W.] beg not from Allah than what the Prophet [S.A.W.] himself had asked for.

8. Protect your Hajj from all unpropitious motives or actions. Beware lest you Hajj should become like the

Hajj of those who will get no share in the Hereafter, because the latter group shuts its eyes from the rewards of the eternal world and begs exclusively for worldly bliss. When they reach the House of Allah, they offer the following prayer:

"Our Lord, give to us in this world. And for such there shall be no portion in the Hereafter."

(2: 201)

Make a plea to Allah for grace and success in both worlds by means of the Hajj and pray to Allah in these words: "Creator, I have come to Thy Presence to supplicate for success and the fulfilment of my righteous desires in both this life and the life Hereafter." Keep saying this prayer also:

"Allah! Grant us goodness in this world and good in the Hereafter (also) and protect us from the agony of Fire." (2: 201)

9. During Hajj avoid transgression of Allah's commands with extreme sensitivity. The journey to perform the Hajj is in fact a passage to the House of Allah. You are the guests of Allah there. You have gone there to renew your covenant of devotion to Allah. By putting your hand on the 'Hajar-e-Aswad' you are in fact taking a pledge of faith and bondage and when you kiss the stone, you kiss the emblem of submission to Allah, you proclaim your fidelity by chanting repeated Takbir (praises) and Tahlil *(La-Ilaha illa Illah)* of Allah. Imagine, then, that in such an atmosphere how disgusting would be the commission of even a minor vice or the blemish of a small transgression. Allah has warned His servants who present themselves in His Court in these words:

"There should be no ungodliness."

10. During Hajj keep away from all sorts of quarrels. In the course of the journey when there is a rush of people

everywhere, when you suffer discomforts, when there is a clash of interests at every step, when feelings are injured every moment, it is the duty of the guest of Allah to display large-heartedness and self-sacrifice and show toleration, liberality and kindness to everybody. Abstain from rebuking your servant even.

"And there should be no quarrels."

11. Safeguard against sexual matters and continue to be vigilant against carnal sentiments in the course of Hajj. In the course of the journey when there is a greater possibility of provocation of sexual passion or of eyes going astray, you should become more alert against the evil promptings of your passions and the devil and try to protect your piety at all costs. In case you are accompanied by your spouse, you should not only avoid indulgence in sexual relationship with her, but also shun all that can stir up sexual passion. In order to warn the pilgrims, Allah ordains:

"The pilgrimage is (in) the well-known month and whosoever is minded to perform the pilgrimage (let him remember that) there is (to be) no lewdness."

(2: 197)

And the Holy Prophet [S.A.W.] has affirmed:

"Any man who comes here to perform Hajj in the House of Allah and keeps away from immoral and sexual affairs and has not indulged in ungodly acts returns in that state of purity and innocence in which he was born from the womb of his mother."

(Bukhari, Muslim)

12. Pay full reverence to the symbols of Allah. The word 'Shariah' refers to the symbol appointed by Allah to remind and bring home to the people some spiritual or meaningful reality. 'Shaair' is the plural of the above

word. All things associated with the Hajj serve as symbols to bring home to you of some reality about devotion to Allah. You should revere them all. The Holy Quran affirms:

"O ye who believe! Profane not Allah's emblems nor the Sacred Month nor the garlands nor those repairing to the Sacred House, seeking the grace and pleasure of Allah." 'Surah Hajj' affirms:

"And whosoever observes the sanctity of what have been ordained as Symbols of Allah, does so because of the piety of the hearts."

13. Perform the articles of Hajj with utmost humility and adopt an attitude of destitution and helplessness before Allah, for above all Allah likes the virtues of humility, modesty and poverty in man. Someone enquired from the Holy Prophet [S.A.W.], "Who is a Haji?" The Holy Prophet [S.A.W.] observed: "The person who has dishevelled hair and is covered with dust all over."

14. Say Talbih with a loud voice after tying the 'Ihram', after each prayer, while ascending a height or descending a slope, on joining a caravan and on waking up each morning. The words of the Talbih are as follows:

"Here I am O Lord. Here I am, Here I am. No partner hast Thou. Here I am. Behold unto Thee belong the Praise and the Bounty; and also the Sovereignty. No partner hast Thou." (Mishkat)

15. On arrival at the plain of 'Arafat', say the maximum number of prayers for mercy and offer penitence. The Holy Quran affirms;

"Then hasten onward from the place whence the multitude hasteneth onward and ask forgiveness of Allah. Verily Allah is Forgiving, Merciful."

(Al-Baqarah)

The Holy Prophet [S.A.W.] has observed:

"The day of Arafa is the best of all days in the view of Allah. On this day, the Lord of the Heavens especially turns His attention towards the world and expresses His Pride before the angels on the humility and misery of His pilgrims. Allah observes to the angels: "O angels, look! my servants stand before me in the sun in a helpless state. They have gathered here from afar and the hope of begetting My Mercy has drawn them to this place, although they have not yet seen the agony of punishment." After expressing His pride, Allah then ordains that these people have been granted salvation from the torments of Hell. On no other occasion are such a greater number of men granted salvation as on the day of 'Arafa'."

(Ibn Habban)

16. On reaching Mina, offer sacrifice with the same passionate zeal and devotion to Allah with which the friend of Allah, Hadrat Ibrahim [A.S.] had placed the knife on the neck of his dear son Hadrat Ismail [A.S.]. Imbibe these feelings of sacrifices and let them be embedded in your mind and heart so that you may be willing to offer sacrifice in every field of life and your practical life reflects an image of:

"Verily my prayer, and my sacrifice, and my living and my dying are for Allah, Lord of the worlds."

(Al-Anam)

17. Occupy yourself continuously in the remembrance of Allah in the days of Hajj and never let, the memory of Allah fade from your heart. Remembrance of Allah is the essence of all worship. Allah affirms:

"Remember Allah during appointed days. (2: 203) Further Allah observes:

"And when you have completed your devotion then remember Allah as ye remember your fathers or with more lively remembrance."

The main purpose of the articles of Hajj is that during the days of Hajj, you should keep yourself completely absorbed in the commemoration of Allah and then memory of Allah should so permeate through your soul that the mundane activities and struggles of life may not succeed in turning your thoughts away from the memory of Allah. In the days of paganism, people used to laud the memory of their ancestors and made loud boasts about them after performing the articles of Hajj. Allah ordained that these days should be spent in the remembrance of Allah and in acknowledging His grandeur alone Who is truly Great.

18. Perform circumambulation of Allah's House with feelings of great love and devotion. Allah ordains:

"And you should circumambulate the House of Allah."

The Holy Prophet [S.A.W.] has said:

"Each day Allah confers a hundred and twenty favours on His pilgrims. Sixty blessings are showered upon those who circumambulate the House of Allah; forty blessings are bestowed upon those who offer prayers in the House of Allah; and twenty blessings are conferred upon such as only keep gazing at the Kaaba (Baihaqi). Furthermore, the Holy Prophet [S.A.W.] observed:

"He who has performed fifty circumambulations of the Baitullah (House of Allah) is purged of all his sins and is transformed into that state of innocence in which he was on the day of his delivery from the womb of his mother." (Tirmidhi)

Reading and Reciting Holy Quran

- The best Muslims are those who learn and teach the

Quran. Knowledge of the Quran and reciting it are two merits.

- The Quran should be held, taken or given with the right hand not the left.
- Women during child-bed or during the menstrual cycle and men and women who are seminally defiled, may neither touch nor read the Quran.
- All chapters of the Quran and all of its words are benevolent and beneficial.
- Gathering in a group to read and study the Quran is recommended.
- Listening carefully while the Quran is being recited or read is not only an act of politeness, but an obligatory duty upon every Muslim.
- Reading the Quran with proper contemplation, thinking and concentration is necessary to understand the meaning fully.
- The Quran is a book of guidance. It is not a book of history, science, geography, etc., in spite of the fact that it contains historical, scientific, geographical and various other facts.
- The Quran is a book of guidance for mankind in every respect of life. It is not meant to be recited only at ceremonial openings and such occasions.
- When buying or selling the Quran and no fixed price is attached, using terms and tones of language usually used when bargaining should be avoided.
- A Muslim's knowledge of the Quran should be refreshed by re-reading it frequently; this applies especially to those who memorize it, for it is difficult to remember it when it is abandoned for a while.
- When reading or reciting the Quran, the established rules of pronunciation and intonation included in an

independent science called al-tajwid should be followed; these rules have been passed down from the time of the Prophet and the Companions.

- When reciting the Quran, it should be beautified with a good voice and the verses chanted, not sung, for a beautiful voice increases the beauty of the Quran. This however should not be done in a way contradicting the rules of al-tajwid. The inclination of some, to recite the Quran with a melodious voice approaching singing, thus contradicting the rules of al-tajwid, is forbidden. The listener should take the first opportunity to correct such a recitation and politely draw attention to its incorrectness.
- When reciting one of the fourteen special verses of the Quran requiring prostration upon completion of the verse, the Quran should be laid aside, and a sajdah (a prostration) made.
- A Muslim should not be hasty to judge others' reciting of the Quran.
- Disputing, arguing or engaging in controversy about the Quran must not be indulged in, for it is the Book of God.

Preparation for Friday

- Though Friday, according to Islam, is the best day on which the sun has ever risen, and the lord of days, it is not the Islamic sabbath, because sabbath does not exist in Islam.
- A Muslim should bathe or purify himself with 'wudu' as perfectly as possible before going to prayer. Though bathing is not obligatory, it has a more cleansing effect; though 'wudu' is good, bathing is more excellent.
- Best clothes should be worn and perfume applied, if this is available, or pleasant-smelling oil should be put on the hair.

- A tooth stick or toothbrush should be used to ensure that the mouth is clean and has a pleasant odour. This is more important on Fridays before leaving for prayer than on other days.
- Before leaving for prayer, nails should be cut and cleaned, and one should ensure that clothes are clean and beard and moustache tidy.
- The Friday prayer in congregation is a necessary duty for every Muslim, with certain exceptions, e.g. children, women, invalids and those too ill to perform prayer.
- If there is more than one mosque available, it is yet better to say the Friday prayer together at one mosque.
- Going as early as possible to the mosque on Friday is recommended. Walking to the mosque, if this is possible, and not riding is also more worthy.
- On entering the mosque, the rules of behaviour in the mosque must be observed.
- Care should be taken to avoid annoying others in the mosque; for example, squeezing between two men or stepping on others.
- Most mosques on Fridays become full of worshippers. No individual has the right to make another get up and then move into his place. He should politely ask those present to make room for him.
- While in the mosque, the worshipper must avoid any sitting position which could cause him to drowse, to sleep, or which would invalidate his 'wudu'.
- If a worshipper should find himself dozing, he should try to change his place. In this case, he should change places with his neighbour.
- A worshipper should avoid taking any position that would uncover his body between the navel and the knees.

- The Prophet Muhammad forbade worshippers to sit together in a circle in the mosque before Friday prayer, because this hinders straight rows, and reduces the available space.
- Facing the imam while he is giving khutbah from the minbar (pulpit) is polite conduct.
- When the imam asks God's blessings, etc. for the Muslims, he should not raise his hands in an attitude of supplication.
- When the Friday prayer is finished worshippers should not rush to leave the mosque, or crowd the exits.
- As mentioned above, a sabbath does not exist in Islam, therefore, it is not required that a Muslim abandons working during the whole of Friday. What is required, is to stop working during prayer time.
- A worshipper should listen to the imam as soon as he starts his khutbah and keep silent until he finishes. To attend prayer with a frivolous attitude is against the aim of the Friday prayer.
- It is undesirable to fast on Friday alone; to fast on Friday, however, in conjunction with Thursday or Saturday is allowed.
- It is neither necessary nor required to abandon travel on Friday.
- Friday is a good occasion to remember the Prophet, peace be on him, and invoke a blessing on him by saying: Allahuma Salli ala Muhammad wa ala ali Muhammad (O God, bless Muhammad and Muhammad's family).
- Reading the Quranic chapter of Al-Kahf every Friday is recommended.

Khutbah at Friday Prayer

- The imam should avoid the custom of always wearing black clothes on Fridays.

- As soon as the imam ascends the minbar he salutes the worshippers, just before he sits or immediately after.
- The imam should face the worshippers while he is delivering the khutbah.
- Topics discussed in the khutbah should be related to current, relevant issues.
- The Friday khutbah is of two parts in each of which the imam must speak while standing; in the interval between he must sit for a short while on the minbar.
- The voice of the imam should be clear, but he should not shout in order to be heard. His language should be simple and understandable.
- The imam should not interrupt his khutbah in order to greet someone or to make an announcement of any kind.
- The imam should not make his khutbah or his prayer lengthy. Each must be of moderate length. In fact, the shortness of the khutbah is a sign of the imam's understanding and knowledge of Islam.
- The second part of the khutbah should not be devoid of information.
- The khutbah is a message and not a performance. The imam should avoid being conspicuously eloquent or poetic; he should also avoid speaking in a voice or in a manner which tends towards musicality.
- The imam's raising his hands in the khutbah while saying 'dua' for the Muslims is not recommended. It is enough that he points with his forefinger.
- The imam should prepare his khutbah beforehand; his 'dua' should preferably be spontaneous and not memorized.
- The imam should not begin the actual prayer until he has convinced himself that the rows of worshippers are straight.

Significance of Mosque

The mosque is where Muslims should pray five times every day, where they seek refuge from the troubles of this world, from its everlasting daily demands, its complications and its vanities.

Design

- A mosque should be built in every residential district.
- The design of the mosque should be characterized by simplicity, as must its furnishings.
- The mosque should be devoid of any lavish kind of ornamentation, representation of anything, pictures or images.
- Extravagance in spending large sums of money to build luxurious mosques should be avoided.
- Members of the Muslim society should neither vie with one another about the virtues or beauties of any particular mosque nor compete in building ostentatious mosques.
- Attaching pieces of gold of silver to any part of the mosque or its furnishings is forbidden.
- The carpets and walls of the mosque should be devoid of a multiplicity of colours for that distracts the concentration of the worshippers.
- Writing on the walls of the mosque, inside or outside, including Quranic verses or God's attributes, should be avoided. The names of the Prophet and the first four rightly-guided Caliphs likewise should not be written.
- The minbar should not be placed in the middle of the mosque. Its height should not exceed three steps.
- Every mosque should have two entrances, one for men and one for women.

- Lavatories should be sited as far from the mosque as practicable, and from the fountains or basins for ritual ablution.
- Raising flags inside the mosque is an innovation.

Cleanliness and Tidiness : The mosque deserves to be the cleanest place on earth. Therefore:

- Muslims must be sure before entering the mosque that their body and clothes are clean and do not smell bad.
- Filth must be removed from shoes and the shoes removed before entering the mosque.
- Although it is not forbidden to eat anything in the mosque, it is not a place for taking meals and drinks.
- Whoever brings in or causes dirt in the mosque has a duty to clean it up and remove it. It is not the duty solely of the mosque caretaker to keep the mosque clean and tidy; it is also the responsibility of every Muslim entering the mosque and seeing any uncleanliness, to remove this from the mosque.
- The mosque should be sprayed or sprinkled with perfume to give a pleasant odour.

9

Regular Practices

The Holy Prophet [S.A.W.] observed that Allah has affirmed as follows:

> "My creatures! Each one of you is misguided, save the one whom I guide. So seek guidance only from Me so that I may instruct you. My people! Each one of you is famished, save the one whom I feed. So apply to Me only for subsistence, so that I may grant you livelihood. My slaves! Each one of you is naked, save the one whom I dress with an apparel, so beseech clothing from Me so that I may dress you with garments. My bondmen! You commit sins day and night and I can forgive all sins. So seek forgiveness from Me so that I may forgive you your sins."
>
> (Sahih Muslim)

1. Never lose hope of acceptance by Allah of your repentance and petition for forgiveness. Whatever the magnitude of your sins, purify your soul by offering repentance and be hopeful of Allah's mercy, Despair is the characteristic of unbelievers, It is the distinctive trait of the believers that they repent the most and under no circumstances do they lose hope of Allah's

clemency. It is disastrous to succumb to dismay and lose hope of Allah's Mercy and clemency considering the magnitude of sins. The most outstanding quality of the favourites of Allah is that they do not stick to the wrong and guilt but admit their fault clearly and unconditionally. They are never supposed to be above faults and omissions, but when they commit any fault and realise the wrong done, they do all within their means to beg forgiveness from Allah and to purify themselves of that fault and misdeed.

"And those who when they do an evil thing or wrong them selves remember Allah and implore forgiveness for their sins. Who forgiveth sins save Allah only? - and will not knowingly repeat (the wrong) they did."
(3: 135)

And Allah affirms in another verse:

"Lo! those who ward off (evil) when a glamour from the evil troubleth them they do but remember (Allah's guidance) and behold them seers." (7: 201)

And the Holy Prophet [S.A.W.] observed:

"All human beings without exception are sinful, but the best sinners are those who repent the most."
(Tirmidhi)

In the Holy Quran, Allah has mentioned it as a distinct virtue of the believers that they offer penances before Allah at dawn and repent and seek His Forgiveness and Allah has urged the believers that they should rest assured that Allah shall cover their sins with His Forgiveness and Clemency, for He is All Forgiving and the Most Affectionate towards His creatures.

"Ask pardon of your Lord and then turn unto Him (repentant). Lo! my Lord is Merciful, Loving."
(11: 90)

2. Always be hopeful of Allah's Blessings and rest assured that however great your sins may be, Allah's Munificence is wider and all-encompassing. When a person who has committed a greater volume of sins than the surf of the sea feels ashamed and offers sincere penance before Allah, He listens to his entreaties and grants him refuge under His Mercy.

"O My slaves who have been prodigal to their own heart! Despair not of the Mercy of Allah who forgiveth all sins. Lo! He is the Forgiving the Merciful. Turn unto Him repentant; and surrender unto Him before there come unto you the doom, when ye cannot be helped." (39: 53, 54)

3. Whenever you feel shame and remorse and at whatever stage of your life, consider this feeling and realisation a special favour of Allah and be sure that the doors are always open for repentance. Allah accepts repentance of His slaves as long as they are alive. However, when they are at the threshold of death and are about to pass over to the next world, the time for offering repentance expires. The Holy Prophet [S.A.W.] observed:

"Allah accepts the repentance of His slaves, but only before the slave has breathed his last."

(Tirmidhi)

The brothers of Hadrat Yusuf [A.S.] pushed him into a dark well and felt sure that he was dead. In other words, they stood guilty of the murder of a Prophet. They soaked Hadrat Yusuf's shirt in blood and presented it as a positive evidence of his death to their father Hadrat Yaqub [A.S.]. They assured him that a wolf had devoured Hadrat Yusuf [A.S.] Many years after the commission of this grave offence when the sense of guilt prevailed upon them, they went to their father remorsefully and requested him: "Dear father, pray to Allah on our behalf and intercede with Him to grant us forgiveness." The Messenger of Allah Hadrat Yaqub [A.S.] did not disappoint his sons by confronting them with the question: "Your offence is grave. Many years have elapsed since you committed this heinous crime, why ask for forgiveness now?" Instead he undertook to offer a prayer to Allah that He should grant them salvation and assured them that Allah would certainly forgive them for Allah is the Most Forbearing and Most Compassionate.

> "They said. O our father! Ask forgiveness of our sins for us, for Lo! we are sinful." (12: 97)
>
> "He said: I shall ask forgiveness for you of my Lord. Lo! He is the Forgiving, the Merciful." (12: 98)

The Holy Prophet [S.A.W.] told a strange tale to his Companions [R.A.A.] with a view to save them from falling a prey to dismay. The tale contains the moral that whenever at any stage of his life a believer feels ashamed of his misdeeds and he sincerely entreats Allah to forgive him, Allah shall bestow upon him salvation and He shall never refuse him His favour.

> The Holy Prophet [S.A.W.] observed: "There was a man in ancient days who had committed ninety-nine murders. He enquired from people: "Who is the greatest scholar of the time?" The people gave him the name of a Allah-fearing monk. The man approached the monk and said. "Respected Sir, I am guilty of ninety-nine murders. Can my repentance and petition for forgiveness be accepted?" The monk replied: "No, you stand no chances for forgiveness." In utter dismay the man killed the monk too. Now he had completed a century of murders. He again went round asking the people as to who was the greatest religious scholar on the earth. The people gave him the name of another monk. The man approached the monk to offer repentance. He related his problem in detail and enquired from him: Sir, I have committed

a hundred murders. Tell me, can my repentance be accepted?" The monk replied: Why not? Nothing stand in the way of acceptance of your repentance. Go to such and such country. You will find a few venerable slaves of Allah engaged in prayer and devotions to Him. Join them and devote yourself to the worship of Allah and never return to your homeland, as this place is no more virtually suitable for you (In other words, it is impossible for you to remain firm upon your vow of repentance and to strive to reform yourself while living in this place)." The man set out according to the directions of the monk. He had hardly covered half the distance when death overtook him. Now the angels of grace and the angels of torment fell into a dispute. The angels of grace argued, "This man repented of his sins and went a long way to offer submission to Allah." The angels of torment countered: "No, he has not yet performed a single act of virtue- thus the argumentation between the angels went on. In the meantime an angel appeared in the shape of a human being. The angels requested him to settle their dispute. He gave his verdict: "Measure the distance on both sides and determine which side is nearer; the place from where he set out or the place where was he going." When the angels measured the distance on both the sides, it came out that the destination was nearer as compared to the distance he had so far covered. Thus Allah had in fact forgiven him. (Bukhari, Muslim)

4. Confess your sins only before Allah; beseech Him only for forgiveness; express your sense of humility, helplessness and guilt only before Him. Humility and prostration is a tribute which you should pay only to Allah. The unfortunate one, who pays this tribute of humility and prostration to other human beings who are as helpless and humble before Allah as he himself,

> becomes insolvent and is left with nothing to pay as tribute to Allah. Such a man is condemned to disgrace and ignominy. He goes to everybody in search of honour and respect but he gets none.

Allah affirms:

> "Thy Lord is the Forgiver, Full of Mercy. If He took them to task now for what they earn, He would hasten on the doom for them; but there is an appointed term from which they will find no escape." (18: 58)

The Quran alarms:

> "And He it is Who accepts the repentance from His bondmen, and pardoneth the evil deeds and knoweth what ye do." (42: 25)

In fact, one must himself be convinced that there is only one way to salvation and whoever is denied that approach, is condemned to ignominy and destitution for ever. The befitting attitude of mind in a believer is that whatever the degree of his offence he should only offer penitence to Allah and shed tears of shame only before Him. There is none except Allah Who only has the authority to grant pardon. So much so that even if someone tries to propitiate the Prophet excluding Allah, he will be deprived of favour before Allah, and will be discarded outright. The Prophet of Allah [S.A.W.] is also a slave of Allah soliciting His favour and mercy. The Prophet has been appointed to the exalted office by virtue of his surpassing humility among the creatures of Allah and he makes greater penances to Allah in comparison with others.

The Holy Prophet [S.A.W.] observed:

> "O People! Seek forgiveness of Allah for your sins and return to Him. Look at me. I offer prayers to Allah for salvation hundreds of times in a day."
>
> (Muslim)

Concerning the hypocrites Allah affirms:

> "They swear unto you, that ye may accept them, Though ye accept them. Allah verily accepteth not wrong doing folk" (9: 96)

The terrible episode of Hadrat Kaab b. Malik [R.A.A.] as related in the Holy Quran gives us a lesson that man should suffer hardships and endure all trials, but he should never think of abandoning submission to Allah. The trials that come in the way of Islam and the maximum pain and suffering he has to bear in the way of Allah are means to purify and illumine the life of man and to elevate his rank. This humiliation is the sure means of securing eternal prestige and he who abandons submission to Allah and seeks dignity elsewhere shall find it nowhere. Such a man will meet with disgrace everywhere and no eye on earth or in the sky shall regard him with respect.

> "And to the three also (did he turn in mercy) who were left behind, when the earth, vast as it is was straitened for them and their own souls were straitened for them till they bethought them that there is no refuge from Allah save towards Him. Then turned He unto them in mercy that they (too) might turn (repentant unto Him). Lo! Allah! He is the Relenting, the Merciful." (9: 118)

The three referred to above are Hadrat Kaab bin Malik Hadrat Murarah ibn Rabi' and Hadrat Halala b. Umayyah [R.A.A.]. The example of their penitence serves as a beacon light for the believers as long as the world exists. Hadrat Kaab b. Malik [R.A.A.] who had lost his eyesight in old age and used to walk with the help of his son, had himself related the instructive episode of his exemplary penitence to his son which has been preserved in the Books of Tradition.

"When the preparations were being made for the battle of Tabuk and the Holy Prophet [S.A.W.] used to call upon the people to join the war I regularly attended all his meetings. Whenever I heard him speak, I made a resolve that I would join the war. However, on returning home I relapsed into laziness. I thought there was plenty of time yet and I had all the provisions of the journey. Moreover, I was in good health and could afford the best mount. There was nothing that could delay me in joining the battle. In this mood, I continued to postpone my departure until all holy warriors had reached the field of battle and I lingered on in Medina entrapped in indecision and lethargy.

"Soon the reports began to pour in that the Holy Prophet [S.A.W.] was returning and one day I heard that he had arrived in Medina and was staying as usual in the mosque. So I went to the mosque. On arrival I found that the hypocrites were trying to convince the Holy Prophet [S.A.W.] of the genuineness of their excuses on oaths. The Holy Prophet [S.A.W.] heard their insincere speeches and indicated his acceptance of their lame excuses by observing 'May Allah forgive you'.

"When my turn came, the Holy Prophet [S.A.W.] enquired: 'Say, what prevented you from coming'? I saw that his smile had a trace of annoyance, so I spoke the truth. "O Messenger of Allah [S.A.W.]! As it happened I had no excuse. I was healthy and prosperous and possessed the mount. It was my lethargy and negligence which deprived me of this privilege.

"On hearing me speak the truth, the Holy Prophet [S.A.W.] observed: "Well, then, go and wait the verdict from Allah." I got up and went among the people of my tribe. The people of my tribe railed at me and said: "Why did you not offer some plausible excuse. You have always been in the forefront in the service of Islam." However, when I found that two other friends of mine had also told the truth, I felt at ease and determined to hold firmly to the truth.

"Afterwards, the Holy Prophet [S.A.W.] issued a general proclamation that no one should speak to us. As soon as this proclamation was issued forth, the attitudes in Medina suddenly changed for me. I became a helpless stranger among my own kith and kin. No one in the society exchanged greetings or entered into a conversation with me. One day, I felt extremely depressed and went to a childhood friend and cousin Abu Qatada [R.A.A.]. I offered him salam, but he did not reciprocate. I, then, said: "Abu Qatada! I ask you in the name of Allah, tell me, am I wanting in love for Allah and His Messenger [S.A.W.]." Qatada [R.A.A.] remained silent. I repeated my question, but he made no answer. When I asked him in the name of Allah for the third time, he said: "Allah and His Messenger [S.A.W.] know better." My heart overflowed with a surge of emotion and I burst into tears and returned home with the burden of my grief enhanced.

It was during those days that a Syrian trader in the bazar delivered to me a letter from the monarch of Ghassan. The Christian monarch had written: "It has come to our knowledge that your chief is subjecting you to extreme repression. You are not a lowly person. We know the worth of a man like you. Come to us. We shall treat you as befits your status and rank." As soon as I read the letter, my tongue uttered: "Here is another calamity that has befallen me." And I threw the letter into the hearth.

"Forty days had passed in this state when a courier of the Holy Prophet [S.A.W.] delivered his command that I should separate from my wife also. I enquired: "Shall I divorce her?" The answer came: "No, just live separately from her." I despatched my wife to the home of her parents and told her: "Now, wait for the verdict from Allah."

"On the fiftieth day after dawn prayers, I was sitting on the roof of my house highly dejected, stricken with extreme grief and considering life as no longer bearable, when suddenly someone shouted to me: 'Kaab! Congratulations'. On hearing this, I understood that the hour of my deliverance had come and fell in prostration to my Allah. Later people rushed towards me. They came in crowds and congratulated me. I rose and went straight to the presence of the Holy Prophet [S.A.W.]. I saw his august face glowing with happiness. When I moved forward and greeted him, the Prophet [S.A.W.] observed: "Kaab! Congratulations! This is the happiest day of your life."I submitted: "Prophet of Allah [S.A.W.], is this clemency a favour from you or from Allah?" The Holy Prophet [S.A.W.] observed: "This is a favour from Allah" and then recited the verses of *Surah Taubah* (9)."

5. Do not delay in offering repentance. Nobody knows when his life will end, and the next moment will bring death to him or his life shall continue. Always remember your fast approaching end and continue to cleanse the impurity of sins from your heart and soul and mind and speech.

The Holy Prophet [S.A.W.] observed:

> "Allah extends His mercy during the night so that the person who committed a sin during the day should return to Him in the night. Allah extends His mercy during the day so that the person who has committed a sin during the night may return to his Lord in the day time and see His forgiveness until the sun rises from the east." (Muslim)

The expression 'Allah extends His mercy' means that Allah beckons His sinful slaves towards Himself and desires to cover their sins with His blessings. If the person has committed a sin under the pressure of a temporary impulse, he should immediately turn towards his kind and All-Forgiving Allah and should lose no time, for sin begets sin. The Satan constantly lies in ambush for the human being and never misses an opportunity to lead man astray.

6. Offer repentance with such true and deep sincerity of heart that the entire course of your life is altered and

after repentance you may appear an entirely different man.

Allah decrees:

"O ye who believe! Turn unto Allah in sincere repentance! It may be that your Lord will remit from you your evil deeds and bring you into Gardens underneath which rivers flow on the day when Allah will not abase the Prophet and those who believe with him." (66: 8)

In other words, offer such sincere and true repentance that not a trace of any temptation to return to the sin remains in your heart or mind. Such a repentance has three or four ingredients. If the sin relates to a transgression of Allah's right, repentance should have three elements:

(i) Man should be sincerely ashamed of his sins.

(ii) Man should firmly resolve to avoid sin in future.

(iii) And man should put his heart and soul in the task of reforming and embellishing his life.

If a man has committed a sin which involves the violation of a human right, repentance should consist of a fourth element also:

(iv) Man should restore the right of another human being or seek forgiveness of the person whose right he has violated.

This is the repentance which really cleanses the man of all his sins. His soul is cleared of sins and adorned with pious deeds, is presented before Allah and is awarded a dwelling place in His Paradise.

The Holy Prophet [S.A.W.] observed:

"When man commits a sin, his heart is stained with a dark spot. Now if he:

(i) renounces the sin;

(ii) is ashamed of his sin and seeks salvation;

(iii) and turns to Allah with a firm determination to avoid sin in future;

Allah illumines his heart. But if he again commits sin, the dark spot is enlarged until it covers the whole of his heart. This is the rust about which Allah affirms in His Book:

"Nay, but that which they have earned is rust upon their hearts." (83 : 14)

7. Take a firm resolve to remain true to your repentance and be vigilant day and night that the commitments you have made before Allah are duly fulfilled. Test the firmness of your resolve by constant efforts to purify and reform yourself. If despite all your efforts to guard against evil, you slip and commit an offence, do not lose hope even then. On the contrary seek refuge in the Mercy of Allah and offer fervent prayers to him: "O Creator! I am weak and infirm. Do not banish me in disgrace from Your threshold. For, I can seek asylum nowhere except in Your Mercy."

Repentance of a wrong-doer invites the pleasure of Allah. Taubah (Repentance) literally means 'return, to turn to'. When thoughts and emotions go astray and one gets entrapped in the quicksand of sin, his connection with Allah is severed and he is so far removed from Allah as if he is lost to Allah. And when such a man returns and turns to Allah in utter shame for his sins, it is as if a lost slave has come back to his master. This situation has been graphically described by the Holy Prophet [S.A.W.] in the following eloquent allegory:

"If one of you loses his camel in a waterless desert with all his provisions of food and water laden on the lost camel and having vainly searched for the camel in all directions of the desert he despairs of his life and lies down under a tree awaiting death and in this

> state he suddenly beholds his camel laden with all the provisions standing by his side, imagine then his happiness! - the happiness of your Lord and Creator far surpasses the happiness of this man when His lost slave returns and having gone astray resumes allegiance to Him." (Tirmidhi)

On another occasion, the Holy Prophet [S.A.W.] elucidated Etiquette of Life in Islam the same fact by means of another impressive allegory:

> Some prisoners of war were brought before the Holy Prophet. [S.A.W.] The group included a woman who had lost her infant. The maternal instinct so overpowered the woman that she found no peace or rest unless she picked up and breast-fed any baby she found near her. On seeing the woman in such state the Holy Prophet [S.A.W.] enquired from the Companions [R.A.A.]: "Can you imagine that this woman will fling her baby into fire with her own hands?" The Companions submitted: "O Messenger of Allah [S.A.W.]! Leaving apart the matter of throwing the child herself, she would stake her life to save the child if it were falling by itself." The Prophet [S.A.W.] thereupon observed:
>
> "Allah is by far even more Compassionate and Kind to His slaves than this woman is considerate towards her child."

8. Offer repentance to and seek forgiveness of Allah continuously. There are countless offences which a man commits from morning till evening; sometimes man is not even conscious of these transgressions. Do not imagine that repentance is called for only when a capital sin has been committed; man needs to repent and pray for his salvation at all times, because he is liable to make a slip at every step. The Holy Prophet [S.A.W.]

himself used to repent and pray for his salvation seventy or even hundred times in a day.

(Bukhari, Muslim)

9. Do not look down upon a sinner who repents and reforms his life. Hadrat 'Imran b. al-Haseen [R.A.A.] has reported an incident of the time of the Holy Prophet [S.A.W.]: "A woman of the tribe of Juhainah presented herself before the Holy Prophet [S.A.W.]. She had become pregnant as a result of an unlawful relation. She submitted: "O Messenger of Allah [S.A.W.]'. I deserve punishment for adultery. Enforce the Shariah in my case and punish me." The Holy Prophet [S.A.W.] sent for the guardian of this woman and observed to him: "Treat this woman well and when she has delivered the child, bring her to me." When the woman returned after the delivery of her child, the Holy Prophet [S.A.W.] commanded that her garments should be tied fast around her body (so that the garments may not slip off during stoning and her physical veil may not be torn off) and when this had been done, the Holy Prophet [S.A.W.] ordered that she should be stoned to death. The order was carried out. The Holy Prophet [S.A.W.] later offered funeral prayers for her. Hadrat 'Umar [R.A.A.] submitted to the Holy Prophet [S.A.W.]: "O Messenger of Allah [S.A.W.]! This woman committed the offence of adultery and you are saying funeral prayers for her." The Holy Prophet [S.A.W.] thereupon observed: "She repented and offered repentance of such magnitude that if it were portioned among seventy men of Medina, it would secure their salvation. Did you see any one better than the one who presented the gift of life to Allah?"

10. Say the 'finest prayer' to Allah. The Holy Prophet [S.A.W.] observed to Hadrat Shaddad ibn Aus [R.A.A.] 'This is the *Sayyed-ul-Istaghfar*' ('the finest prayer').

"Allah! Thou is my Creator! There is no deity except Thee. Thou created me and I am Thy slave. I shall remain faithful to the pledge of devotion which I have given to Thee to the best of my capability. I seek asylum with Thee against the fearful consequences of my sins. I acknowledge all the blessings Thou hast conferred on me and I confess that I am a sinner - Hence, O My Creator, Forgive my sins. Who else except Thee will forgive my sins?"

(Bukhari, Muslim)

Performing Prayers

1. Pray to Allah only. Do not call upon any one else except Allah to fulfil your needs. Prayer is the essence of worship and worship should be rendered to Allah alone.

The Holy Quran affirms:

"Unto Him is the real prayer. Those unto whom they pray beside Allah respond to them not at all, save as (is the response to) one who stretches forth his hand, towards water (asking) that it may come to his mouth and it will never reach it. The prayer of disbeliever goeth (far) astray." (13: 14)

In other words all powers to fulfil prayers and to dispose of things lie in the hands of Allah. All powers vest in Him and no power lies with any one else. All are dependent upon Him. There is none except Him Who hears the petitions of human beings and fulfils their prayers.

"O mankind! Ye are the poor in your relation to Allah. And Allah! He is the Absolute, the Owner of Praise."

(35:15)

The Holy Prophet [S.A.W.] observed:

"Allah affirms, 'My creatures! I have declared tyranny unlawful for Me. So you should also consider acts of oppression and excess on each other as forbidden. My slaves! Each of you is misguided, except the one whom I guide on the right path. So seek guidance from Me alone, so that I may guide you aright. My people! Each of you is hungry, except the one whom I feed. Hence call upon Me for sustenance, so that I may provide for your livelihood. My servants! Each of you is naked, except the one whom I have blessed with garments. So entreat Me to confer dress on you and I shall provide you clothing. My worshippers! You commit sins in the night as well as in the day and I shall forgive all sins"! (Sahib Muslim)

The Holy Prophet [S.A.W.] also observed: "Man should call upon Allah alone to provide for all his needs, so much so that even if a shoelace is broken, man should pray to Allah to provide a shoelace, and if he needs salt, he should beseech Allah to send it to him." (Tirmidhi)

The Implication is that man ought to turn to Allah for the fulfilment of his most insignificant and ordinary needs. None except Allah can hear the prayers and none except Him can fulfil wants.

2. Ask Allah for only that which is lawful and good. To beseech Allah's help for the execution of unlawful purposes and sinful acts is the height of impertinence, immodesty and irreverence. To pray to Allah for the fulfilment of unlawful and forbidden desires and to make vows for such desires is to perpetrate the basest joke on religion. Similarly, do not offer prayers to Allah to change those realities which He has determined once for all and which are now unalterable. For example, a short man should not pray to Allah to make him tall, nor should a tall man pray to Allah to make him short; nor indeed should a man pray to Allah for eternal youth so that he may never experience old age etc.

The Holy Quran affirms:

> "And set your faces upright (towards Him) at every place of worship, and call upon Him, making religion pure for Him (only)." (7: 29)

He, who would present his needs before Allah, should not take to the path of infidelity and pray for the fulfilment of unlawful desire, but should display good character and virtuous passions and beseech Allah for the fulfilment of lawful wants.

3. Say prayer with profound sincerity and a righteous disposition and with the conviction that Allah Whom you beseech is perfectly aware of your condition and is Most Considerate towards you; it is He alone who hears the petitions of His servants and fulfils their prayers. Always offer a pure prayer unmixed with all taint of exhibition, display, deception or polytheism.

The Holy Quran affirms:

> "Call ye then Allah devoting your obedience wholly to Him." (40: 14)

And Surah Baqarah bears the command:

> "And when My servants question thee concerning Me, then surely I am nigh. I answer the prayer of the supplicant when he crieth unto Me. So let them hear My call and let them trust in Me, in order that they may be led alright." (2: 186)

4. Offer prayer with perfect concentration and devotion of mind and heart and with a positive conviction of Allah's favour. Instead of gazing at the enormity of your sins, look towards the unlimited mercy, kindness and the countless bounties and blessings of Allah. The prayer of an inattentive man whose thoughts are not concentrated on Allah and who is only mumbling a few words halfheartedly at a whim without anticipating the favour of Allah is vain.

The Tradition relates:

> "Offer prayer with the firm conviction of Allah's favour. Allah does not accept a prayer sent forth by an inattentive heart." (Tirmidhi)

5. Say prayer in utmost humility with awe and fear of Allah. Your heart should be astir with the awesome majesty, grandeur and power of Allah and fear of Allah should be obvious from your physical posture. Your head should be bent and eyes downcast. Your voice should be muffled, limbs limp, eyes damp with tears and the whole demeanour should present a picture of helpless misery before Allah. The Holy Prophet [S.A.W.] on beholding a man stroking his beard during worship, observed: "Had he the fear of Allah in his heart, his body too would have been overcome by it."

In point of fact while praying a man should tremble with the realisation of his destitution and helpless misery and with the fear that if he were repulsed from the threshold of Allah, he would not find refuge anywhere. He should have deep awareness of the fact that he possesses nothing of his own; everything he has is a bounty from Allah; if Allah withholds, no other power in the world can bestow anything on him. Allah is the Master of everything; He alone holds the treasure of everything; man is only a miserable beggar.

The Holy Quran commands:

> "Call your Lord with humility."

> The dignity of worship consists in the servant calling upon his Creator in desperate humility and in a lowly manner so that his heart and intellect, emotions and feelings and all parts of his body should be bent in homage to Him and the servant's soul and body should bear evidence to his destitution and plea for help.

6. Say prayer in a muted, faint voice. Do present your petition before Allah in a desperate manner, but never display your desperation and misery openly. Man should display his humility, lowliness and the plea of misery only before Allah.

There is no doubt that sometimes you may say prayers in a loud voice, but only in privacy, or amid a congregation so that the others may say 'Amin'. Generally, however, you should say prayer quietly in muffled tones and take full care that your expression of misery and destitution and your supplication is not just a show intended for other people.

"And do thou (O Muhammad) remember thy Lord within thyself humbly and with awe below thy breath at morning and evening. And be thou not of the neglectful." (7: 205)

The Holy Quran praises the beauty of the worship offered by Hadrat Zakriya [A.S.] in these words:

"When he cried unto his Lord a cry in secret." (19: 3)

7. You should execute some pious deed before saying prayer. For instance, make some sacrifice, give alms, feed the hungry one or offer supererogatory worship or observe a fast. In case, Allah forbid, you land in some trouble, offer prayer to Allah reminding Him of all these pious deeds which you have performed with true sincerity of heart for His sake only.

The Holy Quran says:

"Pure utterances ascend towards Him only and pious deed propel them to higher altitudes." (35: 10)

The Holy Prophet [S.A.W.] once related the incident of three men who were entrapped in a cave during a very dark night. They prayed to Allah reminding Him of their truly sincere deeds and Allah rescued them from the calamity.

It so happened that during a dark night a group of three men took refuge in a cave. As Allah willed, a rock slided down the hill and falling over the mouth of the cave closed the passage completely. It was a massive rock and was too heavy for them to push aside and clear the passage. On consultation among themselves, they resolved to pray to Allah reminding Him of their truly sincere deeds in anticipation of His Favour to rescue them from this calamity. In accordance with this resolution, one of them related his pious deed as follows:

> I used to take goats for grazing in the forest and earned my living by means of this occupation. On returning from the forest I used to offer milk first to my old parents and then to my children. One day, I arrived late. My old parents had gone to sleep. The children were awake and hungry. But I could not bear to feed the children before my parents had taken the milk, nor did I wish to put them to inconvenience by waking them up. So I stood all night at the head of their beds holding the cup of milk in my hand. The children clung to my feet and cried for milk all the night, but I remained unmoved and stood there until night gave way to morning.

"O Allah! I performed this deed for Your sake only. Remove this rock from the mouth of the cave in recompense for my deed." And Allah caused the rock to move aside just so much as to let in a view of the sky.

The second man spoke thus: I put some labourers to work and paid wages to all of them except one man who went away without receiving payment for his labour. A short while later when the man returned to claim his wage I said to him: "All these cows, goats and servants are yours. Take them where you will." He said: "For Allah's sake, don't cut joke with me." I answered: "This is not a joke. All this is yours. I invested the money which you had left behind in business. By the Grace of

Allah, the business thrived. All this which you see is the profit derived from that business. Take it with an easy mind. All this belongs to you." And that man went away taking everything with him. "Oh Allah! I acted in this way to earn Your Goodwill alone. Oh Allah! Remove this rock in recompense of my deed." By the gracious will of Allah the rock moved further away from the mouth of the cave.

The third one narrated the following account of his pious deed: I had a cousin sister for whom I conceived an extraordinary liking. She asked for some money which I supplied. But when I sat close to her to satisfy my need, she said: "Fear Allah and refrain from this act." I rose at once and I pronounced that sum as a gift to her. "Oh Allah! You know perfectly well that I did this to win your favour only. Oh Allah! Open the mouth of the cave as a reward for this pious deed." Allah removed the rock from the passage of the cave and liberated the three men from this calamity.

8. Along with offering prayers for the fulfilment of pious purposes, try to reform and adorn your life in conformity with the Ordinances of Allah. Avoid all sins and forbidden things. Respect and observe the Commands of Allah in all matters and lead a pious life. It is the height of folly and insolence to eat and drink forbidden thing, clothe yourself out of unlawful gains and fatten your body on illicit earnings and then anticipate acceptance of your prayer. If you wish your prayer may be accepted, your words and action both should conform to the tenets of Islam.

The Holy Prophet [S.A.W.] observed:

"Allah is Pure and He accepts only pure goods. Allah has enjoined upon the pious the same deeds as He has upon the Messengers. Allah affirms:

"O Messengers! Partake of lawful provisions and perform good acts."

Addressing the pious, Allah enjoins:

"O ye who believe! Partake of those lawful and pure things which We have bestowed on you."

The Holy Prophet [S.A.W.] then referred to the case of a man who travels a long distance and arrives at a sacred spot to pay homage; he is covered all over with dust; he raises both hands towards the sky and says: 'My Lord', 'O My Lord', yet because he partakes of unlawful food and drinks and dresses out of forbidden gains and fattens his body on illicit earnings, how can the prayer of such a contumacious and disobedient person be accepted? *(Sahib. Muslim)*

9. Offer prayers regularly. The expression of one's humility, destitution and sense of loyalty to Allah is in itself a worship. Allah Himself has commanded His servants to offer prayer to Him. Allah has said: "Whenever the servant calls Me I listen to him."

Do not get tired of offering prayer. Do not be tied down by the doubt whether your prayer would change your destiny or not. The obstinacy or flexibility of fate or the acceptance or rejection of prayer depends on the Will of Allah Who is All-Knowing and All-Wise. All the same, it is the duty of the slave to offer prayer to Him like a beggar and destitute person and not to consider himself independent of Him for a single moment.

The Holy Prophet [S.A.W.] observed:

"The humblest person is the one who is humble in prayer." (Tibrani)

In addition to that the Holy Prophet [S.A.W.] affirmed: "Allah considers nothing as nobler and as more honourable than prayer." (Tirmidhi)

The most luminous trait of the believer is that in distress or ease, pain or pleasure, poverty or prosperity, adversity or luxury—under all souls of condition he turns to Allah only and presents his needs to Him alone and prays to Him regularly for grace.

The Holy Prophet [S.A.W.] observed:

"The person who does not pray to Allah invokes wrath of Allah." (Tirmidhi)

10. Put complete faith in Allah as to the acceptance of your prayer. Never commit the blunder of renouncing prayer in desperation if quick results of the acceptance of your prayer are not forthcoming. Concentrate on offering prayer instead of feeling anxious about the acceptance of your prayer.

Hadrat 'Umar [R.A.A.] observed:

"I am not concerned about the acceptance of my prayer. I am only anxious to pray. When the favour of offering a prayer has been granted to me, the acceptance will also be granted."

The Holy Prophet [S.A.W.] observed:

"When a Muslim turns towards Allah to ask for some favour, Allah inevitably supplies his want. Either his wish is granted or Allah adds the thing desired to the balance of reward which the Muslim will receive in the eternal world. On the Day of Judgement, Allah shall summon a pious man to His Presence and enquire from him face to face: "O My slave! I commanded you to pray and promised that I shall grant your prayer. Did you then offer prayer?" The man will submit: "Yes, I offered prayer." Allah will then observe: "I granted whatever prayer you offered. Did you not pray to Me on that day for the alleviation of sorrow and pain which had seized you and I had succoured you." The slave will submit: "True, O Creator." Allah then will observe: "I granted that prayer and fulfilled that desire of yours in the mortal world. But on the other day you were struck by another calamity and you prayed to Me for succour, but you found none and, therefore, continued to labour under pain and sorrow." The slave will submit: "Yes, it is true beyond doubt, My Creator." Thereupon Allah will observe: "In Paradise many bounties have I reserved for you in reward for that prayer,"-and in the same manner Allah shall ascertain other needs and make a similar observation in regard to all of them."

Afterwards, the Holy Prophet [S.A.W.] observed:

"There shall not be a single prayer offered by a pious person concerning which Allah will not state. "I granted this prayer of yours in the world and I added that desire of yours to the balance of your reward in eternity." The pious person will ponder then: "Would that none of my prayers had been granted in the mortal world! Hence the servant should continue to pray under all conditions." (Hakim)

11. Observe all external etiquettes, purity and cleanliness at the time of prayer. Keep your heart clear of all evil passions, illicit designs and absurd beliefs.

The Holy Quran affirms:

"Truly, they are the favourites of Allah who repent most and those others who keep themselves pure and clean."

In Surah Muddaththir, Allah enjoins:

"Thy Lord magnify and thy raiment purify."

12. Offer prayer for others also, but begin with yourself. Seek favour for yourself first and then for others too. The Holy Quran reproduces two prayers offered by Hadrat Ibrahim and Hadrat Nuh [A.S.] which bear the above moral:

"My Lord! Make me to establish proper worship and sons of my posterity (also) our Lord! and accept the prayer. Our Lord! Forgive me and my parents and believers on the day when the account is cast."

(14: 40, 41)

"My Lord! Forgive me and my parents and him who entereth my house believing, and believing men and believing women." (71: 28)

Hadrat Ubay b. Kaab [R.A.A.) reports:

"Whenever the Holy Prophet [S.A.W.] happened to mention some person, he [S.A.W.] used to offer a prayer for that person and commenced the prayer by asking Allah's favour for himself first."

(Tirmidhi)

13. If you are acting as leader in the prayer, you should always offer prayer on behalf of the whole congregation using plural parts of speech. The prayers which have been reproduced in the Holy Quran generally contain plural parts of speech. The leader in fact is the spokesman for the whole congregation. When he utters a prayer using plurals, the congregation should say 'Amin' at the end of each prayer offered by them.

14. Avoid prejudice and selfishness in prayer. Do not fall into the error of considering the vast and common blessing of Allah as limited and thus praying for the grant of His Grace and Bounty to you especially.

Hadrat Abu Hurrayrah [R.A.A.] relates: "A Beduin entered the mosque of the Prophet [S.A.W.] and said his prayer and then said: "O Allah: Grant your favour to me and to Muhammad [S.A.W.] and to none else besides us." On hearing this, the Holy Prophet [S.A.W.] observed:

"You have narrowed the vast limits of Allah's blessings." (Bukhari)

15. Avoid formal and conscious rhyming in prayer. Utter your prayer in a simple manner with profound sincerity. Abstain from singing or rhyming. However, it does not matter if by chance your tongue does utter a rhymed speech or an alliteration. A few such prayers as have an informal rhyme and perfect balance in stress are reported to have been uttered by the Holy Prophet [S.A.W.]. For instance, Hadrat Zaid b. Arqam has reported a very comprehensive prayer offered by the Holy Prophet [S.A.W.]:

"Allah I seek Thy refuge from the heart which is devoid of Thy fear, from the being that lacks contentment, from the knowledge that is unprofitable and from the prayer which is unacceptable."

(Tirmidhi)

16. Offer praise and thanksgiving to the Lord before putting your needs and requirements before Him. Afterwards, say two Rakats of supplementary prayer and say (Darood) 'peace and blessings be on the Holy Prophet' at the beginning and end of your prayer.

The Holy Prophet [S.A.W.] has observed:

"At times when a person seeks the favour of Allah or the assistance of man in connection with some need or requirement, the needy person should perform ablution, say two Rakats of prayer, offer praise and thanksgiving to Allah and say (Darood) 'peace and blessings of Allah be on the Holy Prophet'. (Afterwards, he should put his need before Allah)."

(Tirmidhi)

The Holy Prophet [S.A.W.] affirmed the fact that the prayer of a man which is accompanied by praise and thanksgiving to Allah and by the invocation of Allah's peace and blessings on the person of the Holy Prophet is granted the honour of fulfilment. Hadrat Fadala

[R.A.A.] narrates: "The Holy Prophet [S.A.W.] was seated in the mosque when a man entered, performed the worship and at the end uttered. Allahummaghfirli (Allah grant me pardon). On hearing this, the Holy Prophet [S.A.W.] said to the man: "You were rather quick in offering the prayer. When the worship is over, you should first of all render praise and thanksgiving to the Allah, invoke peace and blessings upon the Prophet and finally say your prayers. As the Holy Prophet [S.A.W.] was speaking to the person, another man came in, offered worship and at the end, rendered praise to Allah and invoked His peace and blessings upon the Holy Prophet. The Holy Prophet, thereupon, observed to him: "Now say your prayer, it shall be granted." (Tirmidhi)

17. Offer prayer to Allah at all times and at every step, for He is never tired of hearing the prayers of His slaves. However, traditions reveal to us that there are certain special times and circumstances in which prayers are accepted very soon. Hence, do not miss the opportunity of offering prayer at these hours and circumstances:

    (i) In the stillness of the latter part of night when most people are enjoying sweet slumber, the man who gets up and engages in communion with Allah and places his needs before Allah in sincere humility shall be blessed with special favour of Allah.

"Allah holds court on the sky of the world every night. When the latter part of the night begins Allah observes, "Who calls Me? I will accept his prayer. Who begs ? I will fulfil his need. Who asks for salvation? I will grant him salvation."

(Tirmidhi)

    (ii) Offer the maximum number of prayers in the night of *Shab qadr,* for in auspiciousness this night is better than a thousand months. Say the following prayer especially:

"Allah: Thou art All-Forgiving. Thou likest showing Mercy the best. Hence Forgive me."

(iii) In the field of Arafat when the 'guests of Allah' assemble there on the 6th Dhul-Hajja. (Tirmidhi)

(iv) At particular moment on Friday which falls between the commencement of the sermon and end of the worship or from the time when the 'Asr prayer is over till the hour of the Maghrib prayer.

(v) At the hour of announcement of the Prayer-Call and at the time when the Holy warriors are being lined up for battle in the field.

The Holy Prophet [S.A.W.] has observed:

"Two things are never repulsed from the Court of Allah. One, the prayer offered at the hour of the announcement of Prayer-Call. Second, the prayer uttered at the time of lining up for battle in the field." (Abu Daud)

(vi) In the interval between the announcement of the Prayer Call and the Takbir.

"The Holy Prophet [S.A.W.] observed:

"The prayer offered in the interval between the Adaan (Prayer-Call) and the Iqamah is never rejected." The illustrious companions [R.A.A.] submitted: O, Prophet of Allah, what should we pray during this period. The Holy Prophet observed: Say this prayer.

"Allah! I implore of Thee forgiveness, kindness and protection in this world and in eternity."

(vii) During the auspicious days of Ramadan and specially at the time of breaking fast (Bazaz)

(viii) After the performance of obligatory prayers whether you offer prayer individually or in a congregation.

(ix) In the state of prostration.

The Holy Prophet [S.A.W.] has observed:

"In the state of prostration, the slave gains the nearest proximity to his Allah. Hence offer the optimum prayer while you are lying in prostration before Allah."

(x) When you are seized by a serious calamity or the deepest sorrow and pain. (Hakam)

(xi) When a religious assemblage takes place for the purpose of remembrance and worship of Allah. (Bukhari, Muslim)

(xii) When a reading of the Holy Quran is completed. (Tibrani)

18. Offer prayers at the following places, especially. On the eve of his departure from Mecca to Basra, Hadrat Hasan Basri [R.T.A.] wrote a letter to the residents of Mecca stating the importance of putting up in Mecca and the favours thereof and also clearly mentioned that prayers offered at the following fifteen places in Mecca are especially accepted by Allah:

(i) Near the Multazim (ii) Below the Mizab (iii) Inside the Kaaba (iv) Near the fount of Zam Zam (v) At Safa and Marwa (vi) Near Safa and Marwa at the place where 'Sai' is performed (vii) At the rear of the 'Place of Ibrahim' (viii) In 'Arafat (ix) In Muzdalfa (x) In Mina (xi) Near the three Jamarat. (Hisn Hassin)

19. Make constant efforts to memorise the same words of prayer to Allah as are contained in the Holy Quran and the Traditions of the Holy Prophet [S.A.W.]. It is clear that no better words of prayer and no better manner of offering prayer can be found than that which Allah taught to His Prophet [S.A.W.] and to His pious slaves

[R.A.A.]. Besides there is no speech which can possibly surpass the word taught by Allah and adopted by His Messengers in effect, sweetness, comprehensiveness, grace and acceptability! The repetition of the prayers taught by the Holy Quran and the Traditions and a thoughtful consideration of their meanings trains and educates one's mind as to what wishes and prayers should a pious person entertain. What deeds are worthy of his striving and what goals should he set for himself. There is no doubt that prayer transcends all barriers of language, style. It is, however, a supplementary Blessing of Allah that He has revealed to us what to ask for and in what manner by prescribing words of prayer. Moreover, Allah taught the pious what attitude to adopt for achieving grace in religion and in secular matters and what wishes and aspirations should a pious man entertain in his heart. There is no religious or secular need as well as there is no aspect of grace, for which a prayer has not been prescribed. It is more propitious, therefore, that you should pray to Allah in those words which are contained in the Holy Quran and the Traditions and you should repeat only those prayers which are incorporated in the Quran or those which were uttered at various times by the Holy Prophet [S.A.W.] himself.

However, until such time as you take into memory the words of the prayers contained in the Holy Quran and the Traditions, you ought at least to reproduce their sense in your prayers.

We reproduce in the following pages some comprehensive prayers from the Holy Quran as well as from the Traditions of the Holy Prophet [S.A.W.]. You should learn these prayers by heart gradually and then repeat only these prayers afterwards.

Special Prayers

Prayer for Mercy and Forgiveness : Our Allah! We have wronged ourselves. If Thou forgive us not and have not mercy on us, surely we are of the lost. (7.23)

No doubt unless Allah absolves man of his sins and showers endless Mercy on him, man will go to ruin.

Prayer for Grace in Both the Worlds : Our Allah! Give unto us in the world that which is good and in the Hereafter that which is good and guard us from the doom of the Fire. (2: 201)

Prayer for Forbearance and Fortitude : Our Allah! Bestow on as endurance, make our foothold sure, and give us help against the disbelieving folk. (2: 250)

Prayer for Protection Against the Mischief of the Devil : My Allah! I seek refuge in Thee from suggestions of the evil ones and I seek refuge in Thee, my Lord! lest they be present with me. *(23: 97, 98)*

Prayer for Protection Against the Torment of Hell : Our Allah! Avert from us the doom of hell: Lo! the doom thereof is anguish. Lo! it is wretched as abode and station. (25: 65, 66)

Prayer for the Correction of Heart : Our Allah! Cause not our hearts to stray after Thou halt guided us, and bestow upon us mercy from Thy presence. Lo! Thou, only Thou art the Bestower. (3: 8)

Prayer for the Purification of Heart : Our Allah! Forgive us and our brethren who were before us in the faith, and place not in our hearts any rancour towards those who believe. Our Allah! Thou art full of pity, Merciful. *(59: 10)*

Prayer for Favourable Turn of Events : "Our Allah! Give mercy from Thy presence and shape for us right conduct in our plight." (18: 10)

Prayer for Salvation : Our Allah! We believe therefore forgive us and have mercy on us for Thou art best of all who show mercy. (23: 109)

Prayer for the Grant of Satisfaction and Peace in the Family : Our Allah! Vouchsafe us comfort of our wives and of our offspring, and make us patterns for (all) those who ward off (evil). (25: 74)

In other words, grant us such a pure and noble life that the pious should take us as a model and emulate our example.

Prayer for Parents : Our Allah! Forgive me and my parents and the believers on the day when the account is cast. (14: 41)

Prayer for Protection from Trials and Tribulations : Our Allah! Condemn us not if we forget or err: Our Allah! Lay not on us such a burden as Thou didst lay on those before us: Our Allah! Impose on us that which we have not the strength to bear: Pardon us, absolve us and have mercy on us. Thou art our Protector and give us victory over the disbelieving folk. (2: 286)

Prayer for Getting Rid of the Disbelievers' Domination : In Allah we put trust. Our Allah! Oh, make us not a lure for the wrongdoing folk. And of Thy mercy, save us from the folk that disbelieve. (10: 85)

Prayer for a Propitious End : Creator of the heavens and the earth Thou art my protecting Friend in the world and the Hereafter. Make me to die submissive (unto Thee), and join me to the righteous. (10: 101)

Our Allah! Lo! We have heard a crier calling unto Faith: Believe ye in your Lord! So we believed Our Lord! Therefore forgive us our sins, and remit from us our evil deeds and make us die the death of the righteous. Our Allah! And give us that which Thou hast promised to us by Thy messengers. Confound us not upon the Day of Resurrection. Lo! Thou breakest not the trust. (2: 193, 94)

Some Prayers of the Holy Prophet [S.A.W.] : The Muhaddithin (Reporters of Traditions) have worked hard and devoted whole of their lives in collecting and compiling the books of Traditions, the prayers which the Holy Prophet [S.A.W.] used to offer during journeys and in camp. Along with the prayers incorporated in the Holy Quran, you should also utter these prayers of the Holy Prophet [S.A.W.]. These prayers are not only comprehensive, impressive and propitious, but also teach the correct thinking to the believer as well as the desires and ambitions he should cherish. In fact, a man's real nature is reflected in his desires, especially moments when he is satisfied that no other human being is present and that his murmur can only be heard by his Creator. Each word of the prayers offered by the Holy Prophet [S.A.W.] in the darkness of the night, in privacy, in the midst and outside the company of the people, is characterised by profound sincerity, devotion and eagerness and one feels that the utterer of such prayers is the most exalted person who is perfectly aware of his status as the servant of Allah and he constantly begs from his Allah as a needy person. Moreover, his eagerness and devotion is constantly increasing in depth and intensity as he continues to offer prayers to Allah. The essence of all his prayers is as follows: "Allah! Draw me closer! Spare me from Thy wrath! Bestow upon me Thy favour! Give me success and grace in Eternity."

Prayers to be Offered in the Morning and Evening : Hadrat 'Uthman b. 'Affan [R.A.A.] narrates: "The Holy Prophet [S.A.W.] observed: No harm can come to a man from anything who utters the following prayer morning and evening":

> In the name of Allah by virtue of Whose name naught in the heaven nor earth doth hurt and He is the Hearer the Knower.
>
> (Musnad Ahmad)

Hadrat 'Abdullah b. 'Umar [R.A.A.] reports: "The Holy Prophet [S.A.W.] used to offer the following prayer in the morning and evening regularly without respite":

> O Allah! Behold, I beg to Thee peace in this world and the Hereafter. O Allah! Behold, I beg of Thee forgiveness and safety in my faith, in my world, in mine household and in my wealth. O Allah! cover my defects and give me peace from my apprehension. O Allah! protect me from my front and from my rear, from my right and from my left also from above me; and I seek refuge in Thee lest I be surprised from beneath me! (Tirmidhi)

Prayer Against Lethargy and Cowardice : Hadrat Anas b. Malik [R.A.A.] states:

"I used to remain in attendance on the Holy Prophet [S.A.W.] and I used to hear him offer this prayer very often:

"O Allah! Behold, I seek refuge in Thee from anxiety and grief, from inability and sloth, from faint heartedness and niggardliness, from the burden of indebtedness and the domination of men. (Bukhari, Muslim)

Prayer for the Attainment of Piety and Purity : O Allah! Behold! I beg of Thee, guidance, piety, purity and contentment. This is the most comprehensive prayer. In these four words the Holy Prophet [S.A.W.] has asked for everything that a believer needs.

Prayer for Protection Against Degradation in this World and the Hereafter : "Allah! End all our activities in grace and protect us from the torment of degradation in this world and in the Hereafter." (Tibrani)

Prayer to be Offered after Worship : Hadrat Muadh [R.A.A.] states that one day the Holy Prophet [S.A.W.] took my hand and observed: "O Muadh! I love thee', and then proceeded to affirm: "O Muadh! I advise you that you should never miss uttering the following words after each prayer:

"O Allah! help me in remembering Thee, in expressing gratitude to Thee and in worshipping Thee in the best manner."

Will of the Holy Prophet [S.A.W.] : Hadrat Shaddad b. Aus [R.A.A.] states: "The Holy Prophet [S.A.W.] advised me: Shaddad! when you see the worldly people busy in amassing gold and silver, you should gather the blissful treasure by uttering the following words off and on":

"O Allah! Behold, I beg of Thee steadfastness in keeping (Thy) command and firmness of resolution in (pursuing) the right course. I beg of Thee (the feeling of) thankfulness for Thy grace and (ability for) adoring Thee best. I beg of Thee a sound heart and a truthful tongue. I beg of Thee the good of that which Thee knowest, and I seek refuge in Thee from the evil which Thee knowest. I seek Thy forgiveness for all of my wrongs thou knowest. No doubt Thou knowest all that is unknown to us. (Musnad Ahmad)

Prayer for Forgiveness and the Favour of Allah : Hadrat Abu Hurrayrah [R.A.A.] states that the Holy Prophet [S.A.W.] while bequeathing a will to Hadrat Salman Farsi [R.A.A.], had observed: "I wish to bequeath a few words to you. Beseech the Most Kind in these words. Rush towards the Most Kind and offer prayer to Him in these words day and night:

"O Allah! Behold! I beg of Thee vigour and health in my faith and effect of faith in my dealings and behaviour and success leading to peace and mercy from Thee; and also security, forgiveness and Thy pleasure." (Tibrani, Hakam)

Prayer for Purification from Sins : Hadrat Umm Salama [R.A.A.] narrates: "The Holy Prophet [S.A.W.] used to offer the following prayer:

"O Allah! clean my heart from sins, just as you clean white cloth of dirt. O Allah! cause as great a distance between me and my faults, as there is between East and West. (Muljam Kabir)

Prayer for the Attainment of Respect Among the People : O Allah! make me patient and thankful to Thee, and make me small in my own eyes, but great in other people's eyes.

A Comprehensive Prayer : Hadrat 'Aishah [R.A.A.] states: "It so happened once that when the Holy Prophet [S.A.W.] came to see me I was engaged in offering worship. The Holy Prophet [S.A.W.] needed me immediately but I was delayed, whereupon the Holy Prophet [S.A.W.] observed: 'Aishah, you should utter brief and comprehensive prayers. When I came to the Holy Prophet [S.A.W.] I submitted: "O Messenger of Allah [S.A.W.]! Teach me a brief and comprehensive prayer." The Holy Prophet [S.A.W.] observed: "You should utter the following prayer:

> O Allah! I ask of Thee all the good which is in the present or in the future, and I ask of Thee paradise, and the works and deeds, which would take me nearer to the same, and I seek refuge in Thee from Fire and the works and deeds which would take me nearer to the same. And I ask of Thee that which was sought by Muhammad, and I seek refuge in Thee from that regarding which Muhammad sought Thy Protection, and that the end of all Thy decrees above me should be good." (Hakam)

Prayer for Holding firm to Islam : O Allah! maintain my faith in Islam, while I am standing or while I am sitting or while I am lying and let not the enemy, the envious pass sarcastic remarks about me.

Prayer of a new Convert to Islam : Hadrat Abu Malik Ashja [R.A.A.] reports: "My father narrated that whenever a person embraced the religion of Islam, the Holy Prophet [S.A.W.] used to teach him Salat and also the following prayer:

"O Allah! forgive me, have mercy on me, guide me, grant me peace and give me sustenance."

Prayer for the Avoidance of Dissensions and Immorality : O Allah! I seek refuge in Thee from evil morals, deeds and desires. O Allah! Behold, I seek refuge in Thee from schism, hypocrisy and evil morals.

Invocation of Peace and Blessings on the Holy Prophet [S.A.W.] : Invoke peace and blessings of Allah upon your venerable benefactor Hadrat Muhammad [S.A.W.]. Truly, we can make no recompense for his countless favours and limitless love and affection. What we can do, however, is to invoke the peace and blessings of Allah on him with the deepest sense of reverence, love, devotion and loyalty to his person. We should pray to Allah, "Creator! Your Messenger [S.A.W.] had to suffer terrible torments in his task of communicating your message to us. He [S.A.W.] took great pains to guide us on the path of righteousness. Creator! We can make no return for this favour. We implore You, O Creator! to shower Your boundless benefactions upon the Prophet [S.A.W.], to exalt him in Your favour; to protect his religion from the onslaught of falsehood; to extend his religion and to bestow upon him a higher rank than all other favourite companions of Yours in the eternal world." The Holy Quran enjoins upon the Muslims:

"Lo! Allah and his angels, shower blessings on the Prophet. O ye who believe! Ask blessings on him and salute him with a worthy salutation." (33: 56)

The Holy Prophet [S.A.W.] observed to Hadrat Ubay bin Kaab [R.A.A.]:

"Ubay! If you devote all your time to invoking peace and blessings of Allah upon the Prophet, Allah shall take it upon Himself to provide for your sustenance in this world and in eternity."

(Musnad Ahmad)

Hadrat Anas b. Malik [R.A.A.] narrates that the Holy Prophet [S.A.W.] observed:

"A person who invokes peace and blessings of Allah on me is recompensed by Allah in the following manner:

> "Allah showers blessings on him ten times. Allah adds ten virtues and erases ten vices from his record of deeds. And Allah elevates his rank by ten grades." (Nasai)

In addition to this, the Holy Prophet [S.A.W.] affirmed:

> "The angels continue to invoke the blessings of Allah upon a man as long as he devotes himself to invoking peace and blessing of Allah upon me." (Ahmad and Ibn Majah)

The Holy Prophet [S.A.W.] observed:

> "The man who hears my name mentioned yet fails to invoke the peace and blessings of Allah on me is a miser." (Tirmidhi)

The Holy Prophet [S.A.W.] declared the person most deserving of the honour of his companionship and attendance in the life Hereafter who invokes the peace and blessings of Allah on him the most.

The Holy Prophet [S.A.W.] observed:

> "The person who invokes peace and blessings of Allah on me the most, will be the best deserving my companionship and attendance on the Day of Judgement." (Tirmidhi)

There is a slight variation in the wordings of the texts of the invocation of peace and blessings of Allah which the Holy Prophet [S.A.W.] taught to the illustrious companions [R.A.A.] on various occasions. You may use any of these texts. The text which is generally recited in worship and which has been declared as the most propitious one by Hadrat 'Abdullah b. 'Abbas [R.A.A.] is as follows:

> "O Allah! Shower Thy mercy upon Muhammad and the followers of Muhammad, as thou didst shower Thy mercy upon Ibrahim and the followers of Ibrahim! Behold Thou art Praiseworthy, Glorious! O Allah! shower Thy blessing upon Muhammad and the followers of Muhammad, as Thou didst shower Thy blessings upon Ibrahim and the followers of Ibrahim. Behold, Thou art Praiseworthy, Glorious."
>
> (Sihah Sitta, Musnad Ahmad)

Hadrat 'Abdullah b. Masud [R.A.A.] observed to the people: "You should invoke peace and blessings of Allah on the Holy Prophet in a proper manner. Who knows this invocation may be presented before the Holy Prophet [S.A.W.]?" The people requested him to teach the proper invocation to them. Thereupon he observed: "You should recite the invocation thus:"

> "Allah! Shower Your favour, blessing and benefactions upon the lord of Prophets, leader of the pious and the seal of Prophets, Muhammad who is Your servant, Your Messenger of Blessings. Allah, elevate him to an exalted position which may be the envy of his predecessors. Allah! Show Your blessings to Muhammad and the progeny of Muhammad as you blessed Ibrahim and the progeny of Ibrahim. Truly, You possess the purest attributes and are Great. Allah! Show Your favour to Muhammad and the progeny of Muhammad as You showered favour on Ibrahim and the progeny of Ibrahim. Truly, you possess the purest attributes and are Great." (Ibn Majah)

Hadrat Abu Masud Ansari [R.A.A.] narrates: "Once Bashir bin Saad [R.A.A.] submitted to the Holy Prophet [S.A.W.]: In what manner should we invoke peace and blessings of Allah on you? The Holy Prophet [S.A.W.] remained silent for a while and then observed: Say these words:

O Allah! shower Thy mercy upon Muhammad and the followers of Muhammad as Thou didst shower Thy mercy upon the followers of Ibrahim! Behold! Thou art Praiseworthy, Glorious. O Allah! shower Thy blessings upon Muhammad and the followers of Muhammad, as Thou didst shower Thy blessings upon Ibrahim in the worlds. Behold Thou art Praiseworthy, Glorious.

Supplication of Sacrifice : Lay down the animal parallel with the direction of the Qibla and utter the following prayer first:

Behold I have turned my face earnestly towards Him Who originated the heavens and the earth and I am not of polytheists. Behold, my salat, my offering, my living and my dying are all for Allah, Lord of the worlds. No partners hath He, concerning this I have been bidden and I am of the Muslims O Allah! (I offer this) to you and You gave it to me.

After reciting this prayer, Say *'Bismillahi Allahu Akbar'*. (In the name of Allah Who is Great) and cut the throat of the animal with a sharp-edged knife. Having performed the slaughter read this prayer:

"Allah' Accept this sacrifice offered by me as Thou accepted the sacrifice offered by Thy friend Ibrahim and that offered by Thy loved one Muhammad. May peace and blessings descend upon both."

Although it is permissible to let someone else perform the slaughter of your sacrificial animal, yet it is better if you perform this act with your own hands. While you perform the slaughter, try to think and feel in the same way as you express through the words you utter at the time of sacrificing the animal i.e., all that we have got belongs to Allah and it is all to be spent in His way only. The act of sacrificing the animal in His name is in submission to His will and if ever required we shall readily sacrifice even our own life in the way of Allah and shall be grateful to Him that He conferred upon us the honour of martyrdom by affording us an opportunity to shed our blood in His name.

Aqiqa Prayer : 'Aqiqa' refers to the goat or ram which is sacrificed on behalf of a newborn child on the seventh day after his birth.

The Holy Prophet [S.A.W.] observed;

"On the seventh day a name should be prescribed for the child. Its hair and all filth should be removed and sacrifice should be performed on his behalf."

Before sacrificing the animal, first make it lie down parallel with the direction of the Qibla and recite the prayer which is uttered at the slaughter of a sacrificial animal i.e. from his wards say and cut the throat of the animal with a sharp edged knife and then recite the following prayers:

> "O Allah! This is the 'Aqiqah of .... Accept it as Thou accepted the 'Aqiqah offered by Thy loved one Muhammad [S.A.W.] and by Thy friend Ibrahim [A.S.]. The blood of this sacrifice is ransom for the blood of the child; its flesh is the ran some for the flesh of the child, its hair are a ransom for the child's hair and its bones are ransom for the child's bones. Allah! Accept it."

The people who possess means must offer sacrifice on behalf of their children. 'Aqiqah is a desirable sacrifice. Two lambs or goats on behalf of the male child and a single goat or lamb on behalf of the female. It is permissible also to sacrifice a single goat on behalf of a boy. However for those who lack means, it is certainly improper to perform the sacrifice by begging loans.

Non-cooked 'Aqiqah meat may be distributed. It is preferable, however, to send cooked meat to the beggars, the poor and your neighbours. On the eve of the *'Aqiqah* of Hadrat Hasan [R A.A.] the Holy Prophet [S.A.W.] instructed: "Send one chopped leg of the animal to the midwife and eat the rest yourself and feed others." (Abu Daud)

Taravih Prayer : The word 'Taravih' is the plural form of 'Tarviha'. 'Tarviha' denotes the period of rest and relaxation at the end of every four Rakats of prayer. It is in this context that this supplementary prayer of the month of Ramadan is called 'Taravih'. Tarviha, i. e. to pause and relax at the end of every four Rakats of prayer, is a Sunnah.

The following prayer should be recited during *'Tarviha'*:

> "Pure is the Ruler and the Sovereign. Pure is the Exalted and the Supreme, the Awesome and the Powerful and the Great Wielder of Authority. Pure is the Immortal Sovereign Who neither sleeps, nor will ever die. Purest and free from all blemishes is our Sustainer Who is the Provider of angels and of Jibbrail.
>
> Allah! Grant us asylum from the Fire of Hell. O Protector, O Protector, O Protector."

Offer the 'Taravih' prayer in congregation and if possible listen to the recitation of the full text of the Holy Quran during *'Namaz'*. Offer 'Taravih' behind a 'Hafiz' (the one who has memorised the full text of the Holy Quran) who recites the Quran with full reverence, devotion and eagerness in moderate pace and with proper pauses and correct accents so that the listeners do not get tired and the Quran may be recited so clearly as to make every word of it audible and distinct. It is a great injustice with the Holy Quran to read it rapidly without understanding as if you are trying to get rid of a burden. The Book of Allah deserves to be read with a will, devotion and concentration pondering over its meaning and implications and trying to grasp its real sense and spirit.

Similarly the 'Taravih' prayer must be offered with ease and concentration showing no haste and hurry. To perform

Ruku and Sajda (Prostration) in rapid succession without knowing what is being uttered amounts to sheer disregard of the objectives of prayer and missing the relish of real taste and enjoyment of worship.

Qunut-i-Nazila : Whenever, Allah forbid, the Muslims are faced with a critical situation and the menace and terror of the enemy has overcome them, they should recite Qunut-i-Nazila during prayers, especially in the course of the dawn prayer (Fajr). In the second Rakat of the morning prayers, after performing the Ruku' recite the following prayer in the standing posture before performing the prostration. Traditions reveal that this prayer was recited during worship by the Holy Prophet [S.A.W.] and his illustrious Companions [R.A.A.] at critical times, they offered this prayer especially during morning worship:

> O Allah! guide us amongst those whom Thou hast guided aright, and preserve us among those whom thou hast preserved. Include us amongst those whom Thou hast taken under Thy protection. Bless us in that which Thou hast bestowed upon us and protect us from the evil of that which Thou hast ordained, for it is Thou Who ordainest and none can ordain against Thee indeed! Never is he abased whom Thou takest as friend and none is respected whom Thou takest as a foe. Blessed art Thou Our Allah and exalted. We ask repentance from Thee and turn to Thee; O Allah! send torment upon the unbelievers, who prevent us from following Thy way and refute Thy messengers, and fight against Thy friends. Allah! grant forgiveness to us and to the Faithful males and females and Muslim men and women and bring reconciliation among them and foster affection (for one another) in their hearts and bless them with conviction and insight and make them firm and unwavering followers of the Holy

Prophet [S.A.W.] and enable them to fulfil the pledge You have taken from them; help them against Thy enemies and against their enemies. O Real Deity! hear our prayers and deal us with these people!"

Prayer for the Fulfilment of a Need : Whenever any need, big or small, arises, you should stand before Allah and offer two Rakahs of supererogatory prayer, (Salạt al Hajat). Afterwards, offer thanksgiving and praise to Allah and invoke peace and blessings upon the Holy Prophet [S.A.W.]. Then utter the following prayer. There is every hope that Allah will not reject your prayer. The Holy Prophet [S.A.W.] observed:

"When someone seeks fulfilment of a need from Allah or man, he should first carefully perform ablution, say two Rakats of supererogatory prayer and then offer thanksgiving and praise to the Lord; afterwards, he should invoke peace and blessings of Allah on the Holy Prophet; [S.A.W.] and finally utter this prayer to Allah:

"There is no deity save Allah the Clement the Bountiful. Glory be to Allah, Lord of the Magnificent Throne! Praise be to Allah, Lord of the Worlds! I beg of Thee the means of (obtaining) Thy mercy and securing Thy pardon; participation in every righteousness and protection from every sin. Leave no sin of mine unforgiven no anxiety unrelieved and let no need of mine unfulfilled wherewith Thou art pleased. O Thou the Most Merciful of Those who show mercy! (Tirmidhi, Ibn Majah)

Prayer for Memorising the Quran : To learn the Holy Quran by heart and to memorise its text for ever you should offer the prayer which was taught to Hadrat 'Ali [R.A.A.] by the Holy Prophet [S.A.W.].

Hadrat 'Abdullah b. 'Abbas [R.A.A.] reports: "Once we

were sitting in the company of the Holy Prophet [S.A.W.] when 'Ali [R.A.A.] arrived and complained about his memory: O Messenger of Allah [S.A.W.]! My mind does not retain the verses of the Quran. I cannot remember what I have learnt previously." The Holy Prophet [S.A.W.] observed:

> "O Abul Hassan! Let me teach you a prayer which will be of benefit to you and to those whom you will teach this prayer and having learnt this prayer whatever you commit to memory shall be retained and you shall always remember it." Hadrat 'Ali [R.A.A.] submitted: "O Messenger of Allah [S.A.W.]! Do teach me this prayer" Whereupon the Holy Prophet [S.A.W.] observed concerning this prayer: "Say this prayer on Friday night and offer it on three, five or seven Thursday nights in succession. By the Will of Allah, this prayer will prove efficacious, I swear by His Name Who has entrusted me with the Religion of Truth, this prayer by the believers never goes unanswered."

Continuing his narration, Hadrat 'Abdullah b. 'Abbas [R.A.A.] says: "Five or seven Thursday nights had passed when Hadrat 'Ali [R.A.A.] came to the company of the Holy Prophet [S.A.W.] and submitted: "O Messenger of Allah [S.A.W.] Before this whenever I memorised four verses, my memory failed me when I tried to I reproduce them. Now, however, the position is that I memorise forty verses and when I wish to reproduce them, it appears as if the Book of Allah is lying open before me. Similarly, I used to hear a tradition and later failed to reproduce it, but now I hear several traditions and retain them so well that I hardly miss a single word while reproducing those traditions."

On hearing this, the Holy Prophet Muhammad [S.A.W.] observed: "I swear by the Lord of Kaaba that Abul Hassan is a true believer."

Giving detailed instructions about this prayer, the Holy Prophet [S.A.W.] observed: "Say this prayer on Friday night. When the sons of my brother Yaqub requested him to pray for their redemption, Ya'qub replied: "Yes, I shall offer a prayer for your redemption shortly." Ya'qub meant that he would pray for their redemption on the next Friday night. So 'Ali! Rise at the hour of 'Tahajjud' on Friday night, for this is the most propitious time for the fulfilment of prayer; one's soul is eager at this time and the heart is fully devoted to Allah. If perchance you are unable to rise in the later part of the night, get up at midnight.

If you can't wake up at midnight, then offer four Rakahs of supererogatory prayer in the first part of the night in the following order: In the first Rakat, recite Surah Fatiha and after this Surah Yaseen; in the second Rakat, recite Surah Fatiha and Surah Ad-Dukhan, in the third Rakat, read Surah Fatiha with Surah Alif Lam Mim Sajdah; and in the fourth Rakat, recite Surah Mulk, after Surah Fatiha. Afterwards, having recited 'Attahiyyat and offered Salam on both sides, offer thanks to Allah and praise Him. Invoke Allah's peace and blessings upon the Holy Prophet and all other Messengers in a proper manner. Implore Him to grant redemption to all the believing men and believing women and offer prayer for the salvation of those brethren who preceded you in faith. And finally say this prayer:

> "O Allah! Be thou gracious unto me by enabling me to eschew sins altogether as long as Thou sufferest me to live; and have mercy upon me lest I concern myself with ought which is of no consequence to me. And vouchsafe me the aesthetic sight which will cause Thee to be well pleased with me."

"O Allah! Originator of the heavens and the earth Lord of Majesty and Glory and of Might is comprehensible! I beseech Thee O Allah' O Beneficent Allah in the name of Thy Majesty and of the Light of Thy countenance to cause mine beau to retain Thy explaint as Thou hast taught to me. And grant that I may recite it in such manner as will cause Thee to be well pleased with me. O Allah, Originator of the heavens and the earth, Lord of Majesty and Bounty and of Might Who is unchallengeable. I beseech Thee O Allah, O Beneficent Allah! in the name of Thy Majesty and of the Light of Thy countenance, to illuminate my sight with Thy scripture, make my tongue fluent with its words to comfort mine heart therewith, to make me fully receptive to it and to wash my body clean with its blessings. For indeed, none aideth me in (attaining) the truth besides Thee and now giveth it unto me besides 'Thee. There is no strength nor power save in Allah, the Exalted, the Magnificent."

Prayer for Gaining Understanding of the Quran : The favourite worship of the pious is to recite the Holy Quran and to meditate and reflect upon its meaning. Love of Quran is proof of attachment to Allah as it is also a means to establish communion with Allah. The believer obtains spiritual bliss by contemplating and meditating on the meanings of the Quran and it is through this process only that he secures access to the founts of wisdom contained in the Quran.

The Holy Quran is undoubtedly an easily comprehensible Book. As regards obtaining guidance from it and carrying out its injunction, the teachings of the Holy Quran are very simple, clear and free of all ambiguity or complexity of meaning. However, to grasp its inner meanings and significance and to derive wisdom from it, it is imperative that you should study the Quran after having fulfilled all the conditions and obligations for gaining comprehension of it; reflect upon its contents with sincere application and never adopt a careless and listless attitude towards the Book, but study it constantly for the rest of your life.

It is quite natural that at certain points during study, you will come across a text upon which you will deliberate long and hard without arriving at any one interpretation which your mind will accept. You will then feel at a loss. But if you are a devoted student of the Quran, don't ever feel dejected or lose heart, nor should you entertain any impudent notion of levelling criticism upon the Holy Book. And feeling hopeless, don't abandon the practice of deliberating and meditating upon the meanings of the Quran.

On the contrary, you should turn towards Allah with full concentration and reposing complete trust in Him you should seek His aid in the unravelling of this problem. Do not make an impudent bid to make a whimsical exposition of the Quran or to give it an interpretation which conforms to your ideas. Like a true seeker of Truth, stick to the meaning which the text of the Quran makes plain and pray to Allah in extreme humility and with a sense of helplessness: 'O Allah! Eliminate my confusion; make the true meaning manifest to me and let my heart be content with that interpretation and meaning which is really true'. For this purpose, recite the Holy Quran rather loudly but distinctly with pauses in the course of supererogatory prayers at night. Offer the prayer reproduced below. It is hoped from Allah that the prayer will prove efficacious.

The Holy Prophet [S.A.W.] observed: "Any person who offers this prayer while in a state of sorrow and distress, Allah shall alleviate his suffering and bestow upon him felicity and rejoicings."

"Allah! I am Thy slave. I am the son of Thy bondman and the son of Thy bondmaid. My brow is in Thy grip. I am under Thy command. Thy judgement in regard to me is just and fair. In the Name of all Attributes applicable to Thee and all Attributes which Thou hast reserved for Thyself, or those which Thou bast revealed in Thy Book, or have transmitted to one of Thy creatures or have kept them hidden in the treasury of the unseen with Thee in the Name of all these Attributes I implore Thee to make the Holy Quran the joy of my heart, the light of my bosom, a panacea for my distress and a cure of my sorrows and perplexity."

The narrator of this Tradition Hadrat 'Abdullah ibn Masud [R.A.A.] states that the people submitted to the Holy Prophet [S.A.W.]: "Shall we learn this prayer?" Whereupon the Holy Prophet [S.A.W.] observed: "Any one who hears this prayer, must learn it and memorise it."

Weekly Sermon: The Friday sermon is an extremely effective and disciplined means of arousing Islamic sentiments, keeping the Faith alive and carrying out the duty of remembering Allah constantly and in an orderly manner. It is a unique religious institution designed to remind the Muslims of their obligations each week in a perfectly natural way and to inculcate in them a sense of the requirements of religion and an impassioned spirit to serve Islam. But you can make an effective use of this institution only when you address the congregation in their vernacular.

As regards the second sermon, it must be delivered in Arabic; however, the first sermon ought to be delivered in a speech which the audience can understand. It is proper for you to prepare a brief but comprehensive address on the requirements of religion in the context of current affairs and try to develop the mind of the people and rouse them to live each week regularly and in a disciplined manner. If for some reason it is not possible for you to prepare an address yourself, you should at least read the Arabic text and deliver its meaningful translation in the vernacular of your audience. Among the Arabic texts, your best choice is a sermon delivered by the Holy Prophet [S.A.W.] or the illustrious companions [R.A.A.]. Below are reproduced quotations from the authentic speech of the Holy Prophet [S.A.W.]. One of these is the historic sermon which he [S.A.W.] delivered on the first Friday after his migration to Medina. The second address contains an eloquent call to the Muslims to acquire a deep sense of the Holy

Quran and to deliberate and ponder over its meanings constantly for it is impossible to hold on to religion without a firm attachment to the Holy Quran.

The First Sermon of the Holy Prophet [S.A.W.] in Medina:

> "Thanksgiving and Praise be to Allah. I pay Him gratitude. I invoke His aid. I beseech His Forgiveness and seek Guidance from Him; and I put my faith in Him; and I disbelieve Him not and I consider him as my enemy who disbelieve Him. And I bear witness that there is no deity except Allah; He is Alone and has no partner; and I bear testimony that Muhammad [S.A.W.] is the servant of Allah and His Apostle. Allah sent him with guidance, light and exhortation and instituted him as His Messenger at a time when the office of Prophethood had long remained dormant; the light of true knowledge had faded; evil was dominant; society was in a state of upheaval; doom was hanging overhead; and death was hovering over the head of each man. Hence he who believed in the Messenger and obeyed Allah and His Messenger was righteous. And he who defied the both went astray, transgressed limits and fell into shortsightedness and having lost the path of righteousness advanced far into wrong. I instruct you to fear Allah.
>
> The best counsel that a Muslim can offer to another Muslim is that a Muslim should persuade the other to make provision for the life Hereafter and urge him to fear Allah. Fear Allah as hath He ordained you to fear Him. Hence no exhortation is better than this, nor can there be a better reminder. The fact is that awe and fear of Allah is the real aid to secure a propitious destiny in the eternal world for the man who passes his life in constant fear of Mighty and the Exalted. Allah affirms: "My word suffers no change and I

> never do the least injustice to any of My people." Hence fear Allah in all the public and private affairs relating to this world or the life Hereafter. Verily Allah redeems the sins of a person who fears His wrath and He enhances the reward of such a person to the maximum degree. And he who constantly fears Him achieves the highest success; and behold, the fear of Allah saves man from His punishment, protects him from His wrath and behold! the fear of Allah makes your faces radiant and lively; it pleases Allah and elevates the man before Allah Almighty.

So, gather virtues of your share and never fail, or lack in submission to His Commands, especially when He has taught you what is right and what is wrong through His Book and has guided you to the right path. This is to differentiate the truthful from those who are liars. Behave well with the people, as Allah has treated you with kindness. Consider His enemies as your own, and strive hard in the way of Allah. He has chosen you and has designated you as 'Muslim' so that one who is to perish should meet his doom with manifest reason and logic and one who is to live, should live with manifest reason and all power and authority rests in Allah and Allah one.

So, ever remember and mention Allah and mind your deeds and actions keeping in view the day to come; for the man who sets the matters between him and the Almighty, Allah suffices him in all the matters between Him and the mankind because Allah decides the fate of the mankind and the mankind wields no authority over Him. Allah is the Master of every thing that men possess; men exercise no power on anything that men possess; men exercise no power on anything divine; He is Paramount and there rests no power but with Allah."

(Al- Tibri, Vol. 12, p. 255)

Advice to Develop Interest in the Quran : "Verily, thanksgiving and praise are due to Allah alone. I offer Him gratitude and praise and beg His aid; and we seek asylum with Him against our misdeeds and wrongs committed by us. Whomsoever He guideth (and he guideth only those who really look for His guidance) no one can lead him astray. Whomsoever He deflects from the right path (and He deflects only those who yearn not the guidance) no one can guide him aright."

I bear witness that there is no deity save Allah. He is Alone. He has no partner.

> Verily, the best word is the Book of Allah. Indeed, successful is he who adorns his heart with the word of Allah and whom Allah has favoured with Islam and turned him away from paganism and who preferred the word of Allah over all the human thinking and theories. Verily the word of Allah is the truth, most impressive and most effective. Love him who loves the word of Allah. Develop real love and attachment with Allah with your heart and soul. Let not the recitation of the word of Allah and remembering Him bore you and let not your hearts be indifferent and adamant to the word of Allah. Worship Allah alone; and attribute none as His partner or associate, fear Him ever to the extent He should be feared. Confirm your pious deeds by your words also i.e. say what is proper and becoming of you; and love each other for the cause of Allah and in total submission to Him. May Peace and Mercy of Allah be upon you!" (Ijaz-ul Quran)

The Second Sermon : "The praise is due to Allah, the abundant praise, and benediction and peace be upon His Messenger whom Allah has sent as a witness, a warner and an inviter towards Allah with His mandate and as a radiant light and may peace and abundant peace be on his progeny, followers and companions.

Thereafter, O mankind, I exhort you to fear Allah, for verily fear of Allah is supermost virtue and incumbent upon you is the obedience. And verily he, who obeys Allah and His Messenger, achieves great success, Allah, the Exalted, has declared in His Dignified Book (the Quran): Verily, Allah and His angels invoke Sense of Devotion benediction on the Apostle. So, O ye who believe, invoke blessings on him and seek abundant peace for him.

Allah! Bestow on our Master and our Guide Muhammad and on his progeny, followers and his companions who obeyed him in adversity. Allah! Shower Thy perfect pleasure on those who excelled (to affirm faith) amongst the emigrants and the helpers, particularly on the unanimously admitted the most excellent of mankind, next to the Prophets the Amir of the believers, our master, Abu Bakr the most truthful [R.A.A.] and on the Amir of the believers, our master Umar Al Farooq [R.A.A.] and on the Amir of the believers, our master, Uthman b. Affan [R.A.A.] and on the Amir of the believers, our master, Ali [K.A.W.] and on his two noble sons, the masters of the youth of the inmates of Paradise Hasan and Hussain [R.A.A.] and on their mother, the leader of the ladies of the paradise, Fatima-Zohra [R.A.A.] and on all companions of the Holy Prophet and their successors [R.A.A.].

Allah! Grant success to those who uphold the way of life taught by the Deen of Muhammad [S.A.W.] and make us amongst them; and humiliate those who humiliate the teachings of Muhammad [S.A.W.] and make us not amongst them. O servants of Allah! May Allah show mercy on you. Verily, Allah enjoins justice and kindness, and giving to kinsfolk, and forbids indecency, abomination and transgression. He exhorts you so that you always remember. Remember Allah, He will remember you (in adversity) Pray unto Him, He will respond to you. And remember Allah the most High, most Excellent, most Dignified most Superior, most Grand and the Greatest."

Birth Ceremony

It is propitious to read a sermon at a wedding ceremony in order to explain the significance of 'Nikah' (marriage contact) in Divine law, and to bring home to the parties the requirements and heavy responsibilities imposed by this contact. With a view to derive the maximum benefit from the sermon, it is advisable for the preacher to translate the sermon and offer a brief exegesis of the text in the vernacular so that the assembly may fully appreciate the sermon. To this end, we reproduce below the text of the Nuptial Sermon along with its translation:

> "Thanksgiving and praise are due to Allah alone, we seek aid from Him alone; and we beseech forgiveness of our sins from Him only; and we consign ourselves to the protection of Allah against the evils of our souls and against all offences: Truly, whomsoever Allah guides on the straight path (and He puts him only on the straight path who sincerely desires to walk along that way), no one can lead him astray. And whomsoever Allah deflects (and He deflects only him who yearn to be deflected), no one can put him on the straight path. And I bear witness that there is no deity except Allah and I testify that Muhammad [S.A.W.] is the bondman of Allah and His Messenger."

O Believer! Fear Allah, as He should be duly feared; and die not save you be Muslims.

O mankind! Fear the wrath of your Allah Who created you from a single soul and from it created his spouse; and from then twain bath spread (all over the world) a multitude of men and women. Fear Allah, in Whom you claim your lights from one another and (be careful in observing your duty to) the wombs (that bore you). So! Allah is Watchful over you.

> O Believer! Fear Allah constantly and utter what is fair and sound. Allah, then, will rectify your deeds

and cover up your sins with forgiveness; and whosoever obeys Allah and His Messenger, he indeed shall secure a glorious success. (Mishkat)

The Holy Prophet [S.A.W.] says:

"By Allah! I fear Allah more than all of you; I save myself from the wrath of Allah more than do all of you; but I observe fast and sometimes I do not keep fast. I say prayers at night and I sleep also; and I also take women in marriage. Hence whosoever turns away from my way, he bears no relation with me."

(Bukhari)

Guideline for Decisions : Do have 'Istikhara' on the eve of such important events of life as journey, Nikah (marriage contract), employment and in commercial matters. 'Istikhara' means 'to beseech goodness and welfare'. When your mind is in doubt as to which aspect of an important and lawful problem is propitious for you, you must perform an 'Istikhara' and, then, adopt the course suggested by your heart, taking it was the will of Allah.

Whenever you are confronted with an issue of extraordinary importance, and find it difficult to reach the correct decision and adopt the right course, perform two Rakats of supererogatory prayer at any hour outside the unpropitious and forbidden timings. Afterwards, offer the 'Istikhara' prayer

Hadrat Sad b. Abi Waqqas [R.A.A.] reports that the Holy Prophet [S.A.W.] observed:

"It is propitious for the progeny of Adam to beseech goodness and welfare from Allah; and it is also propitious for the progeny of Adam to submit to the Will of Allah; and it is most unfortunate for the progeny of Adam if they do not beseech goodness and welfare from Allah and are not happy in the Will of Allah."

(Musnad Ahmad)

The Holy Prophet [S.A.W.] also observed:

> "One who observes 'Istikhara' is never disappointed; and the one who takes counsel is never put to shame; and the one who observes economy does not have to depend on others." (Tibrani)
>
> Hadrat Jabir [R.A.A.] states: "As the Holy Prophet [S.A.W.] taught us the Quran, so also he [S.A.W.] instructed us to observe 'Istikhara' in every matter. The Holy Prophet [S.A.W.] used to observe: When anyone among you is perplexed over an important matter, he should perform two Rakats of supererogatory prayer and then offer this prayer: (Bukhari)

O Allah! I ask of Thee the good through Thy knowledge, and ability through Thy power and beg (Thy favours), Thine infinite bounty. For, behold, Thou hast power; I have none. Thou knowest, I know not; and Thou art the great knower of things hidden.

O Allah! If in Thy knowledge this matter be good for my faith, for my livelihood, and for the issue of my affairs, then ordain it for me, and make it easy for me and bless me therewith. But if in Thy knowledge, this matter be bad for my faith, for my livelihood, and for the issue of my affairs, then turn it away from me, and turn me away therefrom and ordain for me the good wherever it be, and cause me to be pleased there with.

The Submission : The Holy Prophet (S.A.W.) has said:

> "O believers, adorn your lives with the virtues of service. Cover yourselves with the sheet of the fear of Hereafter, make Hereafter the goal of your life; and be ever prepared to make your abode there. Bear in mind, you have to depart from this world and to present yourselves before Allah."

Only two things will save you there; firstly your good deeds done during your lifetime in this world, and secondly that source of charity which you might leave behind, after your death.

Devoted Prayers : Ablution and Cleanliness are Prerequisites of prayers, while performing wuzu, clean your teeth with a miswak also. The Holy Prophet (S.A.W.) has said: "The distinguishing sign of my followers on the Doomsday shall be that their foreheads and the limbs washed in ablution shall glow with radiance. Thus, whosoever wishes to enhance his radiance may do so."

> Offer Prayers in clean and proper dress. The Holy Quran lays down "O the offsprings of Adam! Go to pray adorned with proper apparel for each prayer. (7 : 31)

Prayers should be Offered Punctually.

(Innas salata Kanat, alal-mominina kitaban mauqoota)

> "Worship has been made obligatory upon the Muslims with fixed hours." (4 : 103)

Hadrat Abdullah bin Masud (R.A.A.) once asked the Prophet (S.A.W.) "O Prophet of Allah! Which action pleases Allah the most?" The Holy Prophet (S.A.W.) said: "The act most liked by Allah is to offer prayer at its proper time."

> The Holy Prophet (S.A.W.) has also said: "Allah has made five prayers obligatory. One who offers them with submission and humility having performed the ablution at the prescibed time, becomes entitled for salvation by Allah. But one who fails to do so, may get salvation or may not." (Malik)

Importance of Congregational Prayers : Prayers should always be offered in congregation even if the congregation is missed, the obligatory (farz) (prayers should be offered in the mosque. Sunnah prayers may, however, be offered at home.

> The Holy Prophet (S.A.W.) has said: "He who offers prayers with the first takbir (i.e. immediately on hearing the call) for forty days consecutively in a congregation, is made safe from both Hell and hypocrisy." (Tirmidhi)
>
> And further: "If people come to know the recompense and reward for collective prayers, they would flock to the mosque despite a thousand impediments. The first line of the congregation is like the row of the angels. A two-man party of worshippers is better than one man's and the greater the congregation, the more it is liked by Allah." (Abu Daud)

Prayers should be offered with composure and peace of mind. Perform all the forms (postures) of prayer with an undisturbed mind and peacefulness. There should be a resonable pause between the two prostrations (Sajda) and the following prayer is to be recited during this interval.

"Allah forgive me and bless me with The Mercy, guide me on the straight path, relieve me of my distress, grant me peace, and arrange for my livelihood."

The Holy Prophet (S.A.W.) has said: "He who offers his prayers properly, is in return blessed by Salat in these words, "May Allah protect thee as thou hast protected me."

He has also said: "The worst kind of theft is the pilferage of prayer." When asked by the companions. "Prophet of Allah, how can one steel prayers?" The Holy Prophet (S.A.W.) said. "By performing imperfect postures in prayers."

How to Pray : Offer prayers with concentration, humility, and submissiveness which may inspire you with the majesty and sublimity of Allah. Unnecessarily moving one's hand or feet, scratching the body, combing beard with fingers, putting finger in the nose, and setting clothes right are acts of extreme insolence and should be avoided.

Prayers are a Means of Achieving Nearness to Allah : Offer prayers as if you are before Him; or at least imagine that Allah is watching you. The Holy Prophet (S.A.W.) has said:

> "The servant of Allah is closest to Him when he prostrates himself before Him. Therefore, when you prostrate yourself, pray fervently." (Muslim)

You should act upon the teachings learnt in the prayers in your daily life and let its sublimity reflect in your worldly affairs. The Holy Prophet (S.A.W.) has pointed to this aspect through a beautiful metaphor. He shook a dry twig with some force. All the leaves dropped off. The Holy Prophet (S.A.W.) said: "The sins of persons offering prayers drop off like the leaves of this dry twig." He then recited the following ayat (verse) of the Holy Quran:

> "And establish prayers on the two points of the day (i.e. morning and sunset) and after some time when night has set in. Verily, good deeds erase misdeeds. This is an admonition for those who wish to acquire it. (11:114) (Nasai)

While offering prayers, the Holy Quran should be recited slowly and clearly. This applies to other utterances during the prayer, which should be recited with appropriate pauses and with concentration, ardour, and alertness of mind. If prayers are offered with understanding and care, they become real prayers.

Prayers are to be offered regularly and with punctuality. It is a basic distinguishing feature of the Muslims that they offer their prayers regularly and in time. The Holy Quran says:

> "(And the believers are those) who guard their prayers,"

Optional Prayers : Together with obligatory prayers, the worshippers should also offer nafl or optional prayers. These prayers should be offered as much as possible. The Holy Prophet

(S.A.W.) has said: "For the person who offers twelve rakats of nafl or optional prayers in addition to the five compulsory prayers, has his house built in the Paradise." (Muslim)

Offer Some Prayers at Home Also : Sunnat and Nafl prayers (other than compulsory) should occasionally be offered at home. The Holy Prophet (S.A.W.) has commanded this by saying. "After having offered prayers in the mosque, do offer some prayers at home. Allah will bless your homes on account of such prayers."

The Holy Prophet (S.A.W.) himself used to offer such prayers very often at home.

When leaving your home, for the morning prayers, recite the following supplication:

> "Allah enlighten my heart, my vision, my hearing; creat light on my right, on my left, on my rear and light in front of me. Enlighten me from above and below. O Allah, bestow upon me light, and make it light for me, fill my muscles, flesh, blood, hair, skin, tongue and my breath with light and make light within myself. Give me; Allah! the great light, and make me all light."

Supplication to be Recited after Prayers : Hadrat Sauban (R.A.A.) says that the Holy Prophet (S.A.W.) after completing the prayer with the Salam used to say Astaghfirullah (Allah forgive me) thrice and then recited the following supplication:

> Allah! Thou art peace, and the fountain-head of peace is from Thee. Thou art Blessed, Thou art Great, and Munificent.

Recitation of Holy Quran : The Quran should be recited with full ardour and keen interest, believing that love for the Quran is love for Allah. The Holy Prophet (S.A.W.) has said:

> " The best form of prayer for my Ummah is the recital of the Quran."

Reward for reciting the Holy Quran : A Muslim should recite the Quran very often and he should never feel tired or bored by its recitation. According to the Holy Prophet (S.A.W.):

> "Allah has said that a servant of His who is so engrossed in reciting the Quran that he will not have an opportunity to pray to Him for his needs, shall be granted more than that which He shall grant to those who ask." (Tirmidhi)

The Holy Prophet (S.A.W.) said:

> "Allah's servant gains the maximum proximity to Him through the reading of the Quran." Tirmidhi)
>
> In a beautiful simile, the Holy Prophet (S.A.W.) has compared the individual who reads the Quran daily is like a bottle of musk, perfume of which spreads in all the four directions, while he, who has read the Quran but does not recite it, is like a bottle full of musk which has beensealed." (Tirmidhi)

The Quran should be recited for guidance and inspiration only. It should not be chanted for any other purpose, e.g., for endearing oneself to others or impressing people, or for trying to create an impression of piety. These traits should be eschewed. The are impure motives and anyone who recites the Quran for such a purpose shall not get guidance from the Quran.

Before Recital, Ensure Absolute Cleanliness : Avoid touching the Holy Quran without first having performed ablution and recite it in clean place.

Manner of Recitation : While reciting the Holy Quran, read it with full concentration, ardour and utmost devotion. Allah has said:

> "The Book we have revealed upon you, is full of blessings; so that (people) may ponder upon it and the wise men may receive instructions and inspiration from the same." (38 : 30)

Recite the Holy Quran Distinctly in a Melodious Tone : Read the Quran in a measured and deliberate tone, pronouncing each word correctly and distinctly in an easy tone making sentences quite intelligible. The Holy Prophet (S.A.W.) has directed that the reciter should recite the Quran in a pleasing manner, making it charming with his voice and melody.

(Abu Daud)

The Holy Prophet (S.A.W.) recited the Quran pronouncing each word clearly and each ayat (verse) separately. The Holy Prophet (S.A.W.) has said:

"The reciter of the Quran shall be commanded on the Day of Judgement to recite the Quran melodiously with the same measured tone and sustained pitch, with which he used to recite the Book in the world, and get elevated a step higher as a reward for each ayat. His real abode lies near the last *ayat* he had recited." (Tirmidhi)

Tone of Recitation : The pitch to be adopted in recitation should neither be too high nor too low. It should be intermediate as Allah has set down:

"And offer your prayers neither too loudly nor slowly, instead follow the middle way." (17 : 110)

Best Time for Recitation : Although it is always good to recite the Holy Quran, yet the best time to do so is during late midnight with Tahajjud prayers and at dawn, before or after Fajr prayer. Recitation of the Holy Quran at these hours is very gracious and rewarding. The wish of every Muslim should be to achieve this privilege.

Don't Rush Through the Quran : The recitation of the Quran should never he completed within less than three days. The Holy Prophet (S.A.W.) has said: "One who has recited the whole Quran within less than three days, has not comprehended it."

The Holy Quran is not to be Recited Rapidly : It should be read with understanding and meditation. Hadrat Abdullah Bin Abbas (R.A.A.) used to say that it is much better to read short surahs like Al Quraish and Al-Qadr with understanding and comprehension, than rapidly going through long *surahs* like *Al-e-imran* and Al-Baqarah without following them. The Holy Prophet (S.A.W.) once continued to recite only one ayat for the whole night:

> "(O Allah) if Thou submitest them to Thy wrath, they are Thy servants. If Thou forgivest them, Thou art Most Powerful and All Wise."

Have Due Rregard for the Majesty and divinity of the Holy Quran. And as you care for the visible cleanliness of your person, while reading the Holy Quran, in the same way cleanse your heart of evil thoughts, foul ideas and base motives: A heart that is polluted by evil thoughts and impure motives will neither admit the sublimity of the Holy Quran nor its significance. Hadrat 'Ikramah (R.A.A.), on opening the Holy Quran for recitation, frequently fainted and on regaining consciousness, would say; "This is the word of my Majestic and Dignified Sustainer."

Study Holy Quran in Order to Correct and Remould your Life : The Quran should be studied with the view and the goal that one's life is to be reshaped and remoulded according to the commands contained therein: One should try to wash off wrongs in ones life in the light of the teachings of the Holy Quran. The Holy Quran would show our wrongs to us like a mirror; and now it is for us to cleanse ourselves.

Inspiration from the Holy Quran : While reciting the Holy Quran, one should try to imbibe the effect conveyed by each ayat. When one recites the ayats concerning Allah's compassion, forgiveness, and the eternal gifts of the Paradise, one should feel elated with beer. While reciting ayats pertaining to Allah's wrath and the torture of the Hell, your body should tremble with awe and fear and tears should spill out of your eyes; even your heart should be moved with the emotions of repentance and shame. On reading the accounts of success of the pious Muslims, your face should glow with happiness; and while reading the stories of destruction of nations having gone astray, you should feel sorrow and unhappy. Verses containing warnings and threats of punishments should send a wave of sensation through your body; and verses which bring joyful tidings should make your soul overflow with the spirit of thanksgiving.

Supplication after Recital : After reciting the Holy Quran supplicate to Allah, Hadrat Umar (R.A.A.) has recommended the following prayer after recital:

"O Allah, make me familiar with the wilderness in my grave. O Allah, have mercy upon me for the sake of the great Quran, and make it my leader, light, guide and mercy. O Allah, let me remember what I have forgotten of it, and teach me what I do not follow, and give me capacity to recite it in the parts of night and day and O Lord of the worlds, make it my argument on the Final Day."

Status of Mosque

Love for the Mosque : For Allah, the best part of the earth is that piece of land on which a mosque is built. People who love Allah are identified by their love for the mosque. On the dreadful Day of Resurrection, when there will not be any shade (to escape from scorching heat) such people shall be afforded protection by Allah under the cover of His Throne.

> The Holy Prophet (S.A.W.) has said: "And the man dedicated to the mosque shall be under the cover of the Throne." (Bukhari).

Serve the cause of mosque by keeping it congregated. This is a symbol of Faith. Allah has said:

> "Only those persons who believe in Allah and the Day of Judgement, tend the mosques." (9 : 18)

Mosque Nucleus of your Life : Farz (Obligatory) prayers should invariably be offered with a congregation in the mosque. Congregation and calls for prayers *(Adaan)* should be properly organized, and your daily life be drilled in harmony with the system of the mosque. A mosque is a nucleus round which the life of a Muslim rotates.

Go to the mosque with a passionate desire for prayers. The Holy Prophet (S.A.W.) has said:

"Visit to the mosques every morning and evening is like going for Jihad (i.e., struggle or fight for the sake of Allah)."

He (S.A.W.) has further said: "Those who go to the mosque at the break of dawn, shall have full light around them on the Day of Judgement."

> And further "Each step of the worshipper who goes for the congregational prayers in the mosque, earns a virtue and erases a sin." (Ibn Habban)

The Mosque is to be Kept Clean and Tidy : Incense should be burn inside the mosque, particularly on Fridays. The Holy Prophet (S.A.W.) says:

> "It is the job of the people destined for the Paradise to sweep the mosque, keep it clean, to throw out all the dust and litter outside and to burn incense especially on Fridays" (Ibn Majah)
>
> He (S.A.W.) further said: "Clearing the litter of the mosque is like the meter (payment of dowry) of a Houri with beautiful eyes." (Tibrani)

Sancity of the Mosque : One must not enter the mosque nor should one pass through it unless one is neat and clean. If unavoidable, one should perform Tayammum and then enter or pass through the mosque.

While Entering the Mosque : You should wear a sober and dignified department. As soon as you enter the mosque, call the greeting "As-salamo Alaikum" (Peace be upon you), take your seat and start praying in such a way which may inspire you with the greatness and sublimity of Allah.

Entering the mosque unconsciously, talking and laughing loosely is a characteristic of careless and insolent persons whose hearts do not harbour 'any fear or respect for Allah. Some peoplerun to the mosque in order to join the Imam in the prayer from the very start and not to miss any part. This is against the etiquette of respect due to the mosque. Whether you miss any part of the prayer or not, you should go to the mosque with dignity, poise and humility and refrain from running.

The Mosque is not a Place for Irreligious Business : Be seated in the mosque peacefully and with poise. Making noise in the mosque, cutting jokes, discussing daily life affairs, or asking and telling market prices, etc., amounts to desecration of the mosque. The mosque is the House of Allah; one should pray there.

Small children who do not know about the respect to be given to the mosque and who are likely to urinate, defecate and spit there should not accompany the worshippers to the mosque.

Grown up Children should be Taken to the Mosque : Mothers should encourage their children to go there; this would create love for the mosque in them. Children should be treated very tenderly and affectionately in the mosque. If they do something wrong or commit some mischief, they should be gently advised rather than chided. They should be taught the advantages of good behaviour.

Do not Make the Mosque a Thoroughfare : Once an individual has entered the mosque, it is incumbent upon him to offer prayers there or recite ihe Quran.

If a Worshipper has Lost Something Outside : Its loss should not be announced within the mosque. If such an announcement was ever made in the mosque of the Holy Prophet (S.A.W.) he would feel displeased, and used to say: "May Allah not give thee the thing thou hast lost."

How to Eenter and Leave the Mosque : While entering the mosque, the right foot is to he put in first, and recite the following prayer:

> O Allah! open the doors of Your favours for me.
>
> Two rakats nafl (voluntary) prayer should be offered on entering the mosque. These two nawafil are known as "Tahiyyat al-masjid" (Greetings for the mosque), On returning from a journey, one should go to the mosque first and offer two rakats of nafl prayers, and then go home. This is based upon the Sunnah (practice) of the Holy Prophet (S.A.W.).

When leaving the mosque, the left foot should he put out first and the following prayer be recited.

> Allah! I ask Thee for Thy favours and munificence.
> (Muslim)

Proper arrangements should be made for calls for prayers and congregation in the mosque. Appoint such persons as callers for prayers (Muazzins) and Imams to lead in prayers, who are the best as regards their piety and morality. As far as possible, the callers and the Imams should perform their tasks without any return for the sake of reward in the Hereafter.

Deviors of Imamat : If you happen to be an Imam to lead in prayers, lead the prayers, keeping in view all the requirements of the office of the Imam. Keep in view the convenience of the congregation. The Holy Prophet (S.A.W.) has said:

> "Imams who lead the assembly in prayers well and believe that they are responsible for the prayers of the congregations, are rewarded with the recompense of the prayers of the assembly, and the Imam becomes

entitled for as much recompense as that of the persons praying under his leadership. The recompense of the latter is, however, not reduced. (Tibrani)

The Call for Prayer : Start preparations for prayers immediately after hearing the call, perform ablution and reach the mosque early; sit quietly in the line and wait for the congregation to be formed. It is an action reminiscent of the munafiqs (hypocrites) to show lethargy after the call, mark time and to go to the mosque unwillingly.

Sound the call for prayer with ardour and zeal. A person asked the Holy Prophet (S.A.W.) "O Prophet of Allah! Tell me something that may help me to go to the heaven." The Holy Prophet (S.A.W.) said: "Give call for the prayer." And further: "As far as the voice of the *Muazzin* can reach, people hearing his call will testify in favour of the *Muazzin* on the Day of Reckoning. If a shepherd announces a prayercall in the jungle, all the things which have heard him, on the Day of Judgement shall stand witness for him." (Bukhari)

Prayer to be Recited after the Adaan : The Holy Prophet (S.A.W.) has said that anyone who offers the following prayer after having heard the Adaan, shall invariably have the intercession of the Holy Prophet (S.A.W.) on the Day of Judgement:

"Allah the Master of this perfect call and this assembly of prayer! Bestow upon Muhammad 'al Waseelah' and grant him that high position which Thou hadst promised him."

Adaan and your Response Thereto : When the caller (Muazzin) is calling for the prayer, the listeners should repeat the call and when he says "Hayya 'alass Salah" and "Hayya 'ala al-Falah ", the listeners should respond with, (La ḥawla wala quwwata illa bil lahil-Azim). "There is no power nor strength except that of Allah the Great." When the Muazzin during the early morning call says "As-Salatu Khairum Min An-Naum". Prayer is better than sleep," the listener should say: "Sadaqta wa bararta" "You have uttered the truth and good thing."

When Lining up for Prayer : When the reciter of the "Takbir" says: "Qad Qamatis salah" (verily, the prayer has stood), the listener should say:

> "*Aqamaha-Allaho wa Adamaha*" (May Allah always keep it established)

Line up in Congregational Prayers : Be careful about the alignment while offering prayers in congregation and to stand shoulder-to-shoulder in such a way that there may not be a gap in between. A new row should not be formed until the first has been completed.

Performance of Hajj: When your means permit, proceed to the Holy Land for the performance of Hajj, and the same should not be delayed unnecessarily and should be performed, for nobody knows how long he is going to live. The holy Quran has ordained:

> "And Allah has the right upon people that those who have the means to reach the House of Allah (in Mecca) should go on pilgrimage. And he who refuses to carry out this command, ought to know that Allah is independent of all in the world," (3 : 97)

What greater misfortune can there be for a person than that Allah may forsake him:

The Hadith has it:

> "He who intends to perform Hajj, should do it expeditiously, for it is quite possible that he may fall sick, lose his she-camel (means of transport) or some other contingency may crop up hampering (his journey for) Hajj " (Ibn Majah)

And further:

> "If a person who has no sickness or some (other) genuine excuse and is not, prevented by a cruel and oppressive ruler and still he does not perform Hajj, it is immaterial whether he dies as a Jew or as Christian." (Sunan Kubra, Vol. IV)

And Hadrat Umar (R.A.A.) was once heard saying: "I sometimes feel like imposing Jizya on those who avoid going to Hajj despite having the means for the same; they are not Muslims, they are not Muslims."

Hajj to be Performed for the Pleasure of Allah Only : The House of Allah is to be visited and Hajj performed only in order to please Him, and' ,this pious intention should not be polluted with any worldly motive. In the Quran we are told:

> "And do not obstruct those persons who are going to the venerable house in search of Allah's mercy and pleasure." (5 : 2)

At another place Allah has commanded:

> "Perform Hajj and Umrah for the pleasure of Allah alone." (2 : 196)
>
> The Holy Prophet (S.A.W.) said: "The recompense for Hajj Mabrur is not less than that of Paradise." (Muslim, Kitab al-Hajj)

Hajj Mabrur is that pilgrimage which is undertaken only to please Allah and performed with all the rules and rituals observing faithfully.

Proceed on the pilgrimage of Hajj without any fanfare or publicity. You should leave quietly and return quietly, desisting from all acts that would show publicity and self-advertisement. Although the criterion for a pious act, is the fact that it is done only for the sake of Allah and nothing else, yet, this factor is more pronounced in the case of *Hajj* which is considered as an act of self-purgation, purification of mind and soul, and spiritual refreshing. It is all the more important as it is the last chance for the spiritual treatment for those who are in search of salvation and, if one is not spiritually cured by it, there is little hope for his cure by any other method.

> Yearning to visit Holy Land Even if, it is beyond your means to proceed on pilgrimage, you should still keep your heart inspired with the burning desire of visiting the mosque of the Holy Prophet (S.A.W.) and having the honour of, preforming Hajj, and keel your soul alive with the spirit of sacrifice established by Hadrat Ibrahim (A.S.) The Holy Prophet (S.A.W.) in this context, has said: "Those proceeding on Umrah and Hajj are the special guests of Allah. Allah accepts their prayers and grants them redemption, if prayed for."
>
> (Tibrani)

The best travelling provision one takes with him on Hajj is that of piety. In this holy journey one who fears Allah and tries hard to win His pleasure and avoids His disobedience, shall benefit from the blessings of Huy. The Holy Quran says:

> "And for (Hajj) take travelling provisions, and the best (provision) is piety." (2 : 197)

Once you have made up your mind to perform Hajj, you should start making preparations for the same with all the mental devotion and earnestness. You should recall acid enact the history and traditions of Hajj fonder over every rite and details of the Hajj and try to understand what the religion of Allah want; to create and the heart of a true believer Through these rituals And then a true and conscious Muslim try to imbibe the spirit of Hajj and with full awareness remould your life accordingly.

Allah says:

"And remember Allah as He has guided you to

remember Him. And it is a fact that in the past you I had gone astray." (2 : 198)

To achieve this objective a deeper study of those parts of the Quran wherein are described the spirit and importance of Hajj is useful. A study of the traditions and of literature describing the history and rituals of Hajj is also necessary.

The prayers offered during Hajj contained in the literature on Hadis should be memorized and recited. Supplicate to Allah in the words of the Holy Prophet (S.A.W.)

Do not impair your Hajj by any sinful act. Be careful that your Hajj does not become like a show piece of the people hankering after the world, and who have no regard or interest far the hereafter. Allah has said about these people:

> "Our Lord ! Give unto us in this world"; Such (world loving) people have no share in the Hereafter. (2 : 200)

Hajj is the means through which you should solicit Allah's blessings and munificence in the world and the Hereafter and pray in these words:

> Our Lord ! Give Unto us what is good in this world and also what is good in the Hereafter; and guard us from the agony of Fire (Hell). (2 : 201)

Be very particular to avoid the slightest disobedience of the commands of Allah during Hajj. This pilgrimage is a journey to the House of Allah, and you are His guest. You have gone there to affirm your oath of allegiance and servitude. By touching the Black Stone (*Hajar-i-Aswad*), you are holding the hand of Allah pledging your fidelity, and your kissing the stone is like kissing the Threshold of Allah. By repeatedly chanting Takbir (Allah-o-Akbar) and Tahlil (La ilahail-lal-lah) you are proclaiming your fidelity flow disgusting even the idea of sinfulness in such circumstances. Allah has cautioned those who approach His House in these words:

> "There is (to be) no lewdness nor abuse nor angry conversations on the pilgrimage. (2 : 197)

You should abstain from quarrels bickerings during Hajj. When during the pilgrimage there is large gathering of pilgrims causing troubles at various places, conflicts, annoyance and irritation, you as the guest of Allah, should display broad-mindedness, self-sacrifice, restraint, kindness and magnanimity towards everybody. You should not even rebuke your personal servant.

You should scrupulously avoid all talks and thoughts relating to sexual matters. You should be particularly careful during your journey when there will be chance of getting excited and the eyes becoming freer and covetous. If your mate accompanies you, not only sexual contact but oven things that are likely to whip up sexual sentiments are to be avoided. Allah has cautioned in these words:

> "The months of pilgrimage are known to everybody. And therefore, whoever intends to perform Hajj should remember that there is (to be) no lewdness nor abuse nor quarrel during the *Hajj*." (2 : 197)

And the Holy Prophet (S.A.W.) has said:

> "He who has come to perform pilgrimage to the house of Allah, and has saved himself from immoral or sexual acts and also from lewdness, returns home purified like a newly born baby."
>
> *(Bukhari - Muslim)*

Obey all commands and carry out all rituals that have been ordained by Allah in order to have the awareness and knowledge of some spiritual reality. This thing is known as the Shariah of which the plural is Shaair. Allah has said in the Quran:

> "O ye who believe! Profane not Allah's monuments (the symbols of Allah's worship) nor the sacred

months, nor lay your hands upon animals ear-marked for sacrifice, nor those animals which have been dedicated to Allah and have bands in their necks as distinguishing mark, nor obstruct persons repairing the sacred House seeking the grace and pleasure of Allah. (5 :2)

And in Surah Al-Hajj it has been said:

"And one who honours the symbols of Allah's worship, which have been prescribed by Allah, then this is matter of piety of the hearts."

(22 : 32)

Utmost humility, want and submissivness should be expressed in the performance of the rituals of Hajj. Allah likes the expression of the virtues of humility and submission by his servants. On being asked as to who is Haji (Pilgrim), the Holy Prophet (S.A.W.) said, "a pilgrim is one whose hair is dishevelled and bears a dust-ridden appearance."

Recitation of Talbiyah Having put on the Ahram, loudly recite Talbiyah after every prayer, while climbing every ascent or descending a slope or meeting another carvan, and when waking up each morning. The Talbiyah is as follows:

"Here I am! O Allah here I am! Thou hast no partner, here I am. Verily, all praises are only for Thee. All the gifts are Thine: All sovereignty is Thine. Thou hast no partner."

Prayers and Supplications in Arafat Most Important Ritual of Hajj : On reaching the plain of Arafat, you should supplicate and solicit Allah's mercies and forgiveness for sins to the maximum extent.

The Holy Prophet (S.A.W.) has said:

"The day of Arafat is the best before Allah. He especially directs His attention .to the world on that

> day and takes pride (Pleasure) on the humility and submissiveness of the pilgrims and says to the angels: 'O angels! See how my bewildered servants are standing in the sun in my presence. From afar have they come here, in the hope of my munificence although they have not witnessed My wrath." Having expressed His pride in His servants, He orders their redemption from Hell. On no day are so many persons redeemed as on the Day of *Arafat*."
>
> (Ibn Habban)

Sacrifice at Mina: On return to Mina, you should offer sacrifice with the same sentiments that governed Prophet Ibrahim (A.S.), the friend of Allah, when he placed his knife upon the neck of his beloved sun Prophet Ismail (A.S.) and this spirit of sacrifice should henceforth govern all your activities in life, you should be prepared to offer sacrifices in all fields of your life, and your actual way of living may reflect this picture:

> Verily, my prayers, my sacrifice, my life and my death are for only One Allah, who is the Sustainer of the worlds, and Who has no partner." (7 : 163 - 164)

You should remember Allah throughout the Hajj period and do not let his remembrance go out of your mind. Remembrance of Allah is the substance of all prayers and supplications, as Allah says in the Quran:

> "Keep busy in remembering Allah during the appointed days." (2 : 203)

And further in *Surah* Al-Baqarah:

> "And when you have completed your rituals of Hajj, then remember Allah as you remembered your forefathers, or even more than them." (2 : 200)

It is the aim of the Arkan (rituals) of Hajj that you should be continuously absorbed in the remembrance and so deep into your thoughts that no other worldly activities and attractions may distract you from this remembrance. During the pre-Islamic days, the Arabs, having performed Hajj used to engage themselves in talking tall and boasting about their ancestors. Allah has commanded that (instead of this) He should be remembered in these days, and His Greatness alone is worthy of being narrated, for He is really the Great.

> The *tawaf* (circumambulation) of the House of Allah should be performed with great love and devotion. Allah has ordained, "And you ought to circumambulate the old house (of Allah)."
>
> (22 : 29)

The Holy Prophet (S.A.W.) has said:

> " Allah showers one hundred and twenty blessings each day for the Hajj pilgrims. Out of these sixty blessing are for those who circumambulate it, forty for those who offer prayers (at the Kaaba) and twenty for those who merely gaze at it."

And the Holy Prophet (S.A.W.) has also said:

> "One who has circumambulated the House of Allah fifty times, has been washed all of his sins as if he is born only today." (Tirmidhi)

10

Rules for Mourning

Sufferings and Griefs should be Borne with Equanimity : One should not lose heart, and expression of grief and sorrow should never be allowed to exceed the limits of moderation. There is no person in this world who is immune from some sort of failure, frustration calamity, sorrow and deprivation. The difference between the Muslim and the infidel is that the latter, succumbing to the tide or grief, gives himself up totally to grief; at times even committing suicide. A Muslim bears even greater calamities with composure and gives a good account of himself in forbearance and resignation. He considers that whatever has happened is according to the Will of God: none of Whose commands is without significance and wisdom, and that whatever He does is for the betterment of His creatures, having some positive aspect. A Muslim begins to feel a kind of spiritual tranquility and peace and its soothing effect in the midst of grief, and this aspect of destiny makes things easier. The Holy Quran says:

> "All the sufferings that befall on earth, and all the tribulations which you face, are predetermined and recorded in a book. Undoubtedly it is easier for Allah, so that you may not bewail which has escaped you."
>
> (57 : 22)

The Holy Prophet (S.A.W.) has said:

> "Unique is the attitude of the Muslim. He sees good in every situation. If he is faced with bereavement, ailment, or hardship, he bears it up with resignation, and such a trial proves a blessing in disguise for him. If on the other hand, he gets happiness and prosperity, he offers thanks to Allah and this prosperity becomes a cause of good for him."

Initial Response

When one bears a news communicating a bereavement, death, loss or some other such bad event, one should immediately recite.

Inna Lillahe Wa Inna Ilaihe Rajiun.

Verily we belong to Allah and to Him we shall return.

(2 : 156)

In other words all that we have belongs to Allah. He has given all that we have and He can take them away, We all belong to Him and will return to Him. We are under all circumstances resigned to His Will, all His commands are based upon some purpose, wisdom, and justice, and He does everything for some greater goal. The obedient servant is one who never grumbles at any time.

The Holy Prophet (S.A.W.) has said :

> "When a person recites *'Inna illahe'* in the face of some suffering, Allah mitigates his suffering, grants him with a good end, and awards him in return the thing he likes."

One night a lamp in the room of the Holy Prophet (S.A.W.) got extinguished. The Holy Prophet (S.A.W.) immediately said, Inna Lilahe wa inna ilaihe Rajiun. When someone asked: "O Prophet of God, is the putting out of the lamp a calamity?" The Holy Prophet (S.A.W.) said: "Yes, whatever torments or causes inconvenience to a Muslim is a calamity."

The Holy Prophet (S.A.W.) has also said:

"If a Muslim bears patiently any trouble of the body of heart, ailment, sorrow or bereavement, may it be so minor as pricking of a thorn, Allah forgives his sins. (Bukhari – Muslim)

Allah has said:

"And We shall certainly test you with fear and hunger, loss of life and property, and (O Prophet,) give glad tidings to those who show patience in the face of such ordeals and say, 'We are from Allah and to Him we have to return.' They shall be rewarded generously by their Sustainer and their Lord's favour and blessings on them. Verily, such people are on the true path." (2 : 156)

According to Hadrat Anas, the Holy Prophet (S.A.W.) has said:

"The severer the suffering, the greater would be the recompense. When Allah loves some people, in order to purify them, He puts them under trial. As such those who acquit themselves well in this trial, with them Allah is pleased, and those who grumble and express displeasure with Allah, with them Allah becomes displeased. (Tirmidhi)

Hadrat Abu Musa Ashari quotes the Holy Prophet (S.A.W.) as having said:

"When a person loses his child, Allah enquires from the angels, "Did you take away the life of the child of My servant ?" The angels say, "Yes, O Lord :" Allah asks again: "Did you extract the life of his dearest child ?" The angels reply in the affirmative. He then asks: "What did My servant say'?" The angels submit "In his hour of trial, he praised Thee O Lord, and recited *'Inns Lillahe wa Inna ilaihe rajiun'*.

(Verily we belong to Allah and shall return to Him).

Allah then commands: "Build a house for this servant of Mine, and name it the 'House of Thanks'

(Tirmidhi)

Be Discreet in the Expression of Sorrow : It is but natural to express sentiments of sorrow on some trouble, mishap or bereavement; but it should be borne in mind that the expression should not be unbridled and out of proportion, patience and composure should reign supreme throughout.

And example of forbearance and indomitable courage in the face of heart-rending bereavement is provided by the Holy Prophet (S.A.W.) himself. Hadrat Ibrahim, the son of the Holy Prophet (S.A.W.) was breathing his last in the lap of his august father. In this poignant situation the Holy Prophet's (S.A.W.) eyes started shedding tears, but he only said: O Ibrahim, we are rent by grief at thy departure, but our tongue shall express only those words, Which will be according to the Will of Allah. (Muslim)

Thus one should never complain about the disease or speak ill of it. Fortitude should be shown and hope pinned in the reward of the Hereafter. Bearing ailments and sufferings with fortitude, washes off the faithful's (Muslim) sins, cleanses him, and rewards him on the Day of Judgement. The Holy Prophet (S.A.W.) has said:

"Allah sheds off the sins committed by a faithful (Muslim) when he suffers through a physical affliction or a disease, just as the tree sheds off its leaves."

(Bukhari — Muslin:)

Sickness Purifies a Person : The Holy Prophet (S.A.W.) one day saw a lady shivering. The Holy Prophet (S.A.W.) asked: "O Umm Saib (or Musayyab), why you are trembling. The lady said: "I am suffering from fever. May it be cursed." The Holy Prophet (S.A.W.) said "Do not speak ill of fever, because fever purges the offspring of Adam of sins as the fire purifies the iron by removing its dirt." (Muslim)

Hadrat Ata Ibn Ribah describes an episode thus:

"Once I met Hadrat Abbas near the Kaaba who asked me whether I would like to see a lady marked for Heaven. I expressed my eagerness to see her. Hadrat Abbas, pointing to a woman said: "This blackish woman once presented herself before the Holy Prophet (S.A.W.) and said: O Prophet of Allah, I am suffering from such severe fits of epilepsy which makes me totally unconscious, so much so that I become stark naked. She requested the Prophet of Allah (S.A.W.) to pray for her.

The Holy Prophet (S.A.W.) said: "If you keep on bearing this ordeal with fortitude, Allah shall recompense you with the Paradise. If you wish I shall pray for your recovery and Allah shall make you well. She said 'O Prophet of Allah (S.A.W.). I shall bear this disease with fortitude, but do pray for me that I may not shed off my clothes in the course of a fit." The Holy Prophet (S.A.W.) prayed for her," Hadrat Ata says that he saw this lady, Umme Rafz on the stairs of the Kaaba.

***Do not Exceed the Limits of Moderation in Sorrow* :** When overcome by grief, do not commit an act which may imply ingratitude or complaint, it may be contrary to the Shariah. Among these acts are loud lamentations, rending off clothes, slapping of cheeks and breast. The Holy Prophet (S.A.W.) has explicitly said:

"He who slaps his cheeks, tears off his clothes, and laments like the people of the period of ignorance, does not belong to my Ummah. " (Tirmidhi)

When Hadrat Jafar Tayyar was martyred, and this news reached his home, the women-folk of his house began wailing loudly. The Holy Prophet (S.A.W.) sent words that they should not bewail loudly. But they continued their screaming. He (S.A.W.) again ordered them to stop, but they persisted. The Holy Prophet (S.A.W.) then ordered to stuff their mouths with dust."

(Bukhari)

Once the Holy Prophet (S.A.W.) was attending a funeral. A woman was accompanying the funeral procession with burning fire in a brazier. He (S.A.W.) reprimanded her so severely that she had to run away. He further commanded that nobody should follow a funeral procession with burning fire or any kind of music.
(Sirat Un-Nabi, Vol.6)

There was a custom in the pre-Islamic Arabia that when people walked behind the coffin, they used to throw away the cloak and only kept the shirt. The Holy Prophet (S.A.W.) once saw them in this state and said:

"You are following the practice of the infidels. I feel like cursing you so that your faces become deformed."

The people immediately put on their clothes and never did like this again. (Ibn Majah)

Never Extend the Period of Mourning Beyond Three Days : It is natural to feel sorrow at the death of a relative, but the period of mourning ought not to go beyond three days. The Holy Prophet (S.A.W.) has said:

"It is not permissible for a Muslim to mourn the demise of anybody for more than three days; however, the period of lamentation for a widow is four months and ten days. During this period she should not put on coloured clothes, nor apply scent to her clothes and body nor decorate herself." (Tirmidhi)

When the brother of Hadrat Zainab bint Jahsh, a cousin of the Holy Prophet (S.A.W.) died, some women visited Hadrat Zainab on the fourth day to offer their condolences. She dabbed herself with some scent in their presence and said, "It was not at all necessary for me to do so, yet I have rubbed "it just because the Holy Prophet (S.A.W.) has said that it is not permissible for any woman to mourn for any relation except, her husband, for more than three days."

Condolence : We should try to condole each other on the occasion of a bereavement. When the Holy Prophet (S.A.W.) returned from the battle of Uhud, women presented themselves before Him (S.A.W.) to inquire the welfare of their relations. When Hadrat Hamana bint Jahash appeared, the Holy Prophet (S.A.W.) counselled patience and told her to bear the loss of her brother, Hadrat Abdullah, with fortitude, whereupon she recited *Inna Lillahe wa inna ilaihe Rajiun,* and prayed for her brother's salvation. Then the Holy Prophet (S.A.W.) asked her to put up with the loss of Hadrat Hamza her maternal uncle as well, and she prayed for him too.

> Hadrat Abu Talha had a son who was sick; he had to go to work, leaving him sick. Shortly after his departure the son died. His wife asked Hadrat, Talha's friends that the news of the death of the son should not reach the father. When Hadrat Talha returned home in the evening, he asked about the son. The wife told him that he was more comfortable than before, and served food to her husband. He took his meal in peace and went to sleep. In the morning the noble lady conveyed the sad news to her husband in a sagacious way by telling that if some body wanted his thing back from the borrower, can the latter refuse it ? Thereupon Hadrat Talha said: "How can the borrower claim that right?" The forbearing lady said. "Then be resigned to (the bereavement of) your son."
> (Muslim)

Fortitude : All ordeals that are faced for the sake of the truth and supremacy of faith are to be welcomed, and borne with fortitude and smilingly. Instead of being overwhelmed by feelings of sorrow and disappointment, we should thank Almighty Allah, for his favour for the acceptance of our sacrifices.

The mother of Hadrat Abdullah Ibn Zubayr, Hadrat Asma, (the daughter of Hadrat Abu Bakr) once fell ill. Her son Hadrat Abdullah, came to see her. His august mother, on this occasion said: "O son, it is my prayer to Allah that I be alive till I have witnessed two things: either I should hear the news of your death in a battlefield as a martyr and I should, on hearing this news, secure the blessings of fortitude or that you should be the victor in a battle and I should feel the coolness in my eyes on seeing you as the victor". As it happened, Hadrat Abdullah bin Zubayr died fighting in a battlefield during the life time of Hadrat Asma, and Hajjaj bin Yusuf had his corpse hung from a gibbet. Hadrat Asma had become old by that time, but despite her frailty, she went to see the dead body of her son, and instead of lamenting on the unfortunate death of her son, she addressed Hajjaj and said: "Has the time not yet come for this rider to dismount?"

Participation in the Bereavements of Friends : A Muslim should make it a point to condole and sympathise with each other in sorrow and bereavement. Join your friends and relatives in their tragedies and catastrophies to mitigate their pain and sorrow. The Holy Prophet (S.A.W.) has said:

> "The entire Muslim nation is like a single human body. If the eye suffers pain, the whole body is affected; and when the head aches, the whole body feels the pain." (Muslim)
>
> When the Holy Prophet (S.A.W.) learnt about the martyrdom of Hadrat Jafar Tayyar, he said, "Send

> food to the house of Jafar, because his people, overcome by sorrow, will not be able to cook any food today." *(Abu Daud)*

According to Hadrat Abu Hurrayrah, the Holy Prophet (S.A.W.) once said:

> "A person who offers condolences to a woman who has just lost her child, shall be admitted to Paradise and covered with a sheet from Heaven." (Tirmidhi)

He (S.A.W.) further said:

> "He who comforts a bereaved person, shall have as much recompense as the sufferer himself." (Tirmidhi)

The Holy Prophet (S.A.W.) has commanded participation in funerals. Hadrat Abu Hurrayrah reports that the Holy Prophet (S.A.W.) has said:

> "He who has joined a funeral procession and participated in the funeral prayers shall have one qayrat worth of recompense, and he who has stayed till the burial of the coffin, shall have two qayrats worth of reward." On being asked how much two qayrats would be, the: Holy Prophet (S.A.W.) said: "They would be equal to two mountains." (Bukhari - Muslim)

One must seek solace and succour from Allah, in the face of multitude of grief and sorrow. One should supplicate Allah after prayers with all humility. The Quran hay said:

> "O believers (in the face of ordeals and tests) seek relief through patience and prayers" (2 : 153)

Prayers When Faced with Grief **:** Hadrat Abu Hurrayrah has narrated the following:

Whenever the Holy Prophet (S.A.W.) was beset with worries and anxieties, he lifted his head towards the sky and said: Subhan-All-hil Azim.

"Allah is Glorified and Magnificent."

When, however, sorrow was on the increase and the devotion in prayers also gained the upper hand, he used to say.

"Ya Hayyu Ya Qayyum."

O thou Everlasting and Eternal. (Tirmidhi)

Prayers in Difficult Situations : Whenever one is beset with intense grief and extreme difficult situation, he should recite these supplications. Hadrat Saad bin Waqqas reports that the Holy Prophet Yunus (Jonah) when swallowed by a huge fish, recited the following payer for his deliverance.

"There is no god but Thee. Thou art Glorified and Spotless and indeed I myself have done wrong to me." (21 : 87)

As such, a Muslim who when faced with tribulations, prays to Allah in this way, is surely to be blessed with the acceptance of his prayers.

Hadrat Abdullah Ibn Abbas has said that the prayer offered by the Holy Prophet (S.A.W.) on such occasions was:

"There is no god but Allah, the Lord of the great Throne; There is no god save Allah, the Lord of skies and the Lord of earth, the Lord of the Magnificent Throne."

Hadrat Abdullah Ibn Masud says:

"The Holy Prophet (S.A.W.) said that if a person afflicted with some trouble or difficulty, offers the following prayer, Allah will transform his sorrows into cheerfulness:

O Allah, I am Thy slave and son of Thy slave and the son of Thy slave girl. 'My forelock is in Thy hand, Thy command operates in my matters. All Thou commands in relation to me are just. I beg of Thee in every name which is Thine and with which Thou has taught to any of Thy creatures, or which Thou has preferred to keep among Thy secret knowledge, to make the Holy Quran the spring of my heart, the light of my eyes, and a means of dispelling my grief and a remover for my anxiety."

On the Death of a Person : When you have to see somebody on death bed, continuously recite loudly the Islamic article of faith: (Kalima)

"La-ilaha illal-alru Muham-madur Rasulullh.

"There is no god except Allah and Muhammad (S.A.W.) is His Messenger."

The Holy Prophet (S.A.W.) has directed that "When you go to a man who is on death's door keep reciting the *Kalima*." (Muslim)

When somebody is in the agony of death, recite Surah Yasin from the Holy Quran. The Holy Prophet (S.A.W.) has instructed that: "Recite Surah Yasin by the side of those persons, who are having their last breath."

And when the person has expired and till his dead body is bathed, the Holy Quran should not be recited near the dead body; and those persons not clean and need washing, and the females in menses or passing after birth discharge, should refrain from going near the dead body.

On Hearing the News of Death you should Say

"Verily we belong to Allah and shall return to Him."

The Holy Prophet (S. A.W.) has said that one who recites this verse will have three rewards from Allah:

(i) Firstly he gets Allah's blessings and peace from Him.

(ii) Secondly he becomes entitled to recompense for the search of truth, and

(iii) Thirdly he is indemnified for the loss he has suffered and gets a better replacement of the loss.

As soon as one has breathed his/her last straighten his/her, body, arms and feet, close the eyes, and passing a bandage below his/her chin, knot at the head. The toes of the feet fastened together with a strip of cloth, and cover the body with a sheet. All those present should recite.

"Bismillahe wa ala millate Rasul-ullah."

(In the name of Allah and on the millat of the Holy Prophet of Allah (S.A.W.)

All concerned should be informed of the event. While lowering the body in the grave also recite this supplication.

Only good deeds of the dead person should be recounted and not bad ones. The Holy Prophet (S.A.W.) has directed:

"Narrate only virtues of your dead persons and do not mention their evils." (Abu Daud)

He has also said: "When somebody dies and his four neighbours testify that he was a virtuous man then Allah says "I have accepted your testimony, and have forgiven him for those things which were not known to you." (Ibn Habban)

Once the companions of the Holy Prophet (S.A.W) recounted the good deeds of a person in his presence. The Holy Prophet (S.A.W.) stated: "Gentlemen, since you are the witnesses of Allah on earth (on your testimony) this person has been allotted the Paradise (by Allah). When you call a dead person as good, Allah admits him into the Paradise, and whom you call bad, Allah sends him to the Hell."

(Bukhari - Muslim)

The Holy Prophet (S.A.W.) has further said: "Whenever you pay a visit to a sickman or accompany a funeral procession, always have good words on your tongue, for the angels ditto you and say amen (it may be so).

Wash Entire Dead Body Without Loss of Time : For bathing prepare mild warm water with some strawberry leaves in it, if possible. Put the dead body on a neat wooden plank, remove his clothes and cover the lower part of his body with a sheet of cloth. Cover your hands with hand gloves or a piece of cloth. Then clean his private parts first, and see that the sheet continues to cover the same. Thereafter, perform the ablution of the dead body. In this you need not put water into the mouth and the ears. While giving a bath, plug the ears and nose so that water may not enter into the body through these holes. Then wash the head with soap or any other thing. Then tilt the body a little towards the left, and rush water on the right side from head to feet and repeat this process on the other side. Now remove the water-soaked sheet and replace it with a dry one. Lift the body from the plank and place it on a cot wrapped with coffin.

> The Holy Prophet (S.A.W.) has said "Allah forgives forty grave sins of a person who has given bath to a dead person and kept secret of his or her shortcomings or defects; and one who has lowered the dead body into the pit is like a person who has provided a house to the dead person till the Resurrection.
>
> (Tibrani)

Shroud : A medium quality cloth of white colour should be used for the shroud of a dead person. It should neither be too costly nor of a very low quality. For males there should be three pieces of the shrouds one sheet (*or outer garment*), one piece (or tahband) to cover his lower part, and a pieced to be used as shirt or "*Kafni*" The sheet should be longer in length and a bit wider so as to fully cover the dead body and its ends may be tied covering the head and the feet.

For females, in addition to these three pieces, arrange a piece of cloth (Sarband) a little more than a meter in length and a little less than a meter in breadth, to cover the head and the hair; and another piece called seena band (chest cover) of sufficient length to provide additional covering from the arms-pit to the knee.

> The Holy Prophet (S.A.W.) has said: "Anybody who clothes a dead body with coffin, will get a dress of *Sundus* and *Istabraq* (a fine variety of silken cloth interwoven with silver and gold thread) in the Heaven." (Hakim)

> ***Take the Funeral Procession to he Cemetery with a Bit Fast Steps :*** The Holy Prophet (S.A.W.) has said: "Be quick in taking the funeral procession (to the graveyard)." Hadrat Ibn Masud enquired from the Holy Prophet (S.A.W.) "O Prophet of Allah (S.A.W.), at what speed we should march with the dead to the graveyard?" The Holy Prophet (S.A.W.) replied. "A little less than running. If the dead person was a virtuous man, he should be carried to his good end hastily. If he was not a good person, hasten to remove him from your surrounding." (Abu Daud)

Walk on when Accompanying a Bier : Once the holy Prophet (S.A.W.) was accompanying a funeral procession. He noticed some persons riding. He reprimanded them and said: "You ought to feel ashamed, whereas angels are walking on foot you are riding on the back of animals." You may, however, use some means of transport while returning from the graveyard. The Holy Prophet. (S.A.W.) accompanied the funeral procession of Abu Wahidi on foot and returned riding a horse.

Stand up on Seeing Bier : When you see a funeral procession coming, stand up, and if you do not have time to accompany it, wait for some time till the procession has gone ahead. The Holy Prophet (S.A.W.) has said: "When you see a bier, stand up, and those who are accompanying it should not sit till it is placed (on the ground)."

Participation in Funerals : You should make it a point to offer funeral prayers, and Accompany the funeral procession to the graveyard and lend your shoulders to carry the bier to the graveyard . . . . .

The ·grave should be dug according to the direction of Qibla, and the dead body should be lowered into the pit from the side of Qibla. If the body is not heavy, two persons would be enough to lower it, otherwise, three or four persons may have to be employed for the purpose. While lowering the body, turn its face towards the Qibla. After having laid the body untie the knots of the shroud.

Don't be Desperate : If you get involved in some serious worries and calamities which may make your life quite miserable; even then you should not lose hear nor ever try to commit suicide, for this is not only sheer cowardice but misappropriation of Allah's trust and munificence and this is a sin as well. Under such circumstances have recourse to Allah and regularly recite this prayer;

> "O Allah, with Your knowledge of the Unseen and Your power over Your creatures, keep me alive, as long as You know it is good for me to live, and grant me death when You know, it is better for me to die."
>
> (Musnad Ahmad)

Whenever you see somebody in distress, recite the following invocation, Hadrat Abu Hurrayrah quotes the holy Prophet (S.A.W.) as having said that whosoever recites this supplication on seeing somebody in trouble, he by the Will of Allah, himself remains immune from trouble.

"Thanks be to Allah Who has kept me safe from this ordeal in which you are involved, and has granted me supremacy over many of His creatures."

Observe Purdah to Bury a Female When lowering the body of a female in the grave, arrangements should be made for Purdah (Seclusion or keeping away women from the sight of strangers).

While covering the pit with earth, start from the side of the head. Gather soft clay with both the hands and throw it on the grave three times. For the first time while throwing soil say:

Minha khalq-na-kum (We created you from this very earth;.

While throwing the earth second time say:

Wa fiha nueedu hum (And We are returning you to the same),

And when throwing the same for the third time say:

Wa minha nukh-riju-kum taratan ukhra.

(And We shall raise you again from this earth).

(20 : 551)

Do not build the grave too high nor make it like a quadrangle. Only so much earth should be thrown over the grave, which has been excavated from the pit. When the grave has been filled with the earth some water may be sprinkled over it.

After having finished the burial, stay for some time near the grave praying for the salvation of the deceased and recite verses from the Holy Quran for the repose of the departed soul. Other people should also be asked to join in the prayers for the deceased.

The Holy Prophet (S.A.W.) used to pray for the dead person after his burial and also asked others. "This is the time for the reckoning of accounts. Pray to Allah for the stead-fastness of your brother, and beg for Allah's mercy for him." (Abu Daud)

Send Cooked Food to the Bereaved Family : In case of a death taking place among your relatives or neighbours, arrange to send cooked food for one or two times, to that house, as the bereaved family would be too much grieved and upset to think of preparing food. This is a token of sympathy and love with the grieved family.

Give something according to your means in charity for the peace of the departed soul. But refrain from indulging in irreligious and unauthorised practices and rituals.

The Code of Funeral Prayers

Participation in Funeral Prayers : You should make it a point to invariably attend funeral prayers. Participation in funeral prayers is like beseeching Allah for the peace of the soul of the dead person, and this is an important right of the deceased. In case there is a danger that the prayer is likely to be missed if you have to perform ablution, then you should perform Tayammum and join the prayer.

> The Holy Prophet's (S.A.W.) injunction in this regard is: "Offer funeral prayers, such a prayer may move you and soften your heart. A tender-hearted person remains under the shadow of Allah and he welcomes every good act." (Mustadrak Hakim)
>
> And the Holy Prophet (S.A.W.) has also said " A dead body for which three rows of Muslims offer prayers will certainly go to heaven. (Abu Daud)
>
> The Holy Prophet (S. A.W.)) has further remarked "When a person participates in the funeral of another person, and offers funeral prayers for him, the former will get a recompense equivalent to one qayrat and one who takes part in the burial as well, will get recompense equal to two qayrat. Some one asked about the volume of two qayrat the Holy Prophet (S.A.W.) replied "they will be equal to two mountains."
> (Bukhari - Muslim)

The bier should be set in such a way that the head of the dead person should face North and the feet South; and the face mould be in the direction of *Qibla*.

If you are leading a funeral prayer, stand in such a way that you may be facing the chest of the deceased.

The number of rows of participants in a funeral service should be odd. If there are a few persons, only one row should be formed, otherwise set up more rows, but their number must be odd.

Niyyat (Intention) When you begin funeral prayers, affirm in your heart (Niyyat) that you are praying for the salvation of the dead person from Allah. The Most Compassionate of the compssionates. Both the *Imam* and the followers should make this affirmation.

In a funeral prayer the Imam and the congregation should recite the same supplication. The followers should not remain quite. The Imam may call the Takbir loudly and the followers should repeat them slowly.

***Modus Operandi of Funeral Prayers* :** In a funeral prayer four *Takbirs* (Allah-u-Akbar) are recited loudly. With the first Takbir raise your hands upto your ears and thereafter fold them, and recite the following sana (eulogy).

"Allah! Thou art Pure and sublime alongwith their praise and laudation. Thy Name brings good and blessings; and Thy Greatness and Magnitude are highest, Great is Thy Praise, and there is no god but Thee."

Now recite the second Takbir but do not raise your hands nor make any sign with your head. After the second Takbir the following Salat may be recited:

> "Allah! vouchsafe Thy compassion upon Muhammad and his descendents; just as Thou hadst mercy and Thou sent peace and blessed and hadst compassion

on the descendents of Ibrahim. Verily Thou art praiseworthy, the Great."

The third Takbir is to he said without raising of hinds and the prescribed prayers is to be recited for the dead.

Prayers Prescribed for the Occasion : If the body is of an adult man or woman, the following prayers is to be offered after the third Takbir:

"Allah! forgive our living and dead; those present and those who are not present; our minors and elders; our males and females. Allah! those whom Thou keepest alive, may they be kept alive in the fold of Islam; and those whom Thou deems fit to send death, may they die in faith."

The following prayer is to be recited in case the body is that of a boy:

"Allah make this male child a means for our salvation; and make him a means for our reward a store (for our reward) in Hereafter, and make him the intercessor whose intercession may be accepted.

If the body is that of a minor girl, the prayer to be offered is given below:

"Allah make this female child a means for our salvation, and make her a means for our reward store (for our reward) in Hereafter, and make the intercessor whose intercession may be accepted.

Finally the fourth Takbir is to be said and the Salams are to be said in both directions, (right and left.).

Reflection upon Death : While accompanying a funeral, we should always reflect upon our destiny and consider that just as you are going to bury some one today, so some day you too will be buried by others and a funeral procession will march for you. We should, for that while at least have time to reflect upon (our end) and the hereafter and purge ourselves of the base emotions of the world.

Conduct in the Graveyard : Accompany a bier to the graveyard, and participate in the burial of the deceased. Apart from this, you should visit graveyards quite often, as it revives the remembrance of the Hereafter, as well as helps us prepare ourselves for the journey of life after death.

> The Holy Prophet (S.A.W.) once accomp nied a funeral procession to the graveyard, where he wept by the side of a grave so much that the ground became wet. Addressing the Companions, he said: "Brethren! prepare yourself for this day (of death)."
>
> (Ibn Majah)

On another occasion, sitting by the side of a grave, he said: "The grave daily declares in a very frightening tone: Children of Adam, have you forgotten me? I am the house of solitude; the place of isolation and nightmare; the abode of insects and worms; and shortness and ordeals, (for you) except for those blessed ones for whom Allah make me broad and wide. For all men I am a source of torture".

> And he (S.A.W.) further said: "Either grave is a pit among the pits or the Gardens or the Paradise."
>
> (Tibrani)

Grave as a Source of Lesson : A visit to the graveyard should infuse into you the imagery of life after death.

While entering a graveyard, the following prayer may be recited"

"Peace be upon you, O Obedient faithfuls, the dwellers of this place, God willing, soon we shall join you. We Pray to Allah for you and ourselves, that He may keep us safe."

A graveyard is not a place where you may indulge in irresponsible and loose talks; cut jokes, laugh and chit chat on worldly matters. The grave is the gateway to the Hereafter on seeing which you should feel overwhelmed with the feelings remorse and repentance, which may bring tears in your eyes.

> The Holy Prophet (S.A.W.) has said: "I had asked you not to visit the graveyard to save you from shirk. If you now like, can go (to see the graves) since graves revive the memories of the Hereafter. (Muslim)

Graves not to be Built as Permanent Structures : The Holy Prophet (S.A.W.) has specifically prohibited from making graves as permanent structures or decorating them. When the Holy Prophet (S.A.W.) was near the end of his (S.A.W.) worldly life, and felt much pain and uneasiness so much so that at times he covered his face with his sheet and then uncovered his face alternately. In this state of pain and restlessness Hadrat Aishah heard him saying "Allah's curse be upon the Jews and Christian who had converted the graves of their Prophets into places of worship."

Praying for Dead : You should go to the graveyard and pray to Allah far salvation of the dead. According to Hadrat Sufyan, "Just as the living persons are in need of food and water, so the dead are in great need of prayers."

> According to a tradition, when Allah elevates the status of a virtuous servant in the Paradise by one degree he asks Allah, "O Lord, how did I get this elevation'?" And Allah answers: "Because of your son, who has been praying for thy salvation."
>
> (Tibrani)

Manners at the Death Bed

Things That Need to be Done When Someone Dies

- Notification of a person's death to friends and the public may well be through an announcement in the local press, provided that such an announcement does not praise or commend the dead person or demonstrate his esteem. Instead, the announcement would do better to ask others to pray for the dead person.

- Preparing the corpse for burial by washing and shrouding it is necessary. This should be carried out in an inexpensive way.
- Dead men are washed by men, dead women by women, except in the case of a married couple, where the survivor is allowed to wash the dead person.
- The dead person should be washed with water and, if available, lotus leaves, an odd number of times, three or five, or more if necessary, beginning with the right side and, for the last washing, camphor should be added to the solution. If the dead person is a woman, then her hair should be braided into three plaits and placed behind her back.
- Though shrouding the dead should be done with cloth of moderate quality, extravagance is not recommended and using a coffin is not allowed unless necessary for health reasons.
- The Shuhada' martyrs should be stripped of their jewelry and buried in their clothing without having the blood washed off.
- A Muslim who dies while performing pilgrimage or Umrah should be washed with water and lotus leaves, if available, and shrouded in the same two pieces of cloth with which he covered himself for the pilgrimage or Umrah. No perfume, in this case, should be put on the dead, neither should his head be covered.
- Anyone who has washed a dead body is recommended to bathe himself and anyone who has carried it is recommended to perform ablution.
- It is the duty of those who wash the dead not to mention to others whatever they may have noticed of the bodily

imperfections of the dead person. Mentioning good things is allowed.

- It is recommended that, immediately after washing and shrouding it, the body not be kept long, but rather taken quickly, prayed over, and then buried.

On Way to the Graveyard

- The funeral of a Muslim must be attended by other Muslims. Therefore, a Muslim should not be slow to participate in escorting the funeral, whether or not the dead person or his relatives are known to him directly.
- Escorting a funeral consists of two stages; the first lasts till the funeral prayer is offered, and the second till the dead person is buried. It is recommended, however, that those attending the first stage also wait until the second stage is completed.
- Prayer should be performed over every Muslim who dies, including infants. Taking the dead body into the mosque for the funeral prayers is not recommended. Prayers should be conducted in a place outside the mosque, e.g. in the courtyard.
- It is not proper that some people, especially relatives of the dead, do not take part in the funeral prayers, instead waiting on others to do so in their place.
- The pace of the procession should be neither too quick nor too slow.
- Those following and escorting a funeral on foot should walk either in front of or behind the bier, or on the right or left, keeping near it. Those riding, however, should keep behind.
- Following the funeral with incense or candles, mentioning God's name audibly or loudly, weeping aloud, or reading the Quran aloud, are forbidden when escorting a, funeral.

- Speech should be kept short and light during the funeral procession.
- When a Muslim sees a funeral passing he may stand up.
- Conveying the deceased by car or other vehicle is not recommended, unless the cemetery is far away.
- It is recommended that those who carry a bier perform ablution afterwards. This will help to refresh and reorientate them physically and emotionally.
- Walking when following the funeral is better than riding, unless the cemetery is far away. However, on returning from the burial it is permissible to ride or walk.

In the Graveyard

- It is a matter of great importance that a special cemetery be devoted exclusively for the use of Muslims. Muslims may not be buried in the cemeteries of non-Muslims, nor vice versa.
- No person may be cremated, even if the dead person has specifically requested it. Such a request must not be fulfilled.
- The dead should be interred in the cemetery, except the Shuhada (those killed on the battlefield) who should be buried where they are martyred.
- The dead person should be buried in the locality where he died. It is undesirable that the body be taken back to the person's own country or moved to another city.
- The burial must take place as soon as possible after death, with the following exceptions:
  (a) At night.
  (b) From sunrise until the sun is about 4.5 degrees above the horizon (when it is fully risen).
  (c) At the zenith of the sun (when it is at the meridian) until it passes the meridian.

(d) When the sun pales before sunset until it has set. Burying the dead during these times is forbidden unless there is an urgent necessity.

- Allocating a special cemetery for state leaders or for the rich is utterly forbidden. Islam rejects the class system in life and at death.
- When more than one person is to be buried in a single grave, e.g. in the case of war or a widespread epidemic, then that person who in life read the Quran the most should be buried first.
- The task of placing the dead person in the grave must be carried out by men only. The deceased's male relatives are actually expected to place him or her in the grave.
- It is not proper to hire others to wash, shroud or inter the deceased. It is expected that the person's relatives and family do these things. Islam attaches great importance to strong relations between family members in life and at death.
- The deceased is placed in the grave on his right side with his face towards the Qiblah.
- Whoever places the dead in the grave should say: *Bismillah wa ala millati rasoolillah* (In the name of God, by God's grace, and following the Sunnah of the Prophet). The corpse is lowered into the grave from the rear of the grave.
- Standing up in the cemetery until the body is put into the grave is not required. Except for those who place the deceased in the grave, the mourners may be seated.
- It is recommended that those standing around the grave, after the corpse has been lowered into it and before the covering has been placed over it, throw three handfuls of earth into the grave.

- It is an innovation to admonish the dead person after his death. Admonishing should be done during his dying.
- It is recommended to pray for the dead person.

Post-funeral Acts

- If the person died in debt it is the responsibility of his relatives to discharge the debt as soon as possible, provided that this is within their capacity.
- The deceased's last wishes should be fulfilled except if they contradict the teachings of Islam; if, for example, he instructed his survivors to give an extra sum of money to one of his heirs, as Islam already regulates the inheritance for this group of people.

The Message

- It is a Muslim's duty to offer condolences, comfort, and sympathy to the bereaved. To do so contributes to strengthening relationships within Muslim society. Therefore, mixing socially with the bereaved family for a period following the death is Islamic conduct, helping to get them back to normal life as quickly as possible.
- When offering condolences one's words should be chosen carefully. The right words should be used to convey sympathy and to encourage the bereaved to accept God's will.
- Islamic phrases of sympathy are, for instance: *Ghafarallahu limayyitikum* (May God forgive the deceased his sins) and *Inna lillahi ma akhadha wa lahu ma ata wa Kullu shayin 'indahu ila ajalin musamma* (What God has taken or given does indeed belong to Him and He has an appointed time for every thing).
- Comforting and encouraging the bereaved is required for as long as the necessity remains. Thus, the bereaved should be visited from time to time.

- The bereaved family is not supposed to cook food for or serve visitors. On the contrary, friends, neighbours and relatives are advised to prepare food for them, for the loss of their loved one occupies the family's whole attention.
- Showing sympathy to the bereaved is good conduct, but it should be done without exaggeration. Speeches should be kept short and light; jokes, laughing and anything that may give offence should be avoided.
- All innovative practices following the death of a Muslim (such as holding a 'wake' on the fortieth day, etc.) must be avoided.

No Loud Mourning

- Though mourning over the dead is allowed in Islam, great differences exist between the Islamic viewpoint on this and the practice of Muslims at the present time.
- Women have the right to mourn a deceased relative, for a period not exceeding three days. For widows the period of mourning may extend to four lunar months and ten days.
- No loss, however great, should be permitted to sour one's outlook. Endurance should be shown by the bereaved, who are recommended to praise God and say: *Inna lillahi wa-inna ilayhi rajiun* (We belong to Him, to Him do we return).
- Grief at the death of a relative or friend is normal. It is also normal and usual to see people weeping for the dead, and this is allowed in Islam. What is completely forbidden is to express grief by wailing, shrieking, beating the cheeks and tearing hair or clothes.
- When mourning a dead person, care must be taken to avoid phrases that contradict Islamic principles, e.g. 'What will become of me now?' or 'Now our supporter

is gone.' This implies relying on human beings rather than on Allah.

- It is a Muslim's duty to advise those who wail for the dead in this way to stop doing so.
- Islam prescribes that a widow may not remarry during her period of mourning; it is considered impolite, therefore, to ask for a woman's hand during this period.
- A widow in mourning may not wear clothes of saffron colour, or wear jewelry, or dye her hair with henna or use antimony on her eyes.

11

Rightful Responses

Respect for Mosque

- A Muslim should put on his finest and cleanest clothes when going to the mosque, use perfume if available, and be sure that his shoes are clean.
- A Muslim should refrain from going to the mosque if he has eaten onions or garlic, unless he is completely sure that he is free of odour, as such odour will disturb others.
- It is best to enter the mosque and join the worshippers calmly and quietly without hurrying.
- Pushing and shoving when entering or leaving the mosque should be avoided; those on the right should enter or leave first.
- When entering the mosque, a Muslim should proceed with his right foot, saying: *Bismillah, Allahumma iftah li abwaba rahmatik* (O Allah, open to me the gates of Your mercy).
- A Muslim entering the mosque should, if possible, pray two rakats before sitting down.
- Speaking in the mosque is permitted provided the following rules are adhered to:

(a) Using raised voices in the mosque is not right conduct.

(b) Those who recite the Quran in the mosque, should do so quietly, otherwise they will confuse or disturb those praying or reading the Quran.

(c) The mosque is not the place for selling, buying or discussing other worldly affairs. Therefore, if any one is heard discussing buying or selling in a mosque he must be advised not to do so.

(d) One should not sit beside people who talk about worldly affairs in the mosque.

- Before beginning the congregational prayer, the worshippers should stand in straight lines, first men, then children, and then women. All should ensure that the lines are straight, and should stand close together and erect.
- Entering and passing through the mosque is not unlawful for a menstruating woman or one who is seminally defiled. However, they are forbidden to remain in the mosque.
- Mosques are the best places in this world. Therefore, Muslims should frequently visit them. It is a clear indication that a person is a good Muslim if he goes regularly to the mosque.
- To pass immediately in front of a man who is saying his prayer should be avoided, for it would interfere with his prayer to do so.
- One should not be in a hurry to leave the mosque, and when leaving should depart from the mosque with the left foot, saying: *Allahumma inni as aluka min fadlika* (O Allah, I seek Your favour).
- The movements of those praying in congregation should not precede but should follow those of the imam.

- It is not recommended that a Muslim performs his prayers in the one, same spot in the mosque.
- Using a mosque as a thoroughfare is a detestable act.

Behaviour in Graveyards

- There are two main purposes for a Muslim to visit a cemetery: to pray for the dead, and to remind himself of the Hereafter.
- Visiting graves is recommended. Women are permitted to visit graves, though it is recommended that they do not do so too often.
- On visiting graves a Muslim should say: *Assalamu ala ahlil diyari minal-muminna wal muslimin wa yarhamu Allah al-mustaqdimina minna wal mustakhirin wa inna insha Allahu bikum La lahiqun* (Peace be upon the Muslim and faithful inhabitants of the abodes. May God show mercy to those of us who go before and those who go after and God willing, we will meet you).
- Violating Islamic teachings while at the cemetery is forbidden.
- Nothing is to be said over the grave other than what is mentioned in (3) above, except to pray for the dead.
- It is forbidden to touch any grave with the intention of gaining a blessing from it.
- Putting wreaths on graves is an imitation of alien cultures.
- Lighting candles or placing lanterns on the grave is an innovation.
- Women, when visiting the cemetery, are requested to avoid all kinds of behaviour violating Islam, such as wearing un-Islamic dress, wailing, etc.
- The cemetery is not a place where people gather for collective worship at certain times of the year; Visiting

graves must be an occasion only to be reminded of death, which will have a positive effect on the individual's daily life and behaviour. Using the cemetery as a place of worship or celebration is utterly forbidden in Islam.

- Sitting on the grave is forbidden.
- There is no definite day or time for visiting the cemetery.

Rules for Road

Roads, streets and lanes are public property. The rules of behaviour in these places are of great importance. Observing these rules indicates civilization and progress, violating them indicates backwardness.

- The main principle which should govern the behaviour of the individual on the road is to avoid harming or disturbing others.
- Keeping roads tidy and clean is the responsibility of every member of the society.
- The road is not a place for sitting or meeting, so using it in this way should be avoided.
- Violating the rules of Islam on the roads and streets of an Islamic country is a grave matter which has repercussions for the community. So it is a Muslim's duty, if he sees something objectionable to disapprove it and to recommend what is reputable, provided that he does so in conformity with Islamic teachings and expresses himself with wisdom, restraint and good manners.
- Guiding those who are lost and seeking direction, helping the old or the invalid, is an Islamic duty and reflects good manners.
- Removing anything which could be injurious or offensive or which causes annoyance to people on their way, is an Islamic duty.

- Thinking ill of others one sees or meets on the road is un-Islamic conduct. A Muslim should think well of others.
- Returning greetings on the road is one of the rules of courtesy.
- Men and women should avoid mingling along the road. Women should walk on the side farthest from the road or street.
- To stare at a woman on the road after the first glance is forbidden. So a man should lower his gaze or turn it aside.
- To offer a lift to those who do not have their own vehicles is recommended.
- Among rules for the use of public transport is the requirement that women and the elderly be properly respected.
- When using public transport, a Muslim should confine himself to speaking only when necessary and then in a subdued voice, refrain from smoking, or otherwise being a nuisance to fellow travellers.
- Crowding and rushing onto public vehicles is not civilized conduct. The principle of favouring the right when entering and leaving the vehicle should be observed.
- Shouting when approaching someone on the road from behind is bad behaviour. It is better to come nearer to him before speaking.
- Eating while walking along the road or street is considered un-Islamic behaviour.
- A Muslim's manner of walking along the road is a part of his Islamic personality; it expresses to others and conveys to himself certain sentiments and attitudes.

Walking, therefore, should conform to certain guidelines:

(a) Reeling or swaying when walking are to be avoided; so too walking with an effeminate gait, or with a stance of pride, prancing or strutting; also cowering when walking.

(b) When walking in company, one should consider others and not proceed at a pace too fast for them.

Addressing Others : There is no doubt of the importance in any society of giving names. The following are some rules for giving names in the Islamic society.

Giving Names

- Parents should not delay in giving a name to a recently-born child; they should do so as soon as possible, preferably within seven days of the birth.
- If the parents have agreed on the choice of name, well and good. If not, then it is the right of the father to name the child.
- It is recommended that parents give children good, beautiful and meaningful names.

(a) Some of the best names are: 'Abdullah, 'Abd al-Rahman, and Al-Harith.

(b) Names consisting of two parts, the first of which is 'Abd (slave) compounded with one of Allah's names are considered beautiful.

(c) Children may be given the names of Prophets.

(d) Names of angels, such as Jibbrail, should be avoided.

(e) Names which declare the person as possessing excellent moral characteristics, such as purity, honesty, obedience or piousness, should be avoided.

(f) Names meaning slavery to somebody other than God (such as Abd al-Husayn (slave of Hussain) or

Abd al-Nabi (slave of the Prophet) are forbidden in Islam.

(g) Names indicating sadness, war and similar conditions , such as Huzn, Harb, etc., should be avoided.

(h) The main elements of the full name are first name, father's name, and surname. Every child must be brought into relation to his father and called by his real father's surname. That applies to the married woman who should retain her own family name and not relinquish it in favour of her husband's. That would amount to a humiliation for her and must be avoided.

(i) Having and giving good names is important not only for people, it is also required when naming streets, squares, towns, etc.

(j) Changing names of people or places when necessary should not be rejected. Changing forbidden names is considered a necessity.

Addressing Others

- Calling out to people from a distance in the street, market or other public place is not polite conduct. It is better to approach close to the person before hailing him.
- People can be called either by their names or their agnomens.
- Calling a teacher or parents by their first name should be avoided, as that is a sign of impoliteness.
- Shortening or apocopation of a name is a suitable way of calling others provided they are satisfied with it.
- Calling another person by a certain title or agnomen must have the full approval of the person concerned.

- If someone wants to call to a person whom he does not know, then it is best to use general terms that will not insult him, such as 'friend', 'brother'.
- Calling a non-Muslim or corrupt individual by a patronymic (Abu so-and-so/Umm so-and-so) is an abhor rent practice unless necessary for identification purposes.

Rules for Sports

- To become addicted to watching sports amounts to a waste of time and has hardly any benefit for a Muslim. In Islam, sports are encouraged insofar as they are a means to build strong, healthy bodies. Sport must be treated as a means and not as an end; when sport becomes an end in itself it is prohibited. This does not apply to the case of physical education instructors, or trainers.
- Sports dress should be designed and made in accordance with the rules of Islamic dress discussed above.
- Placing or accepting a wager by contestants on the result of a race or other event is forbidden except in a camel, horse or elephant race. For non-contestants, betting and gambling of any sort is forbidden.
- All kinds of sports which endanger life, as in modern wrestling or boxing, are forbidden.
- All forms of sports which harm any animal, such as oxen, cocks, etc. are forbidden, for this contradicts the humanitarian demands of Islam.
- The most highly recommended types of sports in Islam are those involving some sort of projectile, such as shooting or throwing.

Bibliography

Adams, C.C. : *Islam and Modernism in Egypt,* Oxford University Press, New York, 1953.

Ahmad, Bherhan : *The Mujaddid's Conception of Tauhid,* Feroz Pub., Lahore, 1940.

Ahmad, Imtiaz : *Divorce and Remarriage among Muslims in India,* Manohar Publishers, New Delhi, 2003.

Ahmad, K. N. : *Muslim Law of Divorce,* Kitab Bhavan, New Delhi, 1988.

Ahmad, Manzuruddin : *Islamic Political System,* Kitab Bhavan, New Delhi, 1991.

Ali, Chiragh : *The Proposed Political Legal and Social Reform under Muslim Rule,* Popular Prakashan, Bombay, 1883.

Badrul, S. : *Muslim Behaviour,* Kitab Bhavan, New Delhi, 1991.

Bahedur, Kalim : *The Jamaat-i-Islami of Pakistan,* Progressive Books, Lahore, 1978.

Baksh, S. K. : *Politics in Islam,* Kitab Bhavan, New Delhi, 2003.

Bawer, Raymond : *The New Man in Soviet Social Psychology,* Oxford, New York, 1990.

Berger, M. : *Islam in Egypt Today : Social and Political Aspects of Popular Religion,* MacMillan, London, 1970.

Bernier, Francois : *Travels in the Mogul Empire*, MacMillan, London, 1916.

Bukhsh, S. K. : *Contribution to the History of Islamic Civilization*, Kitab Bhavan, New Delhi, 2000.

Charles, Howard : *The Constitutionalism*, Great Seal Books, New York, 1947.

Chave, F. : *Islamic Histroriography*, Cambridge University press, New York, 1990.

Davids, Waines : *An Introduction to Islam*, Cambridge University Press, New Delhi, 1995.

Durrani, F.K.K. : *Muhammad (PBUH) the Prophet*, Oxford, New York, 2001.

Enayat, Hamid : *Islam in the Political Process*, Cambridge University Press, Cambridge, 1993.

Engineer, Asghar Ali : *A Rational Approach to Islam*, Gyan Books Pvt. Ltd., New Delhi, 2001.

———: *Islam : Challenge in Twenty-first Century*, Gyan Books Pvt. Ltd., New Delhi, 2004.

Guillaume, A. : *The Traditions of Islam*, Khayats, Beirut, 1966.

Hassan, Ali : *Observations on the Musulmauns of India*, Macmillan & Co., London, 1832.

Helmut, Reifeld : *Islam in South Asia : Adaptation, Accommodation and Conflict*, Social Science Press, New Delhi, 1999.

Houtsma, T. : *Encyclopaedia of Islam*, Macmillan, London, 1934.

Irfan, Habib : *The Agrarian System of Mughal India*, Popular Prakashan, Bombay, 1963.

Jafar, Sharif : *Islam in India*, Oxford, New Delhi, 1972.

James, Burges : *The Muhammadan Architecture of Ahmadabad*, Bernard Quaritch, London,1900.

Jha, V. : *Indian Society: Historical Probings*, Rawat Pub., Delhi, 1974.

Joseph, and Bosworth, C.E. : *The Legacy of Islam,* Oxford University Press, New York, 1979.

Karl, Jaspers : *Man in the Modern Age,* Routledge & Kegan Paul Ltd., London, 1997.

Katharine, Scarfe : *Perception of the Islamic Word,* Cambridge University Press, New Delhi, 1992.

Lewin, Roger : *In the Age of Mankind,* Simithsonian Books, Washington, D.C., 1956.

Lewis, Richards : *Universe,* Harmony Books, New York, 1973.

Martin, Lings : *A Sufi Saint of the Twentieth Century,* Century Pub., London, 1971.

Mirza, Waheed : *The Life and Works of Amir Khusrau,* Kaveri Pub., Calcutta, 1935.

Mortimer, Edward : *Faith and Power, the Politics of Islam,* Oxford, New York, 2002.

Muhammad, Iqbal : *Six Lectures on the Reconstruction of Religious Thought in Islam,* Royal Pub., Lahore, 1930.

Nabith, A. : *The Foundations of the Articles of Faith,* Feroz Pub., Lahore, 1963.

Nasr, Seyyed H. : *An Introduction to Islamic Cosmological Doctrines,* Cambridge, 1964.

Nicholson, R.A. : *Literary History of the Arabs,* Kitab Bhavan, New Delhi, 1994.

Nusservanji, D. : *Zoroastrian Civilization,* Oxford, New York, 1922.

Oage, Charles H. : *The Society,* Macmillan & Co., London, 1959.

Padwick, C.E. : *Muslim Devotions,* MacMillan & Co., London, 1960.

Phillips, O. Hood : *Reform of the Constitution,* MacMillan & Co., London, 1970.

Pierce, R.A.: *Russia in Central Asia, 1867-1917,* University of California, Berkeley, 1960.

Qadir, Abdul, : *Criminal Law of Islam,* Kitab Bhavan, New Delhi, 1999.

Qazi A. Qadir : *The Changing World of Islam,* Royal Pub., Lahore, 1992.

Rizvi, Hasan Askari : *Islami Reassertion : a Socio Political Study,* Progressive Publishers, Lahore, 1981.

Robert, D. : *Exploring our Living Planet,* National Geographic Society, Washington, 1989.

Saukat, S. : *Human Rights in Islam,* Kitab Bhavan, New Delhi, 2001.

Sharma, Arvind : *Women in World Religion,* New York Press, New York, 1990.

Syed, M. H. : *History of Muslims in India,* Anmol Publications, New Delhi, 2003.

——— : *Islamic Terrorism : Myth or Reality,* Gyan Books, New Delhi, 2002.

Tarn, W. W. : *The Greeks in Bactria and India,* Cambridge, London, 1938.

Thomas, Arnold : *The Legacy of Islam,* Oxford University Press, New York, 2000.

Thompson, H.R. : *Sculptures and Inscriptions of Darius the Great on the Rock of Behistan,* Oxford, London, 1907.

Tritton, A.S. : *The Caliphs and their Non-Muslim Subjects,* Oxford, New York, 1930.

Tutsch, Hans E. : *Facets of Arab Nationalism,* Wayne State University Press, Detroit, 1965.

Underhill, E. : *Mysticism : a Study in the Nature and Development of Man's Spiritual Consciousness,* Oxford, New York, 1956.

Usmani, J.M. : *The Authority of Sunnah,* Kitab Bhavan, New Delhi, 1998.

Von, Edmund : *Modern Islam,* University Press, Los Angeles, 1952.

Von, Grunebaum : *Unity and Variety in Muslim World,* Oxford, New York, 2003.

Waheed, Akhtar : *Sufi Approach to the Problem of Alienation,* Wilson & Co., New Delhi, 1975.

Weiner, Myron : *Sons of the Soil : Migration and Ethnic Conflict in India,* University Press, Prineton, 1978.

Williams, Michael : *Outlines of World Military History,* Oxford, New York, 1996.

Wilson, Lambron : *Traditional Modes of Contemplation and Action,* University Press, Tehran, 1977.

Wolfson, H.A. : *Glimpses of Medieval Indian Culture,* Popular Pub., Bombay, 1959.

Yahanan, Friedmann : *Tolerance and Coercion in Islam : Interfaith Relations in the Muslims Traditions,* Cambridge, New York, 1990.

Yazbeck, Haddad : *Islamic Values in the United States,* Oxford, New York, 1997.

Zaehner, R.C. : *Hindu and Muslim Mysticism,* Oxford, London, 1960.

Zahid, Malik : *Subjects of Quran,* Kitab Bhavan, New Delhi, 1998.

Zahurul, Hasan : *Tarikb-i-Sufiya-i-Gujarat,* Jamil Academy, Ahmadabad, 1981.

Zaki, Azam : *The Ideas of Arab Nationalism,* Cornell University Press, New York,1956.

Index

B

C

D

E

F

G

H

I

Q

R

S

T

U

V

W

Z

❑❑❑